Journey
to the Heart
of Cuba

Carlos Alberto Montaner

Journey
to the Heart
of Cuba

—

Life as Fidel Castro

3/03
Algora Publishing
New York

Algora Publishing, New York
© 2001 by Algora Publishing
All rights reserved. Published 2001.
Printed in the United States of America
ISBN: 1-892941-61-9
Editors@algora.com

Originally published as *Viaje al corazón de Cuba* ©*Plaza & Janés Editors, S.A.*, 1999.

Library of Congress Cataloging-in-Publication Data: 00-012987

Montaner, Carlos Alberto.
 [Viaje al corazón de Cuba. English]
 Journey to the heart of Cuba : life as Fidel Castro / by Carlos
Alberto Montaner.
     p. cm.
Includes bibliographical references.
 ISBN 1-892941-61-9 (alk. paper)
 1. Cuba—History—1959- 2. Castro, Fidel, 1927—Psychology. I.
Title.
 F1788 .M66 2001
 972.9106'4'092—dc21

00-012987

Dedicated to Carlos Varona, Levi Marrero, Mario Villar, Miguel Gonzales-Pando, Felicito Rodriquez and Enrique Baloyra — six friends who could not make the return trip.

On the next page and the following: the cunning letter written and sent by the 12 year-old Castro to President Roosevelt, trying to get ten dollars.

Santiago de Cuba.

Nov 6 1940.

Mr. Franklin Roosvelt,
President of the United
States.

My good friend Roosvelt
I don't know very En-
glish, but I know as much
as write to you.
I like to hear the radio, and
I am very happy, because
I heard in it that you will
be President for a new
(período)
I am twelve years old.
I am a boy but I think very
much but I do not think
that I am writing to the

President of the United S-
tates.
If you like, give me a
ten dollar bill green american, in the letter, because
never I have not seen a
ten dollar bill green american and I would like
to have one of them.
My address is:—

Dr. Fidel Castro
Colegio de Dolores
Santiago de Cuba
Oriente. Cuba

I don't know very much
English
but I know very much
Spanish and I suppose
you don't know very Spa-
nish, but you know very
English, because I am
an American but I am
not American.

(Thank you very much)
Good by. your friend,

Fidel Castro

If you want iron, to make
ships, I will
show to you the bigest
(minas) of iron of the land.
They will be in Mayari.
Oriente. Cuba.
Cuba.

TABLE OF CONTENTS

I

PORTRAIT OF
THE YOUNG FIDEL CASTRO

No other living political figure provokes so much anthropological curiosity as Fidel Castro. His beard and olive green uniform have entered the iconography of the 20th century along with Hitler's mustache, Churchill's cigar and Charlie Chaplin's bowler hat. He ensconced himself on the front pages of the newspapers and for half a century there has been no way to evict him. His ability to retain his grasp on the scepter has made it into Guinness: no Iberian American dictator — Franco included — has lasted this long. He has been at the helm of the Cuban state for more than 40 years. With a cunning smile, firmly idle, he has watched nine United States presidents file past. Sometimes he has had the patience to sit at the door of his shop and watch the cadavers of his enemies pass by. Others, he has rushed to order executed. Any measure is acceptable if his position of power is at stake.

His infinite eloquence is legendary — especially when there are more than three people gathered and he feels the irrepressible desire to demonstrate his immense erudition. This compulsive urge multiplies exponentially with relation to the size of his audience. The more people, the longer and more convoluted the speeches. If the podium is high and the plaza is large, his loquacity is exacerbated. Then he really lets loose. He arrives at the critical phase of verbal incontinence. His speeches become never-ending. He lectures for eight hours, with nary a concession made to his bladder or that of his desperate listeners. This is not an insignificant fact: it reflects how little he cares about the rest of humanity and how immensely he values himself. He talks about everything: about sugar cane, livestock breeding, neoliberalism, the imminent collapse of the capitalist world, hurricanes and every topic — science, the economy, ethics or sports — that comes to mind. He is a president stuffed full of big words, encyclopedic, oceanic, pedagogic, and moreover in a tone that is usually apocalyptic. Those who have not heard him cannot imagine the devastating power of a word. A power, sometimes, that means life or death.

Those long discourses serve a transcendental liturgical function. There, in that torrent of disordered words, truth and lies are defined; there, jumbled among colloquial expressions, gibes and expressions of rage, amidst complex explanations and foolish simplifications, the outlines of reality are drawn. Public enemies are chosen, and friends, too, as well as what must be believed and what must be rejected. Castro's word is the people's sacred book, the revolutionary bible that serves as a theoretical framework enabling them to make value judgments and to preserve or to condemn certain forms of conduct. It is the dogmatic reference that allows one to determine whether a thought or an opinion has revolutionary content. If Fidel affirmed it, it is correct; if he disapproved of it, it must be rejected. This is the well-known mechanism of scholastic philosophy: as in the religious arena, things are true or false depending on the opinions of the authorities. That is the infallible character of revealed truths.

In Cuba, Fidel is the only moral or intellectual authority. Loyalty to the Chief is demonstrated in the fidelity with which Castro's words and judgments are adopted. To be a revolutionary is to be a *fidelista*; and to be a *fidelista* is to repeat faithfully and blindly Castro's discourses, to assume ownership of his words and to play them back with the loyalty of a record-player. And in the mechanical repetition, in the exactness of the mimicry, lies the talent of his acolytes; this is one of the greatest emotional gratifications relished by *caudillos* — the creation of a choral society.

But it is not that way all the time. Fidel is not the sacred oracle at every moment. Sitting down, he is another person. When his audience is reduced to one, he immediately changes the communication strategy. The danger is that his circadian rhythms, the mechanism that regulates his sleeping and waking, is inverted. Like a tulip, Castro blossoms at night. He

4

comes to life and bursts onto the scene like a verbal vampire who comes out of his coffin to chat for hours on end. It is then that the captivating Fidel emerges, apparently very interested in his interlocutor. He can appear to be refined and attentive. Now, he does less talking; he asks questions. He becomes a punctilious inquisitor, desperate to know exactly how many mayors there are in the province of Málaga, the exact number of automobiles that transit the PanAmerican highway on Thursdays, or how, in detail, a hydroelectric plant works. Castro has a classificatory idea of the world in which he lives, a meticulous, Pythagorean attitude, like those esoteric Greeks who believed that reality could be reduced to numbers. Castro has a head full of numbers. He is a talking almanac who accumulates facts and inconsequential information with which he later ratifies his foregone conclusions.

And here's another characteristic: he is never willing to change his mind or revoke a decision. Mistakes are for other people. He is a nobleman, stubbornly convinced that he's right; he's a proponent of the old aristocratic saying that it's better to persist in an error than to admit it. His greatest psychological satisfaction comes from doing what he wants to do, and from being right. To admit that another person has been more astute, or that he has committed a blunder, would strike him as a horrible act of humiliating degradation. Following the dissolution of communism and the demise of the Soviet Union, a hundred friends and dozens of accredited economists have paraded through his office to explain to him that the Marxist-Leninist state was a blunder, and is now an impossibility. But it has all been in vain. He is indifferent to reality. He suffers from a type of political autism. If the entire world says he is wrong, he thinks that the entire world is living a lie — probably one induced by the CIA. There's no way out.

That inability to accept weaknesses or failures must be understood not only as a pathological deformation of his character; it also has to do with the way in which Castro relates to his subordinates. Here, we are in the presence of a *caudillo* [Commander, or Leader], someone who demands total obedience and submission from others as a consequence of his evident moral and intellectual superiority. The *caudillo* is unique because he never makes mistakes. He is infallible. This is the basis for his followers' reposing in him the ability to analyze, diagnose, and propose solutions. This is also the basis of the obdurate stubbornness of *caudillos*. The moment they show their worries and their lack of judgment, the loyalty of their followers is diminished. They don't want to see, they can't see a teary-eyed leader who bows his head and asks for forgiveness. If they have surrendered to him the ability to think, and with it the right to say what they really believe, it is because of the exceptional qualities of the leader. They no longer use their own words, or even their own gestures; theirs have been substituted by those of their beloved leader. They are victims of an instinctive tendency to imitate the idolized master. They cannot accept that this person who has usurped their way of life is an ordinary human being, capable of making mistakes. The pact is very simple: one surrenders one's soul only to an infallible *caudillo*. Like Castro.

Psychological profiles like Fidel Castro's have been perfectly described by psychiatry. They are called *narcissistic personalities* and they are classified among the most common mental disorders. Narcissists see themselves as grand beings of unique importance. They incarnate the height of human vanity as described in Greek mythology. That's why they expect to be given special treatment, different from that of other mortals. Criticism or censure from a subordinate elicits an angry response, with verbal and physical violence; but criticism from a distant source is met with feigned indifference. They are ambitious and selfish to an extreme degree. Norms are for other people. They feel they deserve preferential treatment, but they don't take into account the needs of others. The word "reciprocity" does not exist in their vocabulary, and so their interpersonal relationships are very fragile and fraught with conflict. They are feared, not loved. It is almost impossible to love a narcissist. It is difficult to appreciate someone who doesn't demonstrate empathy or compassion for the misfortune of his supporters. It goes against nature to love someone who defines loyalty as total subordination to his beliefs, preferences and principles. That would mean loving a person who squashes and swallows you.

Narcissistic personality traits are seldom exhibited in their pure state. They are frequently accompanied by histrionism, a form of exhibitionism expressed through extravagant clothes, eccentric conduct and an evident disdain for what is considered socially acceptable. Fidel, like Hitler and Mussolini (two other textbook narcissists), is a clown. His constant wearing of the active militant's costume, his spasmodic gesticulation, the transfigured expression on his face when he stands at the rostrum, define him as a clown. He not only *is* Fidel Castro, he *dresses up* as Fidel Castro. But the histrionism is also a means of manipulation. Fidel presents himself to Cubans as an irascible and aggressive man. That is his body language. He is always on the brink of blowing up, of declaring war, of doing something tremendous. He not only wants to impress; he wants to intimidate. And he achieves that. Those who surround him, fear him — even his closest associates. In fact, especially his closest associates. They fear his brusque remarks, his recriminations, his screaming. Castro can be extremely delicate, even charming, with a foreign visitor, but he can use the worst vulgarities to censure a subordinate. That is one of the saddest signs of Cuban society. It is a universe in which everyone is afraid. Everyone except for one person. Except for the *caudillo* who, from the heights of power, adorned with his unflagging ego, rules the Cubans as he wishes.

Childhood of a Caudillo

Let's tell the life story of this unique character. Maybe his first twenty-five years will serve to clarify some of the mysteries. The *comandante* was born in Birán, a hamlet without glory or potable water, in Oriente province, in 1926. It was a year, by the way, in which a devastating hurricane razed the island. What an omen. His father was a tall and corpulent Galician named Angel Castro, who came to Cuba at the end of the 19th century as a Spanish army recruit. He was just one of the more than 250,000 soldiers sent by Spain to Cuba in a stubborn attempt to block the island's bid for independence. He was a poor and frightened fellow, one of those who couldn't afford to pay the 300-peseta fee to be released from military service — an innocent victim of the colonizers.

Angel Castro lost the war, but he won a new homeland. After being repatriated to Spain, he managed to find his way back to the island. His Galician village, cold and rainy, was no longer enough for him. He had discovered a promising horizon and a society in the midst of expansion that opened itself to the adventures of political freedom. He was a hard-working man, as were many of his compatriots, and he immediately realized that the young republic — inaugurated in 1902 — provided the perfect terrain for an industrious man. The price of the fertile Cuban land was very low and there were plenty of opportunities for work. So much so that in a few years, as the price of sugar went up, during World War I, he was able to make the transition from laborer to supervisor and then to proprietor. That would have been out of the question in his native Lugo, a village of church steeples and little farm-steads, quickly and forever forgotten.

The young immigrant married, in his first nuptials (what an archaic phrase that is), a teacher named María Luisa Argote, and with her, he had two children: Lidia and Pedro Emilio. This good lady fell ill and died young; she was replaced by a humble girl known for her fervent Catholicism and good heart. She was named Lina Ruz and had come to the Castro home as a housekeeper. From that new union came seven children: Ramón, Angelita, Fidel, Juana, Emma, Raúl and Agustina. As time passed, the factious, fractured politics that have divided Cuban society would also affect the brothers and sisters. Lidia was a *fidelista* all her life. Pedro Emilio, a lawyer and an extravagant poet — now deceased — was imprisoned for his inconvenient political opinions. Ramón and Raúl have always been devoted followers of the family hero. Angelita seems to be more dedicated to small commercial activities than to the national battlefield. Juanita has been exiled since the early 1960s, and has been unwavering and energetic in denouncing the country's condition. Emma lives in Mexico, discretely horrified by the disasters generated by her brother. Agustina, Catholic and sentimental, survives in Havana, amiable and without privileges, while she prays day and night on behalf of her unfortunate compatriots.

The same divide persists among their descendants, including those of the "maximum leader" of the revolution. There are pro-*fidelistas* and anti-*fidelistas*. Some live in internal exile; some secretly leave and return to the island, and others have managed to become expatriates. The only truly democratic thing about Cuba is precisely that: families are free to become deeply divided. It's shocking to hear one of Castro's daughters, a son, a granddaughter, a nephew or an in-law say that their relative is the person who has done them the most harm — as people and as Cubans. At moments like those, political hatred reaches a furious human dimension that can only be witnessed in little domestic hells.

From this peculiar start, three facts stand out. The first has to do with what today we would call ethnic origin. Angel Castro was a Galician, and despite the flood of Spanish immigrants who came to the island in the first quarter of the 20th century, or perhaps because of it, the native Cubans (*criollos*) were not very hospitable to the new arrivals. Nationalism, even in a moderate form, was beginning to make itself felt, and was expressed in various aggressive ways. One of them was humor. Galicians, even though they were hard workers, were the butt of jokes. They were always portrayed in the local theater, and later on radio and television, as a kind of imbecile whom the *criollos* could easily fool. In addition, the entire structure of the political power — although not the economic — was in the hands of Cubans who had fought in the wars of independence, or who at least had favored autonomy. Those wars were the source of social legitimacy and gave birth to the political lineage. If Fidel Castro planned on being a national hero, he definitely had chosen the wrong family.

The second important point relates to the political ideas that Fidel Castro began to assimilate, from birth. Angel Castro was probably not a man obsessed with ideological matters, and he was not even considered communicative or open — he was, above all, a tireless worker — but as a Spaniard of 1898, and a soldier defeated by the *gringos*, he could not have had a good opinion of the United States. That was the understandable judgment of Spaniards of his generation. Business relations with the Americans were not easy, either. His farm in Birán bordered on vast, Yankee-owned sugar properties, and disputes over property lines were frequent.

Thus from the cradle, in his rustic but prosperous home, Castro began to hear criticism against Washington. While a sizable number of Cubans perceived Americans as allies who had helped wrest control of the island from Spain, the Castros, naturally, saw the Americans as arrogant and powerful adversaries who had sunk Admiral Cervera's fleet in Santiago de Cuba Bay. There, in the heart of the young Castro, an uncomfortable dissonance must have taken root. It would not be easy to resolve these conflicting impressions. At school, he was taught that the Americans had contributed to freeing Cuba from the Spaniards. At home, his father would tell him that the Americans had savagely and illegitimately attacked them with canon.

The third point stems from the rivalry between city and country that permeated the social relations of Cuba. Fidel Castro was not only a Galician peasant. He was a *guajiro*, a hick, a *"paleto,"* as the Spaniards say. He was a country yokel raised in a rural ambiance in one of the most backward regions of Cuba, and the more educated and cosmopolitan *habaneros* [people of Havana] made fun of such images. Castro's home, his first house, despite the good economic position achieved by Don Angel, was not an orderly and elegant residence like those in Miramar or El Vedado. It was a large house without much grace or esthetic distinction, the kind that was available to a Spaniard, industrious and probably intelligent but without any more schooling than his experience as a worker. Fidel Castro's mother, Lina — according to Pardo Llada, one of Castro's biographers — sometimes called them in to dinner by firing a rifle, and the diners rarely sat around a table. A modern psychologist would see all of this as an unstructured home. At best, it was a primitive way of communicating. Anyway, Fidel Castro was never able to escape those backcountry origins of sugar cane and horses. Maybe that explains, for example, his scorn for bourgeois formalities — that hateful suit and tie — or his cold lack of response to the absolute decay of Cuban cities. The impressions of his infancy, that eye with which he began to perceive reality, has kept him from feeling scandalized by the systematic and cruel destruction of Havana. He is not capable of seeing it, much less feeling it. The rubble doesn't bother him. The universe of his infancy was a dusty farm environment. In his childhood, he was sometimes known as a Galician and at other times as a peasant. Those two qualifiers foretold a pejorative streak.

There is no point in going over the first years of Castro's childhood unless we adopt a psychoanalytic outlook, and we are not going to do that, but we can highlight a couple of facts nonetheless. He was a restless and intelligent child. So much so that a letter Fidel wrote, when he was ten years old, to President Roosevelt, is still kept in

White House archives. He tries to trick Roosevelt into giving him a $10 bill because, supposedly, he has never seen one, and in exchange, he promises to show him where there are some iron mines that could be used to make American ships. What a child.

His mother Lina, like all Cuban mothers with at least some education, considered good schooling to be essential. She sent him to Santiago de Cuba, the province's capital, so that priests could give him a good primary education. She did the same with all his brothers and sisters, who attended the best schools in the country, although Ramón, the oldest, preferred to stay on the farm with his father.

After elementary school in Santiago came the Havana experience. While the girls were enrolled at the Ursulines', Fidel, and when his turn came, Raúl, were sent to do their secondary studies at the Belén school, run by Jesuits — one of the most prestigious schools in Cuba, and arguably the best Company of Jesus school in America. Only, in that institution, in addition to getting a good education and learning sound principles and values, the adolescent Fidel received his first political vision of the world, one that confirmed certain judgments that, in a more rudimentary way, he had heard from his father's lips. The Spanish Jesuits who educated him came from the trauma of the Civil War. They were Franco supporters, *franquistas*. They believed in order and authority above all things. They were suspicious of bourgeois democracies and of liberal, Masonic and Jewish influences. They were anti-Communists, naturally, but also anti-American and (as often happened among the Phalangists) they were suspicious of Western humanist values.

Apparently, two Jesuit priests took charge of Fidel's spiritual development. One was Father Armando Llorente, a kind and energetic Spaniard who ran the many outdoor activities — field trips to the countryside, which Fidel enjoyed — and the other was a Cuban, whose last name, by coincidence, was also Castro. Alberto Castro was very intelligent, a Phalangist, extremely eloquent and talkative, with a good mind for theology. He created and led a small clique of outstanding students, which he baptized the *Convivium,* and he recruited the peasant Castro to join. There, for the first time, Fidel heard the name José Antonio, and there he was told that Spain and Ibero-America, gloriously

11

linked in Hispanic heritage and the Catholic tradition, had a univocal destiny. There, in addition, he learned to sing *Cara al Sol (Face to the Sun)*, while he dreamed that Hitler's army would never be defeated by the decadent democracies of Europe. Those were the years of World War II and Fidel, a tall young man, traced on a map the smashing successes of the Nazi tanks. Even back then, the *gringos* were already the bad guys, for him.

The Jesuit education — as is well-known — intends to build character. Sometimes it achieves that goal; sometimes it fails. The imponderable genetics of the student is probably what determines that, or the quality of the teachers who take him under his control, or the family ambiance during the first formative years. Who knows? What is certain is that the Belén school left its imprint on Fidel. He participated, for example, in the debate club, and he learned the art of organizing and delivering speeches. He participated in various sports — baseball, basketball, track and field — without having an excess of natural coordination, according to Roberto Suárez, his classmate and team-mate. He learned to overcome this limitation with his height, his strength and his tenacity, this last being a trait he cultivated until he incorporated it into the very core of his personality. He learned to overcome any complex about his Galician origins, and above all, about being a peasant in a school where most of his classmates came from the most refined homes of well-to-do natives; he displayed an early and vigorous urge to establish his leadership. He wanted to rule — and it showed. He wanted to be the boss in every activity he joined. His self-esteem was enormous. It also was evident that he brought from the countryside the *machista* values of Cuban rural society: the boastfulness, the readiness for a fist-fight, the personal bravado. In that period he was bitten by the political bug, and like many adolescents, he began to think that someday he would be president of the republic. He even mentioned it to one of his classmates.

The Jesuit teachings had less success in the spiritual realm. Castro himself has reported, with a certain malice, that the temptations of the flesh — very strong in tropical adolescence, when the hormones surge uncontrollably — kept him from taking too seriously the religious scope of his Jesuit education. Chastity and abstinence were too high a price to pay for achieving perfection. Catholicism as a religion, with its eternal punishments and its gentle heaven, were not convenient for him. To him, the Sacred History was neither history nor sacred. The faith of his infancy slipped away as he bumped up against reason and his instincts. The Jesuits also failed at turning him into an intellectual, that is, someone who approaches reality from the world of ideas. He was, fundamentally, a man of action. A dynamo. A builder and an executor of projects. He read, he was intelligent, of course; he was not a bad student, and he accumulated information with his excellent memory, but according to his classmates, he was closer to St. Ignacio than to St. Thomas.

Gangsters and Revolutionaries

When Fidel finished high school and entered Law School at the University of Havana, he wanted to be first, whatever the price. World War II had just ended and the Allies had triumphed. Phalangism and the Jesuit priests were relegated to an anecdotal past that no longer impressed him. Castro's objective was no longer sports, but the leadership of the Federación Estudiantil Universitaria (University Students Federation, FEU), an organization that had a tremendous influence in Cuban political life since the 1930s, when it became the key factor in toppling the dictator, Gerardo Machado. Eighty percent of the young politicians who were leading the nation had come from the FEU, but that influence was two-way: as the university had been introduced into public life, politics had also been introduced into the university, and even into the official high schools. There was corruption, violence, and armed chieftains; the reign of the revolutionary bully prevailed. It was the university of the gangsters — the student leaders walked around with guns at their waist — and to rise to the top, it was essential to take refuge within some of the most powerful and feared factions.

To complicate things further, in that tumultuous university of the 1940s — arising from the insurrection against Machado in the 1930s — two other sources of violence converged: the veterans of the Spanish Civil War, in which more than 1,000 Cubans had fought (nearly all of them in the Communist ranks of the international brigades), and the veterans of World War II. Thus, there were heroes and villains to suit anyone's taste, and all of them had their own affiliate groups inside the university. Fidel, for example, immediately tried to cozy up to the Movimiento Socialista Revolucionario (Socialist Revolutionary Movement, MSR), which was headed by a lawyer named Rolando Masferrer and by an engineering student, Manolo Castro. Masferrer was an ex-Communist and a veteran of the Spanish Civil War, where he was wounded in battle; Manolo Castro was president of the FEU and coincidentally was a friend of Ernest Hemingway. Fidel's aim, at the outset of his career (December 1946), was to get Manolo Castro — to whom he was not related — to support him in becoming the leader of the Law School. To gain his sympathy he did something really monstrous: he tried to assassinate Leonel Gómez, a student leader in high schools who was said to be an enemy of Manolo Castro. Instead, in the fracas, he wounded another student (according to Enrique Tous, a classmate of Fidel's at Belen and at the university).

It's worthwhile to pause over this bloody anecdote. Fidel was not a child of 13 or 14 years of age, but a young man of 20. He was studying law and he had come from a religious school where, for a long time, they had endeavored to inculcate in him compassion and love of others. Leonel Gómez was not his personal enemy. They hardly knew each other. Castro could not have hated him, and of course, he did not attempt to assassinate him in a fit of fury. It was a premeditated act, cold, bold, and conceived in order to obtain the favors of a person he felt it was convenient to serve, even at the price of committing murder. But he failed twice: Leonel Gómez did not die, and Manolo Castro was not grateful of the "favor." On the contrary, he sent a rude message via José de Jesús Ginjaume: "Tell this guy that I'm not going to support a shithead for president of the law school." Fidel never forgave him.

Unable to find refuge in Masferrer's and Manolo Castro's MSR, Fidel turned to another gang, Ginjuame's own, known as Unión Insurrecional Revolucionaria (Insurrectional Revolutionary Union, UIR). This group was anti-Communist and anarchistic; its first leader was a parachutist in World War II, Emilio Tro, a man of almost suicidal temerity, who sympathized with Fidel and forgave him — since Leonel Gómez was also a UIR militant. Once inside the UIR, Castro, gun tucked into his belt, gained a reputation as a quick shot and a violent man. But he still didn't have a coherent political history. He was only a big-talking shoot-'em-up type without an appreciable personal legend.

All of a sudden, a golden opportunity emerged: Masferrer and Manolo Castro, with the assistance of half the government, were preparing an invasion to finish off the Dominican dictator, Leónidas Trujillo. They were training on a northeastern islet off Cuba, Cayo Confite. The leader was the storyteller Juan Bosch, exiled in Cuba and president of the Dominican Revolutionary Party. He was backed by the Venezuelan Rómulo Betancourt, the Guatemalan Juan José Arévalos, the Costa Rican José Figueres — a kind of international revolution of the Caribbean. (Indeed, Castroism did not invent the internationalist concept later on; Castro learned it in his years as a subaltern). Fidel visited Bosch and asked him to allow him to participate. He sent a peace message to Masferrer and Manolo Castro. He got them to promise not to kill him. "Let him come," Masferrer agrees. "In these matters, you can always use more balls."

They were not needed. The failed episode lasted just a few weeks. The government of President Harry Truman, already embarked on the beginnings of the Cold War, asked his colleague in Havana to disband the camp and send the expeditionaries home. The Caribbean oven was not right for that kind of conflicts. The enemy was Moscow, not the local dictators. So Fidel lost the opportunity to craft a revolutionary biography that would match his youthful warring zeal. However, he did not allow himself to be trapped with the rest of the troops. When the warship that brought them home (under detention) came close to shore, he jumped overboard and swam. Legend would have it that it was a rebellious gesture to avoid capture. The truth was otherwise: he was afraid that, the invasion aborted, his enemies Manolo Castro and Rolando Masferrer would take advantage of the confusion to eliminate him. His protector in the UIR, Emilio Tro, had already been assassinated by gunmen associated with the MSR on September 15, 1947, precisely when Fidel was training in Cayo Confite. He could well have become the next dead gangster.

But he didn't; Manolo Castro did. On February 22, 1948, on a street in Old Havana, a group of UIR gunmen riddled Manolo with bullets and killed him. The press immediately pointed to Fidel Castro. Their rivalry was well known. And it was true, in addition, that Fidel Castro had schemed with the UIR to execute Manolo Castro and Rolando Masferrer — whom they did try to assassinate, with several shots that missed. But the historical truth is that Fidel didn't kill Manolo. When they telephoned to ask him to participate in the attempt, they could not reach him. When they went to pick him up, they didn't find him. If he had any share in the responsibility, it was in an intellectual capacity: he instigated the crime, but he did not commit it. Fidel could prove his alibi, without much difficulty; although Hemingway, for one, didn't believe it. He wrote a short story, *The Shot*, about his dead friend, basing the character of the assassin on Fidel Castro. That would not be the only time young Fidel would serve as the model for a turbulent literary figure: in the same period, the novelist Rómulo Gallegos, exiled in Cuba, selected Castro as the inspiration for his profile of one of the gangsters in *Una brizna de paja en el viento (A bit of straw in the wind)*.

In less than eight weeks, young Fidel Castro was in the newspapers again, this time in the middle of a monumental revolt. On April 9, 1948, *el Botogazo* took place. The capital of Colombia was shaken by fires, crimes and violent popular uprisings as a consequence of the assassination of the leader, Jorge Eliecer Gaitán, a popular and charismatic politician of the Colombian Liberal Party. What was Fidel Castro doing on that remote stage of death and isolation? He had attended a student congress, as part of a Cuban delegation secretly financed by Juan Domingo Perón. The delegation was led by the FEU president, Enrique Ovares, then a leftist leader close to the Communists — later a political prisoner of Castroism. Also participating in the delegation were Alfredo Guevara, a Communist and president of the School of Philosophy, the first Marxist who instructed Fidel in the ABCs of the doctrine, and Rafael del Pino, another violent student and a friend of Fidel; many years later, he would end up committing suicide in a Cuban prison after suffering all kinds of mistreatment by guards in the service of his former colleague.

The reasons why Perón financed that congress of radical students can be traced to his confrontation with the United States. At the time of Gaitán's assassination, the Organization of American States (OAS) was re-founded in Bogota under Washington's anti-Communist orientation, and the Argentine president, a champion of the "third way", wanted to balance the American right with a good revolutionary demonstration of leftist/nationalist inspiration. No one thought that anything as dramatic as the assassination of the principal leader of the opposition could occur, and much less that — as a result of that act — a fierce civil war would erupt that would consume thousands of lives and millions of dollars in destroyed property. Fidel Castro, curiously, had asked Ovares to be included among those invited on the trip so as to cool off in the aftermath of Manolo Castro's death. His purpose, in this case, was to avoid violence and try to project himself as a university leader into the political arena, because he had not been able to obtain the support of his law school colleagues during the student elections.

But Castro had a special affinity for conflicts. Thus, shortly before Gaitán was to have greeted the delegation of Cuban students, an assassin shot him dead, and as soon as the news was made known, disturbances erupted. It is here that Fidel experienced his revolutionary baptism, and it is interesting to note what this young man of 22 years of age did: instead of staying in his hotel (given that he did not know his way around the city), or getting in touch with his country's embassy, he joined the popular insurrection, walked into a police station and urged the troops to join in the uprising. The fact that he was a total stranger or that he knew nothing about the Colombian situation did not hold him back in the least. He found himself in the eye of the hurricane, and instead of seeking refuge, he took the opportunity to call for a revolution. Naturally, no one paid him any heed. Shortly after, he was arrested; but the Cuban authorities, more preoccupied with Ovares — the real student leader of the group — negotiated the evacuation of the university students, and managed to get them out of the country on livestock transport airplane. Fidel returned to Cuba in a state of great excitement. He had smelled Revolution, up close. He had seen houses and cars on fire; he had watched shootings and executions. And all of this stirred his adrenaline. The man of action inside of him was giddy with the strongest and most gratifying emotions he had ever experienced.

It was not only a physical sensation. Like many young people of his generation, at the age of 22, Fidel was a revolutionary. That is the key word. He already had a vaguely Marxist perception of society. Not that he had read *Das Capital* — at that age, very few people had done so — but he thought capitalism was an exploitative system, the cause of people's poverty; and he felt profoundly anti-imperialist, given that the malevolent Yankee imperialism embodied the ills of the economic system and the colonial arrogance imposed by its canons. He was thus more than an aggressive young man armed with a pistol. He was that, too, but he also saw himself as a crusader for a cause that would redeem humanity. He was ready to shoot his way clear to power and political fame, in order to lay the foundations of a better world, a more just world, and of course, a world that would stand up to the despicable Americans.

It was at this moment that Fidel began to come closer to national politics, and he did so by registering in the populist *Partido Ortodoxo*. The Orthodox Party, of a social democratic bent, was led by the beloved senator Eduardo Chibás, who with a broom as his symbol was carrying out energetic campaigns against corruption. Chibás came from a rich and educated family, and he was firmly anti-Communist, but he also proclaimed his anti-imperialist and nationalist stance. In reality he was, as the Communists of the time would say, an honest and reformist bourgeois, but inside the party, especially among the youngest members, there was a radical faction in which Fidel moved with agility; and there, he began to exercise some influence.

Fidel continued, of course, to pursue his career as a lawyer, but without the least academic distinction. His father, who did nothing all his life but work for the good of his children, supported him generously. Fidel was one of the few students who owned a car. He secured passing marks thanks to his phenomenal memory and by virtue of his obvious capacity to organize his thoughts in written and oral form; but he has discarded the idea of becoming a great lawyer. The law is not his passion. It is merely his instrument. In Cuba, the politicians were either lawyers or military men. Fidel never thought of dedicating himself seriously to law. He wanted to get into Congress, but only as a stepping-stone on his unstoppable march to the presidential palace.

At a given moment, he even tried to accelerate the process. The chilling tale reveals much about young Castro's will to seize power. It was 1948 and President Ramón Grau San Martín, in the last year of a government that was as democratic as it was corrupt, agreed to receive a delegation of students who were noisily protesting the high price of transportation. Fidel was in that delegation. There were half a dozen university students waiting in the foyer to see the president, on the third floor of the palace; the room where they are waiting had a balcony. All of a sudden Castro stood up and made a preposterous proposal to his colleagues: "Let's throw Grau off the balcony and proclaim a revolutionary republic; in 1933 the students took power. We should do the same."

"You're nuts, Fidel," his friends replied in a tone of disbelief. At that moment, the door opened and Grau walked in, smiling and conciliatory. Fidel was the first to greet him. The president did not notice anything unusual. He never would have thought that one minute earlier, the one who was shaking his hand had suggested his assassination.

Struggling and always cramming the night before his exams, Fidel got through his law studies. It was now the middle of the century. Two years before, a colleague in the law school who also had vocational and political talents, Rafael Díaz-Balart — later his archenemy — had introduced Fidel to his sister, a beautiful girl named Mirta, a philosophy student. They fell in love and married. Shortly after, they had a son. There is nothing unusual about that, except that old Angel Castro, through Fidel's brother Ramón, continued to support him. Castro had no work experience and was quite incapable of supporting a family. His passion was politics, debating, party intrigue, and *la tertulia* (bull sessions).

After graduation, he tried to work as a lawyer, but he barely could handle procedural law, and besides, he was not interested. Inside the Orthodox Party, however, he was climbing to higher and higher positions. He talked on the radio every time he could, he wrote press articles, he got his name around. He took a courageous step: he publicly separated himself from his gangster past, and chose to do that through a dangerous procedure that again put his name in the headlines: he denounced his former colleagues and his ex-adversaries, in the press. He traveled to New York and for several weeks he toyed with the idea of studying political science at Columbia University. In reality, he did not want to be in Cuba. He was afraid (and with reason) that the political gangsters would kill him. And he wanted, really, to distance himself from that lethal and criminal world. His purpose now was to confirm his serious political profile. Chibás found the gangsters repugnant and Fidel wanted to show him that he had left all that behind. He used every method at his disposal to attack corruption (which he attributed to the government of Carlos Prío, Grau's democratic successor). Now he was every bit the lawyer who intended to reach the House of Representatives. The elections were to take place in 1952. Fidel fought to become a candidate. Chibás didn't accept him within his intimate circle, but he allows him to participate.

On August 5, 1951 something strange happened. Chibás ended his Sunday radio program with the most dramatic and spectacular gesture — he shot himself in the stomach, right in front of the microphones. He wanted to shake the Cubans' conscience. It was — this is what he called it — the "last time he was knocking." Why such an attempt to commit suicide? He was upset that he had not been able to prove the accusations of corruption he had levied against a Prío minister; he had lost credibility and felt ridiculous. Was he trying to inspire pity? Maybe. Did he really want to kill himself? It's not clear. A shot in the heart or in the head would have left no doubt. In the stomach, it was grave but not necessarily mortal. Nevertheless, it ended up being so. Poor treatment ended up killing him.

The agony lasted a few days. The country was in upheaval. The popularity of the government was nonexistent. Chibás's burial was the largest such ceremony in the history of Cuba. Even so, Fidel's instinct for power was not dimmed. In the hospital, while the chiefs of the Orthodox Party were planning the route of the funerary procession, the aphonic and somewhat nasal voice of the young congressional candidate was heard to say: "Why don't we draw the crowds toward the palace and stage a coup d'etat against Prío with the dead man?" No one paid any attention to such an indelicate proposition, coming at such an inopportune moment.

Chibás was buried. The Orthodox Party elected Roberto Agramonte, a prestigious sociologist, as his substitute, and it looked as though the country was holding to a democratic course through the upheavals of a nervous society that had never know political tranquility. The elections were to take place in the summer of 1952 and Fidel had a good chance of being elected to Congress. But such was not to be. Fulgencio Batista, the former sergeant turned general, the strongman of Cuba between 1933 and 1940 and legitimate president from 1940 to 1944, facing the impossibility of regaining power through electoral means — opinion polls gave him barely 10 percent of the votes — staged a preemptive coup on March 10, 1952, that sent the government fleeing and began a dictatorship of seven years.

The day of the military mutiny, two colossal changes took place that had transcendental significance for Cuba. Batista once again became a dictator; and Fidel Castro stopped acting as a politician moving within the democratic institutions and turned himself into an armed revolutionary.

In some strange way, hearing that Batista had taken over the garrisons, what came to Castro's mind was a powerful memory of *el Bogotazo*, the Colombian uprising. He smelled the gunpowder. . . He accused Batista before the tribunals of violating the Constitution of the Republic, and he began to plan the resistance. It was time for the Revolution. He felt strangely happy. In truth, he was a revolutionary, not a politician.

II

SETTING THE SCENE

Naturally, the figure of Fidel Castro could only have come to life in a specific country and under concrete circumstances. The world-view acquired by Castro in his formative years was only possible in Cuba. And if one does not grasp the fundamentals of that story, even vaguely, then one's understanding of later events on that island will always be flawed — especially given that Castro explains his political doings not as an exceptional phenomenon linked to his own era, but as a logical continuity of a long historical process rooted in events that occurred at the beginning of the 19th century, when Adams, Jefferson and Monroe were speculating on how they might take over Cuba, to incorporate it into the American Union. Let's try to picture that stunning flight of fantasy.

Columbus called Cuba "the most beautiful land human eyes have ever seen." That may have been an overstatement. The Genoese displayed a certain tendency to hyperbole; he said much the same about Puerto Rico and the shores of Venezuela. His diary is a kind of public relations manual — and justifiably so. The Admiral was determined to convince the Spanish King and Queen — his commercial partners, in a way — of the benefits of his discoveries. And he was not so far off the mark.

Cuba is, indeed, a beautiful island of palm trees, sunshine and pleasant beaches. In fact, maybe we should not even call it an island, but an archipelago. Everything is confusing and ambiguous in that country. Sometimes, the news programs make it sound as though it were little more than some geological secretion that has surfaced in the Caribbean. And that's not accurate. The territory is not as small as it seems. It has, all told, an area of 68,750 square miles, and it is 750 miles long. If one end of the island were situated at Lisbon, Portugal, the other end would reach Marseilles, in France. It is approximately as long as Austria and Switzerland combined. Belgium, the Netherlands and Denmark would fit within its borders, and its perimeter is not very different from that of the neighboring state of Florida. Its population, including exiles, boat people and other political refugees, is 13 million (11 million struggling along in their native land and 2 million who, overwhelmed by nostalgia, drift across the planet — although the majority has managed to settle in the United States).

The history of Cuba differs from the rest of Latin America's — at least, a good portion of it — in several crucial ways. There was no complex indigenous civilization in place, like the Mesoamericans or the Andeans. The Indians who were found by the Spaniards belonged to the vast family of the Arawaks, poor and underdeveloped, and had no significant urban settlements nor dense social structures. They added a few words to the Spanish language — *huracán* (hurricane), *canoa* (canoe), *bohío* (a typical Cuban peasant house built of palm leaves) and a couple of others — and their only contribution to the world seems to have been tobacco and the custom of rolling up the leaves, placing them under their noses, and lighting them to inhale the smoke. They supposedly did this to provoke certain altered mental states associated with religious experiences. In any event, they were promptly exterminated by mistreatment and by diseases brought by the Europeans, for which the Indians had no natural defense. Or they were assimilated, by incontinent young invaders who (for the most part) had left their women behind in the Old World. Two hundred children are attributed to just one of them, Vasco Porcallo, a cruel man with raging hormones who conceived with dozens of frightened and obedient Indian women.

The island, which soon was deprived of its Indian population, also very soon was left without gold and other metals that occurred in miniscule quantities compared to the incredible mines of Mexico and the Andean Altiplano. Thus, Cuba was soon consigned to a specific and limited role: it became a huge base of operations from which expeditions were launched into the continent. It served as a pit stop and a mess hall; a maritime port. And it also became, gradually, a sugar plantation, as the unusual custom of sweetening the food spread throughout Europe and the British colonies in the Western Hemisphere.

Growing and processing sugar cane was one of the most arduous activities in the agricultural world, and the Spaniards, without the Indians to do the hard work, resorted to black slaves from Africa. Cuba then became the tragic destination of hundreds of thousands of captive blacks who arrived on the island only to be crushed as severely as the sugar cane they harvested in 20-hour days of forced labor. The numbers are shocking. Over the duration of slavery, from the early 16th century to the late 19th century, one million blacks were ground into the earth by Cuban society. The "useful" life — the only one they had — of these sugar cane slaves, was calculated with terrifying cold-heartedness by the landowners of the time at little more than five years.

Its privileged geography — it was called the "Key to the Gulf" since the times of Phillip II — conferred strategic importance on Cuba; it had other consequences as well. Cuba was both shipyard and warehouse, giving life simultaneously to trade and to smuggling, and a few important urban centers were built. But there were disadvantages as well: sailing in the wake of the Spanish fleet that docked in Havana or Santiago, in between trips to and from the Americas, were dangerous pirates, corsairs and ships from enemy nations. This led Spain to fortify the island, building large fortresses to house thousands of soldiers.

Bureaucracy grew and the Spanish-based society began to generate titles and dignified ranks to administer it. Thirteen great dukes, marquises and other noblemen roamed throughout the country in luxurious carriages. Impressive palaces blossomed. Trains were used in Cuba even earlier than in Spain — the line from Havana to Bejucal was inaugurated in 1837. The church used its enormous influence in a positive way — it created educational institutions and, among them, the first university. A priest, Félix Varela, became the most important intellectual source of the first independent natives. The colony quickly became very rich. A native (*Criollo*) bourgeoisie emerged as a spin-off of the Spanish bourgeoisie, but since they could not hold state positions they gravitated toward the plantations and the liberal professions, where they became richer and wiser.

By the late 18th century, Cuba's history was nothing but an eccentric fragment of that of Spain. Yet it cannot be properly understood unless we know what occurred in Spain. A few years later, with sweet rhythm, a Havana woman would affirm that "Havana is Cádiz with more black children/ Cádiz is Havana with more spice." An accurate synthesis. The truth is that the Cubans strongly resemble the liberal Spaniards. They read the same books, and they see and judge the world in a similar fashion. Like them, they accept the French influence, favoring free trade and believing, like them, that knowledge can be attained by means of reason.

In 1762, Havana was captured by the British. A few months later, the island's sovereignty was returned to the Spanish King in exchange for other Spanish possessions in North America. During those months of British occupation, Cuba opened to international trade and a bright period of economic expansion began which, with its ups and downs, lasted one long century. It was perhaps the golden century of Cuba's history, and not only due to the British drive for openness. The enlightened despotism of Charles III had a major effect, as did the savvy advice of men like Floridablanca and Jovellanos.

Natives, Liberals and Annexationists

In the early 19th century, Napoleon invaded Spain, and shortly thereafter, wars for independence broke out throughout the Americas. The Cubans were not yet psychologically ready to join in such an adventure. Very few were demanding separation from Spain, and the Spanish authorities responded to them with great severity. The natives (*criollos*) were still very much Spaniard. Rather than secession, the majority were asking for self-government, lower taxes and free trade. They wanted freedom, but not independence — they feared it. Plus, they had both practical and self-interested reasons: they were afraid that independence would prompt a revolt by the black slaves. Acts of rebellion among the slaves already had been repressed with fire and blood. The native landowners had seen what happened to their neighbors in Haiti and in Santo Domingo. In fact, they had benefited from it, because thousands of white tenant farmers from those places had been forced to flee to Cuban territory, and even those who had not been able to save their fortunes in cash had brought valuable technical know-how, for example, in coffee production.

As the 19th century progressed, tensions increased between the natives (who had become increasingly educated and powerful) and the government of the metropolis. Ferdinand VII, who would have nothing to do with the topics of constitution and freedom in Spain, had no intention of treating the Cubans any differently. Spain had already lost almost all its empire in the Americas and was determined to save the *pearl of the Antilles, the ever-faithful island of Cuba.*

The colony was declared "under siege." The captain-generals were nearly omnipotent. Those who happened to be benevolent and enlightened treated the Cubans accordingly; those who were authoritarian and cruel responded according to their instincts. Among them all, however, the idea prevailed that it was dangerous to loosen their grip. The veterans of the Continent, those defeated by Bolívar and San Martín (many of whom were sent to Cuba), were convinced that Spain's power had begun to break down when the authorities slackened their control. "A strong hand" was the advice they gave Madrid: "the stick and the whip" was the most common expression.

Under those circumstances, many natives, representing what could then be called *la cubanidad* (Cuban identity), began to look in another direction: the flamboyant United States, whose independence epic they had not only admired, but had fostered with money and soldiers. In fact, economic relations with the United States were greater than with Spain. Some Cubans preferred to send their children to schools in Philadelphia or Boston rather than in Madrid; Charles IV tried to prevent that, by royal decree. The American development was impressive. Schools, trains and judges arrived with the Americans. They represented modernity, progress.

But Cubans had seen something more prodigious still — the quickness and the agility with which the young nation had swallowed up French Louisiana and Spanish Florida. They had seen it again in Texas and in the northern half of Mexico. The United States, endowed with a powerful metabolism, seemed to have no difficulty in absorbing neighbor populations which it immediately incorporated into its overwhelming development. And if the native white Cubans yearned for freedom — without giving up the slavery of blacks, of course — and if they had no plans to create an independent state, would it not be more reasonable to annex themselves to the emerging young power than to go on being part of a decadent empire?

Besides, how could anyone even think of independence when the Latin American outlook at that moment, plagued by tyrants and civil wars, confirmed that independence was like "plowing in the sea" as Bolívar had said? It was obvious what needed to be done — and so, the annexationist movement was born. Cuba emerged as a nation in search of another more hospitable state to which it could incorporate. And that was not even a uniquely Cuban phenomenon. Similar movements also occurred (and still occur) in all the islands and other territories of the Caribbean basin. The Yucatecs and the Dominicans asked to be annexed to the United States. In fact, some decades later, during the confusion of the First Spanish Republic, even the leaders of the Cartagena revolt in Murcia sent a telegram to Washington asking to be incorporated into the star-spangled banner. Everyone in the State Department had to run to a world map to find out where the damned Cartagena canton was located.

In the mid-19th century, the first armed struggles emerged on Cuban territory. The United States had just snatched away from Mexico half of that country's northern territory, to the applause of the progressives. The imperial spasm of "Manifest Destiny" had many followers back then. Marx, for instance, considered it good news for the proletariat.

The annexationist Cubans fomented the first expeditions against Spain. They were launched from U.S. territory under the command of the Venezuelan General Narciso López, a former officer of the Spanish army. His troops, to some extent, were made up of veterans of the Mexican War, and the first cries of *"Viva Cuba libre"* were spoken with English and Hungarian accents. To them, "free" was not equal to "independent". The people remained indifferent. The expeditionaries were foreigners without roots in the country and without any skills at rallying support. The Spanish troops, including many Cubans, crushed the invaders; the survivors were executed at dawn. Rather than patriots in the conventional sense, they fitted the definition of those then known as *filibusters*. The American William Walker, an invader invited in by the Nicaraguans, was the most famous *filibuster*. His charging army was formed by 200 Cuban exiles commanded by General Domingo Goicuría, an annexationist filibuster, and a proven Cuban patriot. Those were times of exceptional adventures and strange ideological combinations.

A decade later, the Cubans' perception of the United States changed. Between 1861 and 1865 the U.S. Civil War took place, and Lincoln ended slavery. On the island, everybody had known that the end of that monstrous institution was only a matter of time; the only questions were how and when — and how much the slave owners would be compensated. In the U.S., hurt by these internal conflicts, the imperial vocation waned. The Mexicans then considered Washington an ally against the French-Spanish invasion that attempted to crown Maximiliano, an Austrian nobleman. The annexationist movement weakened and the autonomists gained strength. The Cuban liberals and their Spanish comrades tried to come to terms. The Cuban natives wanted freedom and self-government. They wanted to be heard in the Spanish Parliament. They wanted to copy the Canadian model. The Spaniards based in Cuba, the fundamentalists, viewed every concession made as a dangerous step toward independence. Spain feared losing Cuba. It was one of the richest territories on the planet. It had plenty of poets, novelists, playwrights, scholars — even one or two wise researchers. The society had generated a sufficient surplus to support a culture of a certain depth and richness. With rents paid by Cuba, the Spaniards financed the Carlist War and other Spanish excesses. The economic ties between Madrid and Havana were very strong. A few Spanish fortunes were minted in Cuba. Many Spanish politicians and members of the military sojourned in the colony simply to get rich — stealing, while abroad, seemed less of an indignity when at home. The island was prosperous and inclined toward modernity. The best European singers and artists performed at the luxurious Tacón Theater in Havana. In that same location, an ingenious Catalonian tested the first telephone in history. But he neither patented it nor pursued further research.

Liberals and Independentistas

In 1868, both the war in Cuba and the revolution in Madrid began, just a few days apart. On the island, the insurrection leader was a lawyer from the city of Bayamo (Oriente province), named Carlos Manuel de Céspedes, owner of a small sugar mill. The two events were clearly related, but the leaders on both sides of the Atlantic Ocean could not reach an agreement. The conflict known as the Ten-Year War began.

Two attitudes prevailed among the insurgents — some, who favored independence, wished to break their ties with Spain and found a republic; others, who favored annexation, wished to make Cuba a state in the American Union. Gen. Ignacio Agramonte, the most visible figure among the *mambises* (as the rebels were known in the early war years), took to the jungle with the American flag sewn to his jacket. The Constitution that they immediately sat down to write was inspired by that of the United States. In the beginning, the issue of freeing the slaves didn't even come up as a salient point. Yet, as the conflict grew, the pro-independence and abolitionist tendencies were strengthened. The blacks were liberated and many joined the rebels. Many others joined the natives who did not want independence, and they fought on the side of Spain. The colonials even had a black general from Santo Domingo. It was a cruel and devastating war, governed by an excruciating political paradox: it was fought between liberal elites on both sides of the confrontation.

In 1878, exhausted, the adversaries signed the peace treaty at a place named Zanjón. The terms were honorable and there was probably no other way out. Some *mambises*, led by Antonio Maceo, tried to go on fighting but, several weeks later, they had to surrender. The Cubans could not win. They made huge sacrifices and staged heroic events, but internal dissent and the fierce resistance from the Spanish army brought about the final outcome. The dead could be counted by the tens of thousands and the country lost a large measure of its resources, especially in the eastern provinces.

The war, however, proved three fundamental points. It contributed to forging the Cuban nationality, eliminating the annexationist option from the political outlook; it integrated the blacks under that nationality; and it created a cast of heroes, led by the Dominican Máximo Gómez and the mulatto General Antonio Maceo, whose memory and example would influence the Cuban society for decades — from a moral standpoint, perhaps until the present day.

This was in the 1880s. While annexation to the United States had ceased to appear desirable, and the military achievement of independence did not seem plausible, the concept of Cuban-ness, much strengthened, would turn to another channel of expression that already had been present in the 1860s: autonomy.

Many who favored independence switched to favor autonomy. In today's world they would be called *possibilistics*. The autonomy movement was the greatest level of independence that realistically could be envisioned, given the circumstances. Those who favored autonomy registered in a liberal party that pursued, again, liberties and self-government, and insisted in proposing, as model, Canada's successful example. They would not have to break the ties with Spain nor interrupt trade. All they had to do was to cement those ties in mutual consent and in democratic procedures. In Spain, as in Cuba, such a reasonable proposal began to pick up a response.

But along with the support came the usual protests. To many Spaniards, and to some natives, Cuba was more than a part of Spain, it was a property of Spain. It was something they had discovered and civilized, and therefore it belonged to them as a house belongs to the person who builds it. There was, thus, no political space open for the Cubans to conduct their own affairs.

This unfair situation gave way to a new impulse toward independence. Now its architect was a young lawyer, poet and journalist, a remarkable speaker who mastered a nervous and complicated prose style, that was both classical and modern. José Martí, the offspring of Spanish parents, was born in Havana in 1853. Except for a brief parenthesis, he lived all his adult life in exile, mostly in the United States(a nation he admired profoundly and, at the same time, feared for its appetite for continental dominance. Liberal and romantic, Garibaldian,

31

Martí wanted to found an independent, democratic and pluralistic republic, conceived within the Jeffersonian formula of numerous agricultural owners. He rejected disorder and appreciated businessmen who were entrepreneurial and successful. Toward this goal — that of organizing the new and final war of independence — he founded in the early 1890s the Cuban Revolutionary Party, in New York, Tampa and Key West. He summoned the veterans of the previous struggle and the younger generations (whom he dubbed the "New Pines"), to launch together the final attack against Spain, although always making clear that his pronounced nationalism was neither exclusive nor anti-Spanish.

The results of Martí's endeavors could be considered mixed. He managed to persuade the old heroes to reach an agreement among themselves — something short of a miracle — and organized the clandestine insurgence within Cuba. But the first crucial expeditions were intercepted by the U.S. Navy under the Neutrality Act, and large quantities of weapons were lost. Even under such circumstances, overwhelmed by the feeling of abandonment and failure, he landed in Cuba with a small group of followers, in a small boat, in an area where the insurrection was already taking place. He was killed in the first battle in which he took part. However, he had left behind, in exile, a kind of active rearguard — an effective group that favored independence and was capable of carrying out two difficult tasks: raising funds to provide the rebels (through numerous clandestine expeditions) with new troops, weapons and ammunition, while keeping alive a sort of political lobby, tough and talented in intrigue, intended to destroy Spain's image and obtain from Washington the status of legitimate "belligerent," in accordance with international law.

The war was extremely intense and swiftly extended throughout the island. In an effort to crush the rebellion, Spain resorted to the harshest officer among its military. A puny, frail general, though full of spit and vinegar, Valeriano Weyler had served as a military attaché in Washington during the Civil War and later served in the Ten-Year War in Cuba. He had learned that the tactics of terror and scorched earth were most effective in this type of irregular conflict, in which the population supported the enemy. He therefore embarked on a devastating military campaign. Although his adversaries were far from being disadvantaged, he had some initially successes and his troops managed to kill the legendary General Antonio Maceo in combat.

Yet the news of his ruthlessness, selectively picked up by the tabloid press, and the horrific photos of the concentration camps where he confined entire peasant populations, horrified American society. People started to call for intervention, to stop the carnage. Some of those voices were genuinely moved by compassion; others masked a certain inclination to annexation. The *jingoists*, ultra-nationalists, convinced that they would fare better under the United States than under Spain, had hopes of taking over Cuba — a dream that was shared by others, including the Mexicans, under the eternal dictator Porfirio Díaz, who also coveted the island. In those days, a very persuasive book was circulated among the Americans, claiming that only nations with a global naval fleet, like Great Britain, could prevail. But steam navigation required a network of coal bases to keep those ships sailing. To achieve that objective, what better formula than to snatch up from tired old Spain the remains of its empire in the Caribbean and the Pacific?

By 1898, the war in Cuba had lost its intensity, but it was far from extinguished. In the political arena, however, certain spectacular changes had occurred, indicating exhaustion on the part of the metropolis. Antonio Cánovas del Castillo, the Spanish chancellor, who staunchly resisted giving in one inch to Cuba, had been murdered at the end of the previous year by an Italian anarchist (paid by Cuban rebels). Now, the government in Madrid was headed by the liberal Práxedes Mateo Sagasta, much more flexible and prone to make concessions. The first — received by the Cubans with a sigh of relief and by the fundamentalists with a furious uproar — was to replace Weyler. The new Captain General was instructed to empower the Cuban autonomists, some of whom had to be called from exile, and to begin discussing peace formulas with those favoring independence. To counter this "wimpy" attitude — as it was labeled by the media — the Spanish fundamentalists began a series of protests and acts of vandalism against *Criollo* newspapers and against American interests accused of having sided with the Cuban "traitors." Under the circumstances, the United States proposed to the Spaniards — to appease them and to warn them — that one of its warships visit the port of Havana. In exchange, Spain would send a similar one to New York. The intention was not to aggravate Madrid but to intimidate the pro-Spain intransigents who were obstructing a peaceful outcome of the Cuban conflict.

The boat that arrived in Cuba was a Class B battleship, built at a U.S. shipyard — the first one built with genuinely American technology. They had christened it the *Maine*, after the northeastern state. It wasn't the best ship in the Armada, but it was a good warship, with impressive canons. On the night of February 15th, 1898, it was blown up, killing several officers and some 260 sailors. The captain, who was on board, survived unharmed.

What was the cause of the explosion? There are more than 60 hypotheses, none of them proven. At that moment, Spain gave all sorts of explanations and, citing an investigation conducted by experts, assured that its forces had not been involved, since, according to them, the explosion had originated inside the ship. The U.S. Navy immediately opened its own investigation and reached the opposite conclusion: that the explosion had been caused by a mine or a torpedo, since, according to its naval engineers, it had come from outside the ship. Although Washington did not officially blame Spain, the American public did. The old war cry against Mexico — "Remember the Alamo" — became "Remember the Maine."

Military preparations began. The United States sent an ultimatum to Spain, demanding it give up Cuba. In a last attempt, the U.S. offered Madrid a reward of $300 million if it abandoned the island. Spain, offended, did not accept the offer, among other reasons because in Madrid the superstition prevailed that losing Cuba would bring about the fall of the crown. Since the war seemed unavoidable, the Cuban lobby in favor of independence was quickly mobilized to prevent the United States from taking over Cuba. The U.S. Congress approved a joint resolution stating that Cuba had the right to political freedom and independence. The Cuban insurgents notified the White House of their enthusiastic willingness to collaborate with the invading forces. Shortly afterward the Spanish-American War began.

The Spanish fleets anchored in Santiago de Cuba and in Manila, Philippines, were sunk in what must have been more of a target practice than a maritime combat. The Spanish troops stationed near Santiago fought bravely but futilely. Within a few weeks, the Spanish surrendered and the U.S. army occupied the island. Four centuries of Spanish rule came to an end.

The Cuban autonomists, the only natives who didn't seem pleased with the American presence, were ironically the ones summoned to hand over the keys to the city of Havana. With few exceptions, those favoring independence — as historian Rafael Rojas has indicated — applauded enthusiastically. However, their situation was ambiguous. The Spaniards had lost the war — not to them, but to the Americans. The Liberation Army, as the *mambises* were called, had neither power nor money, and soon was forced to disband. Its political arm, The Cuban Revolutionary Party, met a similar fate. The Government of the Republic in Arms had not been a party to the Paris Treaty, a document establishing the conditions for peace, signed by Washington and Madrid in December 1898. In that meeting, Spain had asked the United States not to grant independence to Cuba, just as it was not granting independence to Puerto Rico. The United States explained that it had a public commitment to Cuba's independence and could not revoke it. The Spaniards feared retaliation and thought their interests would be better protected if Cuba became an American state, instead of an independent republic. A curious irony: at that moment, it was the Spaniards who were advocating annexation.

What the Americans were really concerned about was whether they should take on responsibility for the lives and properties of the Spaniards living in Cuba. They had guaranteed them. Yet, how could they maintain such guarantees if Cuba became a sovereign state, capable of ignoring the U.S.? The solution was to pass a law legitimizing U.S. intervention in Cuba in the case of certain behavior contrary to law and social stability. More than a law, it was a sword of Damocles threatening the Cubans and forcing them into "good" behavior. This law, which the Spaniards celebrated, was requested by President Theodore Roosevelt and presented by Senator Orville Platt as an amendment to a bill containing the U.S. military budget. Afterward, the infamous Platt Amendment had to be incorporated, albeit reluctantly, to the Cuban Constitution approved in 1901. That was the condition imposed by the United States for transferring the sovereignty of the island to the Cubans. It created a protectorate of sorts. What Platt and the American politicians didn't know was that the Cubans would soon utilize the weight of that threat in their own political battles.

The Rebellious Republic

The republic was finally inaugurated on May 20, 1902. The situation in the country was difficult, but very promising. Its population was approximately 1.3 million. Nearly 100,00 exiles had returned, and many had brought capital or had acquired valuable experience abroad. The level of literacy was higher than in Spain proper, and hundreds of teachers were invited to Harvard for training in pedagogy. The nearly four years of U.S. intervention had served to organize the public administration and to establish the foundation for a health system that was, at the time, the most efficient in Hispanic America.

A Cuban scientist, Carlos Finlay, had identified and described the complex way by which yellow fever was transmitted, and American doctors, sacrificing their own lives, had demonstrated the validity of his hypothesis (though without giving the Cuban native the scientific credit he deserved). That terrible disease — the biggest scourge in Cuba — began to disappear.

The President-Elect was a strict, punctilious Protestant, a former colonel of the Ten-Year War (during which his mother had died of malnutrition in a Spanish prison). He was ex-President of the Republic in Arms, a teacher who had owned a school during his long exile, and he succeeded José Martí — who respected him highly — as the head of the Cuban Revolutionary Party. He was the preferred candidate of the United States; his name was Tomás Estrada Palma. He governed honorably despite all the difficult circumstances and despite being surrounded by a power-hungry leadership clique, composed mostly of battle-hardened war veterans with no political nor administrative experience. In 1906, however, Estrada Palma resorted to dubious means in his attempt to get reelected, and this prompted a rebellion of vast proportions — the War of 1906. This, in turn, led to a second intervention by the U.S., which this time was dragged to the island by the two conflicting groups. Teddy Roosevelt — a former fighter in the Cuban war, now President of the United States, more mature, less impulsive, and winner of the Nobel Peace Prize for his mediation in the Russian-Japanese conflict — tried to keep his country out of the Cuban conflict. He failed, and began to realize that the sword of Damocles represented by the Platt Amendment was a two-edged weapon that also hung over the Oval Office at the White House.

The United States pacified the island once more, but this time it used less orthodox methods. The U.S. began buying horses and weapons from the insurgents — an ingenious tactic, indeed, but hardly honorable — and later continued to "appease" them with privileges and sinecures. Martí's only son, a brave youth who had fought in the war under Calixto García, became the aide-de-camp of William Taft, the American Secretary of War who later became president of the United States. This placed the young Martí on a path to becoming a general and, eventually, head of the army. This was not a surprising turn of events, since nearly all those who had been part of the older Martí's inner circle — Estrada Palma and Gonzalo de Quesada — were considered *pro-Yanqui*, perhaps because of their American experience.

Corruption, with its deep and old Iberian roots, flourished again immediately after the second intervention. In the 1909 elections, a very popular general from the last war was elected — José Miguel Gómez. He was one of the *mambises* who had fought in the most battles, once taking part in 17 combats in one day, and was famous for his ability as a military strategist. He had never been defeated; but he was known as "The Shark" for his political trickery. Gómez succeeded Maceo after he died in combat. In a way, he was an heir to the aura of prestige surrounding the Cuban Revolutionary Party founded by Martí, which he and his colleagues claimed as their legacy, since most of the structure of that organization had merged with the Liberal Party founded by "The Shark" in 1905.

In the economic arena, the country was in pretty good shape. Foreign investment continued to flow, generally from the United States, while a continuous stream of Spanish workers — immigrating mostly from Galicia, Asturias and the Canary Islands — found opportunities in

Cuba that they didn't have in Spain. The Cuban government encouraged this influx with the purpose of "whitening" the Cuban society, seeking to maintain a higher proportion of whites than mulattos or blacks. The racial balance had been one of the whites' biggest concerns since the colonial times.

The conservatives accused Gómez's liberal government of corruption — a bipartisan political structure had developed, only tempered by the uncontrollable tendency of the liberals to break up into factions — but the most serious and shameful event of those years was The Little War of the Blacks. It broke out in 1912 when a group of colored veterans first attempted to register a party founded on race. When they were prevented from doing so, they rebelled in arms. The incident was settled after the death of 3,000 blacks, three quarters of whom were removed from their houses and murdered by the army. Three persons gained notoriety for being tough during that unfortunate conflict: General José de Jesús Monteagudo, who led the repression; General Gerardo Machado, Minister of Government, and Arsenio Ortiz, an implacable officer who years later would come to be one of the greatest political criminals in Cuban history. The massacre of blacks was stopped by pressure from the United States, which threatened to intervene once more if the massacre was not ended.

Gómez was succeeded in the presidency by another general, Mario García-Menocal, a conservative leader, an engineer graduated from Cornell University, and a successful sugar magnate. During his first mandate (1913-1917), Menocal saw the economic bonanza prompted by the price of sugar during World War I, which made Cuba the country with the highest index of foreign trade per capita.

This period was known as the *dance of millions*. The national currency was created. Entire neighborhoods were developed, with magnificent palaces and mansions. Electrical power and telephone lines spread throughout the country. Exclusive clubs and night clubs were opened, and the number of large hospitals and schools was multiplied. Havana was remarkably beautified.

But there were also scandals. The conservatives' accusations of corruption against the liberals were now reversed, and with justification. Just as serious as the lack of honesty was the political violence by leaders who, protected by cronyism and government connections, re-sorted to guns or machetes with unprecedented frequency and impu-nity. In 1917, in an almost identical repetition of the episode of 1906, albeit with a different outcome, the conservative Menocal got himself reelected on a vote that his liberal opponents seemed to have won — though it could never be clearly proven.

This prompted the beginning of another dangerous civil war (known as *la Chambelona*, after a very popular song). The United States immediately threatened to intervene. Already immersed in the Euro-pean war, the United States had no intention of allowing its main sugar supplier to crumble into chaos and disorder. U.S. President Wilson supported Menocal and forced the liberals to accept the alleged elec-toral fraud. The fighting engineer, nicknamed *el Mayoral* (the foreman), was able to finish his term and transfer the presidency to the attorney and writer Alfredo Zayas, a smart, unscrupulous character to whom a journalist, without mentioning his name, dedicated a book with a re-vealing title: *The Handbook of a Perfect Scoundrel*.

Brother of the famous General Juan Bruno Zayas, Alfredo was the first president who had not come up from the high-ranking commands of the Liberation Army, although he was identified as an opponent of the Spanish rule. He was probably no more corrupt than Gómez or Menocal. But the Cubans, while they appreciated his intelligence and his good nature, were suspicious of his intrigues and his reputation as a restless political turncoat. He had cut deals with Estrada Palma, Gómez and Menocal, had fought with all three and had changed sides. He wanted to reach power at all cost, and when he did, in 1921, the sugar price plummeted, suddenly cutting in half the nation's budget and drastically constraining the economy. Contrary to Menocal's ex-perience (he only experienced one year of crisis), Zayas's term was four years of economic agony and political dispute with the constant inter-ference of a U.S. ambassador who even attended the cabinet meetings.

During this time, the young intellectuals had begun to forge a pressure group demanding sound and serious government with what we should probably call a leftist perspective. The Russian revolution had taken place and the first communists were showing up — and they were well-organized. The university was under their influence. Julio

Antonio Mella, a young and charismatic Marxist, was very much the subject of conversation. Labor disputes were widespread and so was racketeering.

The society had developed a certain level of xenophobia and wrongly attributed the crisis to the constant arrival of Spaniards. Some 800,000 had crossed the Atlantic Ocean after the establishment of the republic. Proportionately, Cuba was the country that took in the most immigrants in the 20th century. The Cuban leadership had secretly achieved its purpose of a nonviolent ethnical cleansing: 70% of the census was now reported as *white* (although the term did not have the same meaning in Havana as in Berlin). By 1925, the last year of Zayas's term, the Cubans were fed up with politicking, violence, the uncontrollable arrival of foreigners, and corruption. There were armed uprisings. The people attributed the nation's acute economic crisis to the latter two factors. In 1925, Cubans wanted a strong-arm president, honest and nationalistic, one capable of putting an end to all the excesses. The chaos had to stop. They believed they had their man in another liberal, a political heir of José Miguel Gómez, in whose cabinet he had served. His name was Gerardo Machado. He caused the first great catastrophe of the republic.

Gerardo Machado Morales was one of the youngest generals in the war against Spain. He was fundamentally honest in economic affairs, and progressive on labor issues — he reduced work hours and raised the minimum wage — and profoundly nationalist. He formed a very capable cabinet, and was the first president to publicly confront Washington — his predecessor had governed under the tutelage of the U.S. ambassador. He vigorously demanded that the Platt Amendment be abolished, signed laws against immigration, and favored the national industry with protectionist tariffs. He was also made remarkable strides forward in the area of public works. He built the central highway, and the Capitol building — a taller and more luxurious replica of the emblematic palace that houses the U.S. Congress in Washington, added new buildings to the university, increased the number of schools, and improved the lighting and water systems. He believed that government was responsible for building infrastructure.

But he had serious defects. He was authoritarian, gave little consideration to human life, and had no respect for democratic methods. He ordered the murder of journalists and political adversaries. He considered it his destiny to rule over Cubans. He mocked the Constitution in order to prolong his presidential term. He tried to limit Cubans' participation in political life, and created a police force that began using repressive means — copied from those used by Mussolini at that time: beatings, confinement and strong laxatives — against his adversaries. Machado was the first dictator of the republic.

This prompted a violent reaction in the society, but one that was totally different from the uprisings of 1906, 1912 or 1917. This was no longer a revolt. It was revolution. Its leaders proposed fundamental and sweeping changes in the system of government and they claimed to be heirs of the movement headed by Martí in the 19th Century, which was later betrayed by the "generals and doctors." There was talk of class struggle and anti-imperialism. A striking anti-Yankee movement emerged. Paradoxically, a segment of the opposition sympathized with fascist nationalism. Another saw communism as the solution to every ill. The democrats began to lose their influence in the society. In any event, Cuban political life had turned radical, changing the paradigms by which the nation judged its problems.

The insurrection against Machado intensified during 1930 and culminated in 1933. There is no doubt that the American stock market crash of 1929, which caused a massive economic depression, precipitated the end. There were military expeditions against Machado, as well as terrorism and assassination attempts. Heading the revolt were the students and the professional bourgeoisie. Machado struck back fiercely. But he gradually lost the support of Washington, of the powerful economic groups and, above all, of an army that could not even collect its wages because the public administration was bankrupt. Besides, his last year coincided with the first year of Franklin Delano Roosevelt, a president determined to limit U.S. military interventionism. Roosevelt announced the "good neighbor policy," because, among other reasons, after the interventions in Cuba, Haiti, Nicaragua and Dominican Republic, the White House had learned that foreign powers cannot impose order and good government conduct with the barrel of a gun. Every intervention turned into a costly, bloody and counterproductive trap, and to the beginning of another dictatorship.

The United States opted, thus, to replace military force with aggressive diplomacy that would achieve the same objectives — regional control and stability. With that in mind, it sent a brilliant diplomat to Cuba. He was to mediate between the government and the opposition to obtain Machado's resignation, without major trauma, to achieve an organized transfer of authority without public disorder and without jeopardizing U.S. economic interests — this was, in the end, the ultimate objective. The mediator, Sumner Welles, performed his work with dedication and skillful maneuvering, but he failed. Suddenly and unexpectedly, a conspiracy gained strength among the students and the army's low-ranking officers — the *sergeants' revolution* — and forced Machado to flee. He accused the *gringos* of betraying him, and those in the opposition blamed the *gringos* for trying to betray them, too.

At the moment of Machado's downfall, there were talks of taking over sugar-mills and of peasant *soviets*. It was merely anecdotic, but it revealed a certain social and political undertone quite fitting to the times.

The Batistianos, the Autenticos and the Ortodoxos

The revolution of 1933 brought forth the name and image of a "strong man" named Fulgencio Batista. He was a sergeant and a stenograph clerk whom fate placed at the right place at the right time. He was a part-Indian mulatto, smart and intellectually curious, but basically lacking in culture. He was corrupt and had no clear idea of the concept of the State. Yet he was prudent, could keep quiet when convenient, and knew how to choose good collaborators to manage the country. Years later, a desperate biographer, in an effort to embellish his professional life, wrote with admiration that "Batista, at 17, was an expert in the arcane secrets of shorthand."

His limitations, however, were minor compared with his instinct for power and his remarkable ability to appear useful to important people. The local bourgeoisie and Washington saw him as the military officer who could establish order. The United States, with a certain relief, abolished the humiliating Platt Amendment as a good-will gesture toward the new era and to rid itself of the burdensome responsibility. Certain leftist elements perceived Batista as an offspring of popular origins — he considered himself a man of the left — and society, tired of turmoil, grudgingly accepted him, although under his rule there was never a lack of abuse, mistreatment and assassination of opponents.

From the barracks, he virtually ruled, from 1933 to 1940, appointing and removing civil officials at his convenience. During this period, the country gradually stabilized and the economy began to overcome the difficulties of the earlier part of the decade. However, the political game had changed. The generation of the War of Independence had given way to the generation of the 1930s, which in turn brought a different reading of the society's problems. Batista had removed the Criollo military aristocracy that used to control the military command, and now the army had deteriorated, with sergeants and soldiers rising through the ranks in accordance with how close they were to the chief. Batista, a *mestizo* who had worked as a sugar-cane cutter, a railroad laborer and a humble conscript soldier in an army controlled by the ruling class, was, by the time he left power, a very rich and socially "polished" man, though the white high society, relentlessly racist, never accepted him as its own. He was just a "good-looking mulatto" — as they used to call him — who had moved up with the point of his bayonet. The revolution of 1933 was about that, too: those at the lower levels superimposed themselves over the usual suspects.

In 1940, after seven years of a dictatorial interregnum, Fulgencio Batista, in alliance with the communists — he named two of them to his cabinet — ran for president and won, without fraud. He benefited from the Cuban people's exhaustion after Machado and the post-Machado chaos. And he particularly benefited from the fruits of the sound government of his latest straw man, Colonel Laredo Bru. Bru's biggest sin — and, indeed, it's not a small one — was that he had not allowed the landing in Havana of nearly 1,000 Jews fleeing Nazism aboard the boat *St. Louis*, despite the fact that they had visas. He forced them to return to Europe, where almost all were exterminated during the Holocaust. It should be noted, although it is no consolation, that the government of Franklin Delano Roosevelt did not allow them to reach American soil, either.

In that same year of 1940, the Cubans abolished the excellent Constitution of 1901, which had hardly had a chance to be of use, and, under the leadership of an upright and brilliant politician, Carlos Márquez Sterling, wrote a new constitution in more social-democratic terms. The new charter was drafted in accordance with the interventionist mentality of the times, heavy on state control; even the teachers' salaries were established. The following year, the United States went to war against the Axis powers, and the sugar price began to rise. The island's economy gained momentum. Things were looking up; there was a certain amount of euphoria in the air. The opposition, composed principally of the groups that toppled Machado and later opposed Batista, was headed up by a brilliant and cynical medical doctor, a professor of physiology, a well-mannered bachelor who had become the most loved and popular figure in Cuba after serving in the government for a few months after Machado's fall and before being brought down after losing Batista's (and Washington's) favor. His name was Ramón Grau San Martín, and the peasants loved him so much that they placed his image on altars and lighted candles for him. His personal guard, however, was made up of former student leaders who had taken part in the revolts of the 1930s, now grown up and hastily graduated from the unfortunately degraded university.

Curiously, Grau represented to the Cubans something already seen in Machado's election: the hope of an honest head of government, who would not steal and who would establish order in the nation. Yet now, as a consequence of the Revolution of 1933, there were other factors. From Grau and his Cuban Revolutionary Party — to which name the word *auténtico* had been added to indicate that they were indeed the true heirs of Martí and the *mambises* of the 19th century — the Cubans expected social justice. They expected a government that would distribute the wealth in a society distinguished by a remarkable contrast between the haves and the have-nots (called the *desposeídos*). That term, which was then widely used as a synonym for "the poor", masked a complex set of economic relations. The "poor" were not people who had nothing, but people who had been *dispossessed*; those who had lost something that they once had, or those who had not been given that which belonged to them. Grau was expected to govern in favor of the large majorities and to do it in a populist fashion, which suited him to perfection. His campaign promise was that during his government every Cuban would have a 5-peso bill in his pocket — and in those days, the Cuban currency was on a par with the U.S. dollar.

The frustration was enormous. In 1944, after a clever campaign, Grau came to power; the Cubans soon discovered that order and rectitude were not going to characterize his government. Although there was never a shortage of competent and ethical persons, among his collaborators there was a large group of professional revolutionaries, some of them pathologically violent, whose merit was basically the courage with which they had fought Machado and Batista, and who demanded their share when victory came. Grau, with his paternalistic concept of government, meted out power to the leaders and the groups that had helped him reach the presidency. He placed revolutionaries who hated each other in different repressive forces. It was not long before this translated into murder and frequent shootings staged by the very persons responsible for enforcing the law. Dozens of deaths resulted, and the situation resembled more than anything else the Capone-like scene of Chicago. Worse than such savage acts were the scandals related to corruption. Government offices were rife with the infamous practice of paying salaries to people who never showed up to work — they were called *botellas* — and many influential people controlled dozens, even hundreds, of such mythical jobs. The Minister of Education, José Alemán, was accused of stealing a fortune estimated at $200 million, while the theft of another $175 million was attributed to the president himself, although it was never proven in court. "What will you do if this is proven?" he was once asked. "I will give it back," he answered, with a mocking smile.

The *Autenticios* were buoyed along by the economic bonanza going on throughout the country, and by a job well done in the area of public works, and it had the support of the powerful labor unions. Thus, despite the lack of scruples and the proliferation of violence, the party managed to win the elections again in 1948, albeit after suffering a serious split.

"Authentic" Senator Eduardo "Eddy" Chibás abandoned the party to create the *Ortodoxos*, the "Orthodox" movement, aimed at rescuing the flag of honesty, denouncing corruption and fighting against social injustice. The Orthodox Party picked up the ethical vision that everyone attributed to the *mambises* — despite their blunders of the first third of the century — and accused the "Authentics" of betraying the pure ideals of the Revolution of 1933.

In any event, the president-elect representing "authenticism" was Carlos Prío Socarrás, an intelligent and likable lawyer. He had been a student leader in the struggle against Machado and had suffered political prison, and was respected for his personal courage and moderation. While many of his fellow students had been allured by Marxism, Prío always remained within the ideological framework of freedom. Although he had other remarkable virtues, his most striking character trait was his cordiality. He made certain efforts to stop the infamous behavior attributed to the Grau government. Yet there his effort seems to have lacked conviction, for his own brothers were soon accused of stealing from the nation's treasury. Like Grau, Prío had to govern with his fellow-fighters, many of whom were, frankly, thugs and killers. Consequently, under his administration, the political gangsterism that marred Grau's term was repeated, albeit at a lower scale, and well-justified allegations of corruption were vehemently publicized by Chibás's Orthodox opposition in the radio, in the press and in Congress.

Prío had, nonetheless, a clearer and more modern sense of government than his predecessor, and he passed laws and created credit institutions to stimulate economic development from the seat of government. This was the heady heyday of Keynesianism and it was believed that the state should be the engine of collective progress. In 1948, the Argentinean economist Raúl Presbich visited Havana and advocated the replacement of imports and the utilization of public expense to manage the economy. This was the seed of what would later be called the CEPAL school of thought, after the Spanish-language acronym for Economic Commission for Latin America, officially created some time later. In Cuba, the economic and political intelligentsia was, sometimes without realizing it, Keynesian and Cepalist. Prío's entourage certainly was.

In many respects, Prío's administration could be called progressive. However, there was one enemy that it had to face that Grau never had to confront with such intensity — the communists. Ambiguous and opportunistic in the struggle against Machado, the communists had been Batista's allies, and Batista was the archenemy of both the Authentics and Orthodoxes. At the time, 1948, with the Soviets blockading Berlin, the Cold War had been declared and Washington was recruiting allies. Since the competition would be carried out worldwide and Latin America could not escape it, the State Department strategists concluded that the best local allies for this fight would be those within the *democratic left.* This meant parties and leaders with a populist message, with socialist overtones, including those of Marxist origins, that upheld popular interests — provided they showed respect toward the democratic formalities and were, of course, enemies of Moscow. In this category were the parties *Acción Demócratica* of Venezuela, *Liberación* of Costa Rica, Víctor Raúl Haya de la Torre's *APRA* of Peru, and Grau's "Authentics" and, of course, those of Carlos Prío. Prío, thus, gave his administration a strong anti-communist brand, coordinated his foreign policy with that of Washington and the Latin American democratic left, and removed the "comrades" from the unions, resorting at times to measures of dubious legal basis, although his administration always respected the fundamentals of human rights.

In 1952, Cuba was blessed with a period of economic bonanza brought about by the Korean War, and the nation enjoyed levels of prosperity similar to that of Italy, while its per capita income was twice that of Spain. The sugar production exceeded 7 million tons. There were, however, pockets of poverty in rural areas and a high index of unemployment or partial employment related to the cyclical nature of the sugar harvest season. In any event, according to contemporary indexes compiled by the United Nations, Cuba ranked just after Argentina and Uruguay as the third most developed nation in Latin America, twenty-first in the world, judged not only by impersonal economic data, but in terms of social factors as well, such as literacy, education, nutrition, fuel consumption, cement production, newspapers, etc.. Havana was a fun, brightly lit city that welcomed tens of thousands of tourists, and had a busy commercial infrastructure. Industry was growing, and 10,000 different kinds of items were being produced (although sugar continued to be the main source of revenue).

Shortly before the end of his term, however, Prío's administration reached a new low in terms of popularity. The Orthodox movement, even after Chibás's suicide, seemed destined to win the imminent elections, since Batista, the alternative candidate, was attracting hardly any voter interest. His time had passed. Yet the General, facing inevitable defeat, used the excuse of political crimes — Alejo Cossío del Pino, a popular congressman and former cabinet member had been murdered — and accused Prío of corruption and of an improbable conspiracy with the military to ignore the results of the upcoming elections on June 1. He led a coup that had been planned by junior military officers, and on March 10 toppled Cuba's legitimate government.

During the early hours of the day, Prío struggled feverishly to pull together an effective resistance; to no avail. Few military officers responded to his call and, furthermore, a very disheartening fact became clear: the majority of the people, de-sensitized by the allegations of corruption, tired of unfulfilled promises, and fed up with "politicking," met this kidnapping of its freedoms with indifference. Only a small group of students seemed willing to put up an armed defense of democracy, but encouraging them to fight would have amounted sending them to their death, and that was not Prío's style.

"All politicians are the same," was the phrase most often heard throughout the disillusioned Cuban towns and cities. Perhaps Batista, who had been feared (though never loved) by the Cubans, would at least bring certain level of order to the country. And it was with this mixture of resignation and skepticism that his ascent to power was received. His name was identified with the authority of the whip and the prison. The coup only cost two human lives. Prío and his family went to exile. In Miami, many years later, like Chibás, Prío shot himself to death. Although no one had noticed, he was profoundly depressed. Cuban historiography owes him a full-fledged biography. He was a gentleman to the last minute of his life.

III

THE INSURRECTION

The U.S. embassy and the labor organizations were alarmed by the overthrow of Prío, while for similar reasons the comrades of the Marxist *Partido Socialista Popular* (Popular Socialist Party) entertained certain favorable illusions. They all thought that, with Batista, the Communists would return to power — at least as minor players — as they had during his first government. But it didn't happen that way.

A realist and a pragmatic man, he discarded any vestige of subordination to principles. Batista had taken note of the existence of the Cold War (actually, in Korea, very hot) — and he hastened to assure the U.S. State Department of his absolute support in its war against Moscow and against its proponents within the Cuban Communist Party. That was not entirely accurate description, because the Cuban Communists, victims of a certain inferiority complex, were quite dependent on the *American* Communist Party and were convinced that the Bolshevik Revolution could not arrive on the island until the proletariat of its great neighbor to the north broke the chains. That thesis, a type of leftist Plattism, was called *browderismo*, because it was related to the North American Communist leader Earl Browder.

After guaranteeing Washington that his government would be as anti-Communist as Prío's — which three days before the coup had signed a treaty with the United States to coordinate the anti-Soviet strategy — he soon proved it by allowing some of the planes that were to bomb Arbenz's Guatemala to take off from Cuba. After coming to an agreement with union leaders, assuring them that they would not be persecuted and the labor gains would not be annulled, Batista left the door open to political evolution within his regime and proposed to hold elections in 18 months. This clever maneuver immediately divided the opposition — of every shade in the country's political rainbow — into two camps that persisted throughout the next seven years: the electoralists and the insurrectionalists.

There were electoralists and insurrectionalists in every party, so that a bitter division arose within the anti-Batista ranks. Debates erupted between the "traitors" who would dare to negotiate with the tyrant and the "irresponsible ones" who were ready to drive the country into a violent revolution without pondering the consequences. That dispute, however, did not appear to affect the bulk of a mostly apathetic citizenry, who, looking at the neighboring states, did not see a substantially different picture. Practically all of Central America was living under military control. In Venezuela, Pérez Jimenez ruled; in Colombia, Rojas Pinillas; in the Dominican Republic, the bloody Trujillo. In the 1950s, it seemed as though democracy had not been conceived for the delight of the afflicted Latin American people.

Batista's papers, from the days after his military coup, make for interesting reading. He and his top aides suspended the Constitution of 1940, putting in its place several statutes in which they proclaimed a historical affiliation to what, at certain moments, had also been called a "revolution." The revolution of March 10, 1952 was supposed to have taken place in order to pursue the ideals of the *mambises* and of the Revolution of 1933, to end the gangsterism and the corruption, and to establish a regime of social justice. There was talk of agrarian reform, and of building thousands of houses for the poor. There were promises of more public beaches and a profound educational transformation. In addition, certain salaries were increased, starting, naturally with that of the military men. At the same time Marta Fernández, the dictator's second wife, a tall and elegant lady, tried to imitate Evita Perón, handing out thousands of donations and food packages to poor families.

While the electoralists, amid major disputes, practiced forging alliances and reinstituting their parties (which had been dissolved by decree), in order to try to oust Batista at the voting booth, the insurrectionalists secretly prepared for armed battle. And the first concrete attempt was carried out by a lawyer who loved philosophy, Rafael García Bárcena, professor of the Advanced School of War, who managed to organize some talented young people who later would reappear next to Fidel. Among them were Frank País, Manolo Fernández, Carlos Varona Duquestrada, Faustino Pérez, Armando Hart and Mario Llerena. Castro was not among them, even if he had been asked to conspire with the group. He was only invited as one of many collaborators, not as a leader, and he was certain that his moment had finally arrived. He declined the invitation and went on pursuing his personal plans.

The coup led by García Bárcena — to whom both friends and enemies attributed authoritarian whims that bordered on fascism — was characterized by astonishing naivety. He and a group of his followers presented themselves, flags waving, at the Columbia garrison, the largest in the country, where apparently some of the conspiring officers were stationed. They tried to convince those in charge to do with Batista what had been done with Prío. The result was predictable: the failed conspirators were apprehended, and some of them, like García Bárcena himself, suffered atrocious tortures. The *Movimiento Nacional Revolucionario* (National Revolutionary Movement) — their organization's name — sealed their failure with 70 detained, 12 of them later sentenced to a year in prison and two years for their chief. This occurred on April 27, 1953, a year after Batista's coup, and there were already signs that the opposition was beginning to regain its strength. In Montreal, Canada, members of the Auténtico and Orthodox parties, represented by Carlos Prío and by Emilio "Millo" Ochoa respectively, put aside their differences and on May 24 signed a pact to coordinate their forces.

Fidel Castro was not satisfied with the agreement and he denounced it, on the pretext that it had not included the Communists. The truth is that he had been preparing a group of followers for some time, to try to overthrow Batista through an armed uprising. It was not convenient to have one of the centers of the opposition, in which his fledgling and fluid organization had no influence, come together in strength. Officially, he was still a member of the Orthodox Party, as were 90% of the young men he had recruited; but his secret objective was to take over the militant young Orthodoxy, which as at that time under the influence of a high-minded journalist named Mario Rivadulla, and to set up a separate camp, very far from the Chibasista leadership (which did't think much of him). Intuitively, Fidel Castro understood that he was the only figure in the Orthodox Party with the guts to lead an armed insurrection, and he did not plan to share the leadership with politicians who were less prepared for revolutionary violence.

The Attack on Moncada

In January of 1953, on the eve of the 100-year commemoration of Jose Martí's birth, a few dozen young people marched through Havana brandishing torches and wearing typical Fascist attire (which did not keep them from proclaiming that they were *la Generación del Centenario*, The Generation of the Centennial). Castro himself, like nearly all the Cubans (including Batista's supporters), had declared himself a devoted follower.

Who were these young people? Fundamentally, they were idealist members of the young sector of the Orthodox, generally from the middle and lower strata of the party, whom Castro recruited with the promise that they would soon enter into combat. Among them was a young labor leader, taking his first political steps. His name was Mario Chanes de Armas, and decades later, he would make history — not for the revolutionary actions in which he participated — the attack on the Moncada garrison, or the Granma expedition on which he accompanied Castro — but for being the longest-held political prisoner in Latin America: 30 years in captivity, and still not long enough to find out why his former friend had chosen to treat him so cruelly.

In any case, they were insurrectionalists, and among them there was no more ideological link with the worship of Martí — whose work the group read and discussed — than a certain diffuse and simplified radicalism in the analysis of social problems, and the conviction that

Batista must be removed from power by force. To begin the work of military training, they relied on a peculiar handbook: the one that José Antonio Primo de Rivera had used to train the Spanish Phalangist militias. No one seemed to find the detail repugnant.

The insurrectionist project as conceived by Castro was simple, but it had some historical background: attack a couple of big garrisons, take them over, deliver weapons to the people, call for a general uprising and force the government to surrender unconditionally. Something like that had been tried in the 1930s by the revolutionary Antonio "Tony" Guiteras with the San Luis garrison, but with little success. Under Castro's plan, after the garrisons were overrun, a provisional government would be named. The Constitution of 1940, a rallying cry for all the opposition, would be restored; and the elections that Batista had foiled with this assault on the institutions would be held. Castro thought that, if successful, that kind of action would catapult him into the first ranks of the political scene, even if his young age — barely 27 — would prevent him from taking on the Presidency because the Constitution required a minimum age of 35.

This precipitous plan, with so little chance of success, displays one element that is characteristic of all the big decisions Castro would make throughout his life: staging risky actions without taking into account the unpredictable reactions and factors over which he would have little control, and trusting above all in his lucky star and in his knack for improvisation. Castro would fail in everything that he planned, and would succeed in everything that he improvised. That seems to be the theme of his life.

In the improbable case that he managed to capture the garrisons, what made him think that the Cubans would support him and start a generalized revolution, when he himself had observed during Batista's takeover was that the society was generally apathetic to public affairs? Castro was a "*voluntarista*," a willful man who predicted the future according to his wishes, without taking reality into account, making his decisions with an astonishing boldness that was limited neither by prudence nor moderation.

When Fidel started to seek economic support to carry forward his military plans, just about everyone turned his back on him, including his own father (who barely contributed $140 of the $3,000 Castro had requested). However, among his own conspirators a truly admirable sense of sacrifice prevailed. One prosperous doctor, Mario Muñoz, sold his private airplane for $10,000 and made a substantial donation to the cause. Jesús "Chucho" Montané donated his termination compensation from the enterprise where he had worked. They even made money through fraud: they bought a car on credit and sold it as if it had been totally paid for. Why hesitate over such bourgeois niceties, thought Castro, when the country's freedom was at stake?

With such scanty funds, the weapons they were able to buy were ridiculous. Old rifles from the turn of the century, revolvers, hunting rifles, 22-caliber carbines (used at fairs, to compete for stuffed animals), and a few pistols or machine guns from Castro's old gangster friends. The enemy, by contrast, was armored, and well-armed with automatic weapons, and they were well-trained because in the last years Cuba had been toying with the fantasy that it was ready to send thousands of military men to join the Korean conflict — where the peace agreement was signed, coincidentally, during the days of the Moncada attack — and the army had recently received weapons from North America. Obviously, when the conspirators in Castro's circle inventoried their weapons, and when they got their objectives and plan of attack from Fidel, sensible voices tried to stop the lunacy. Mario Muñoz and Gustavo Arcos were the most eloquent. An Orthodox like most of the others, Arcos was a courageous and straightforward young man to whom his colleagues accorded the moral leadership. But then one of the conspirators cited a verse from the national anthem, "to die for the homeland is to live," and suddenly, it seemed as if opposing the absurd plan only demonstrated cowardice and lack of fortitude.

So the operation was put to work with a certain sense of euphoria and jubilee, even if the most responsible members embarked on it with a certainty that they were being led off a cliff. Nine of the revolutionaries, counseled by prudence, decided not to participate; but none betrayed the operation.

July 26, 1953. The chosen garrisons were in Oriente province. El Moncada, the second in importance and size in the entire republic, was in the city of Santiago, and the other was in Bayamo. The attack against the Moncada was directed by Castro himself; the Bayamo attack was led by Raul Martínez Araras, an insurrectionalist Orthodox who was starting to have profound doubts about Castro's character. There were some 160 assailants and they arrived by private car or via public transportation; they met at a farmstead near Santiago. Many did not know the city. None was familiar with the garrisons they planned to attack, with the exception of Pedro Miret, a member of Castro's intimate circle, who had been brought in to handle the precarious job of intelligence (which ended up being totally useless). There were unanticipated stairs to climb and sentry posts to get past. There were more soldiers ready to defend the garrison, and they were more alert, than expected. There were unidentified security mechanisms. Some of the assailants got lost in the twisted streets of the unfamiliar city. This took place at night, during carnival season, which added to the confusion. The worse misgivings of Mario Muñoz — who was killed — and of Arcos, gravely wounded, were replicated in excess: in both garrisons, the attack was a complete disaster that cost the lives of dozens of young men, both revolutionaries and soldiers, because both sides fought with courage. Yet, many of the assailants were able to escape — among them, Fidel and Raúl Castro.

In the fight, 8 assailants and 22 soldiers were killed, but 56 prisoners were savagely tortured and assassinated by the soldiers, even though there some instances of chivalry among officials and army doctors who did not allow prisoners to be killed under their watch. Fidel and a group of his followers, once they had escaped, fled to an isolated area on the side of a mountain. The Catholic church, mobilized by the opposition, interceded on behalf of the survivors and they extracted from Batista the promise that if they gave themselves up or were captured, they would not be killed but would be given a fair trial. The wizard who concocted this arrangement was the bishop of Santiago, Monsignor Enrique Pérez Serantes, a friend of Fidel's father. The results of his mission were seen almost immediately: Fidel and his men, surprised by the army, give up without a fight.

Their captors kept their word, and without being mistreated, the young men were jailed and their trial was prepared. Secretly, however, the army's high command gave orders to an official named Jesús Yanes

Pelletier to poison Castro. He refused, and exposed the government's perverse intentions, saving the young leader's life. Only Yanes Pelletier, not very well-versed in psychology, did not realize that sentiments of gratitude and reciprocity are non-exist in narcissist personalities. After the triumph of the Revolution, and after spending a certain period in Castro's personal guard, Yanes Pelletier was sentenced to twenty years in prison.

Thirty-two assailants were brought to trial. Two strong emotions stirred the public; one was intense horror. One prisoner's eyes had been pulled out, in front of his girlfriend and his sister. Another had been dragged to death behind a Jeep. Almost all the dead assailants had been savagely beaten before they were gunned down or shot in the neck, and the cadavers had been manipulated to cover up the tortures. The citizenry was disgusted. The other emotion was admiration for the survivors, and especially for the young lawyer, Fidel Castro.

Suddenly, his gangster past had vanished and he appeared in public opinion as a new Martí, or at least, as a new Antonio Guiteras, that violent revolutionary idealist who was killed in the shoot-out with Batista's army in 1935. Fidel Castro, who had not achieved his objective of taking over the garrisons, much less provoking a popular uprising, had become the most renowned person in all the insurrectionalist sector. Even if he still was not considered "presidential," he had become a figure of national political stature who could offer hope to a large part of the country. (Not to the whole country — and indeed, among the exceptions were the Cuban Communists who hastened to condemn the assault in New York's *Daily Worker*. "We condemn the *putchista* methods, typical of the bourgeoisie, in the Santiago de Cuba and Bayamo actions. . . The stand of the Communist Party and of the people has been to combat the Batista tyranny seriously and to unmask the *putchistas* and the adventurers who go against the interests of the masses."

The brusque attack on Castro and his compatriots did not take into account that the assailants were jailed and could not defend themselves, nor that Raúl, Fidel's younger brother, was a militant in the Socialist Youth, a fundamental but hopeful Marxist who had even been to Prague (along with other comrades) to attend one of the customary international youth festivals organized by Moscow in order to create solidarity and discipline among its sympathizers with the purpose of using them in the Cold War. During that trip, by the way, Raúl met a young member of the KGB, Nikolai Leonov, today a retired general, whom he would casually see again in Mexico, and with whom he would forge the relationship that is a key to understanding the process of Sovietization in Cuba.

Finally, there were two trials, and in both of them Batista's government made the political mistake of giving Fidel Castro a prominent stage from which to speak. In the first, all of the assailants were tried except Fidel, who assumed the defense of his compatriots and made a brilliant five-hour statement against Batista's dictatorship and about the people's right to insurrection when their freedoms are curtailed. The second took place behind closed doors, in a room at the military hospital; Fidel was the only defendant and he served as his own defense attorney. No one has an exact account of what was said in that room, but long after the trial, in the relative peace of his jail cell, Fidel reconstructed his speech according to his own interests, and that text (generously revised by Jorge Mañach, a well-versed intellectual who added quotations, improved the grammar and entitled it "*History will absolve me,*" a phrase taken from Hitler's own defense when he was charged before the German courts with having caused grave public disturbances.

Of those words, there are a few in particular that we should not overlook. One is a paragraph, almost at the end, where Castro is preparing to sum up his statements and describes with considerable precision the state of the country's mood in confronting the nation's problems: "Once there was a republic. It had its constitution, its laws, its freedoms; a president, Congress, and courts; everyone was free to get together, to join organizations, to speak and to write. The government was not satisfactory to the people, but the people could change it, and there were only a few days left until that could be done. There was public debate, which was respected and heeded, and all of the problems of collective interest were freely discussed. There were political parties, educational radio, controversial programs on television, public events and palpable enthusiasm among the people. These people had suffered a great deal and while they were not happy, they wanted to be and had a right to be so. They had been lied to many times and they looked back at the past with real terror. They blindly believed that it could not return; they were proud of their love of liberty and believed that those freedoms would be respected as sacred; they felt an ennobling confidence in the certainty that no one would commit the crime of attempting to destroy their democratic institutions. They wanted a change, an improvement, a step forward, and they could see it drawing near. All of their hopes were placed on the future."

To that impeccable summary of the formal freedoms lost to the Batista coup, Castro added an entire political platform of five points that he would have undertaken if his project had triumphed:

1. Restoration of the Constitution of 1940

2. Distribution of land, in small farmsteads, to peasants

3. Allotment of 30% of business profits to the workers

4. The granting of a majority participation in the sugar industry to the agricultural workers, at the expense of the sugar barons, and

5. Confiscation of the assets wrongfully obtained by dishonest politicians.

Castro played cleverly. Under the cover of his legal defense, Castro had outlined a governing plan in the most rabid populist tradition in Latin America, intended to whet the appetite of nine-tenths of the population. His followers outside the prison immediately started to distribute tens of thousands of copies of the speech among the populace. The packaging appeared to be Castro's defense at the Moncada trial; the real message was pure political propaganda. His defeat in the Moncada attack was turned into a propitious event from which to assault power; he used the court as a podium and began to polish his image as a national leader.

The sentences handed down were severe. Castro got 15 years and his followers, just less, while the women in the group were acquitted. Quickly, they were all transferred to the Isle of Pines prison, where Castro, even though he was isolated from his compatriots in the infirmary, was the object of almost courteous treatment. He was permitted to receive visitors, books, wines, cheeses and very expensive cigars — of which he was a great aficionado. He had access to facilities where he could cook sumptuous meals, which he described in detail in his letters.

In the meantime, he was directing, from prison, through clandestine correspondents, a furious political campaign of public opinion intended to force Batista to grant them all pardon. The barrage of publicity was successful, partly because of the intensity with which his friends took it on: the Orthodox journalists Luis Conte Agüero, José Pardo Llada, Ernesto Montaner, José Luis Massó, and another long list of influential communicators. In addition, one of Castro's former classmates, the Orthodox militant lawyer Manuel Dorta-Duque, contacted a member of the CIA (apparently named Lawrence Houston) who was stationed in Cuba and convinced him of a most ironic theory: that if Castro was not freed, the Communists would become the ringleaders of the anti-Batista movement — something that was totally against the interests of democratic Cubans and North Americans. It is probable that the U.S. embassy also pressured Batista to grant Castro amnesty.

Guevara, Guatemala and the Rise of Radicalism

While this drama absorbed the Cubans, another episode was playing out in another country in the Caribbean basin, and it would eventually intertwine closely with the island's destiny: the overthrow of Jacobo Arbenz, in Guatemala. Colonel Arbenz, at the helm of a legitimate government, was standing up to Washington for two fundamental reasons: the first was his increasing closeness to the Communists, and his purchases of weapons from Czechoslovakia (when the United States refused to sell them to him); and the second, his confrontation with the North American banana companies who were adversely affected by the agrarian reform taking place in Guatemala. Given the circumstances, and with the approval of the so-called democratic left of Latin America (which considered Arbenz less a follower of President Juan Jose Arevalos than a "Napoleon of the Caribbean", and suspiciously pro-Soviet — as he was described by the writer Raúl Roa, who later became a Castro minister) — the CIA staged a successful conspiracy. The Agency enrolled various Guatemalan soldiers and adventurers from the Korean War, who with every little effort destroyed the government of that Central American nation and drove out its president.

The "Cuban" consequences of that operation were many and long-reaching. A young Argentine doctor had arrived in the Guatemala of those revolutionary days to lend his professional and political support to the radicals who installed themselves in power. His name was Ernesto Guevara. He was intelligent, he came from a well-to-do family, and was highly cultivated for his young age — barely 28 years old. He suffered from asthma, which probably contributed to forging his tenacious personality through the constant effort required to overcome the asphyxiating attacks. He was also a Marxist.

Above all, he was a tough-minded and serious man, not given to frivolities, with vestiges of moral fanaticism, convinced that he knew who were the enemies and how they should be treated (i.e., mercilessly) if one meant to triumph in battle. Not by accident, in his prior correspondence, half-jokingly and half-seriously, he had signed himself "Stalin II". This shows a cynical or provoking facet, a person who doesn't mind scandalizing others if he does it in defense of his deep beliefs. For Ernesto Guevara — he was not yet "*el Che*" — the battle against the bourgeoisie and the unfair capitalist system was a life-or-death combat in which you could neither ask nor give a break. "The revolutionary," he later wrote, "should be a cold and perfect killing machine." He had not yet been trained as the executioner of his enemies, but his Guatemalan experience reaffirmed his worst instincts. He had seen how "the Yankees," associated with the "local peons," wrecked with one blow a reformist government that had been unable to defend itself. From there, he deduced that only a Marxist revolution could properly deal with the United States, rapidly decapitating the national bourgeoisie and simultaneously seeking the protective alliance of Moscow, which had the power to neutralize the enemies.

While Guevara was reaching certain conclusions that he later applied to the Cuban picture, the exact same thing was happening at the Central Intelligence Agency. The CIA agents and high-ranking officials who planned and executed the operation against Arbenz were not only promoted and congratulated by the Eisenhower Administration (which saw this as a triumph against communism in the context of the Cold War), but they created a pattern by which to confront the revolutionary efforts of the disdained "banana republics". Therefore, a few years later when Castro took power and started to look to Moscow for shelter, the same CIA officials who previously had toppled Arbenz dusted off their old battle plans and started acting more or less in the same way as before — without realizing that this enemy was substantially different. The Cuban bone was definitely a tougher chew. And that was, among other reasons, because the Cubans knew the Guatemalan experience firsthand and were able to predict how the CIA would act.

Finally, Batista signed the pardon in April of 1955, and on May 15 Fidel and the *Moncadistas* abandoned the Isle of Pines. They had been in jail a little less than two years. The circumstances in the world outside, however, were not the same as before. In November of 1954, under conditions that were unacceptable to the opposition, Batista had celebrated his victory in an election that had been thoroughly manipulated. He behaved like a legitimate ruler and he was proud to receive visits from Vice President Nixon and the chief of the CIA, Allen Dulles (who probably later induced the ban on the Communist Party). The electoral opposition was fractured and baffled, while the insurrectionalists, outside of Fidel Castro's group, were beginning to coalesce into two groups: the university students and the *priístas*, followers of President Prío. Batista's police continued its sporadic crimes, sometimes against prominent people linked to the opposition. Some of those figures were killed — including Mario Fortuny and Jorge Agostini, former revolutionaries from the fight against Machado, friends and collaborators of Carlos Prío and Manuel Antonio "Tony" de Varona (Prío's former prime minister, reputed to have been an honest man) and a good friend of Aureliano Sanchez Arango, an ex-Communist and a professor of labor law, with a gift for political savvy, who tried to organize the insurrection against Batista from the ranks of the *autenticismo* (the Authentic Party). Prestigious Cubans like the lawyer Mario Villar Roces and the historian Leví Marrero were obliterated.

In the weeks that he spent in Havana, Castro maintained a frenetic schedule of political activity, but that did not mean he neglected his sentimental links. He had divorced Mirta Díaz-Balart while in prison, and now he maintained amorous relations with various women. He seemed to feel a special affection for Naty Revuelta, who was married to a distinguished doctor, and who at around that time became pregnant by the famous ex-prisoner. The child of that love affair, Alina Fernández (she never chose to take the last name of her biological father), when she was able to escape from the island, wrote a talented (and humorous), sad and destructive book about her relationship with her father. As a result of his fruitful amorous encounters, and also with a certain legitimate fear that Batista's police would try to assassinate him, Castro frequently changed his address, sometimes sleeping in his sisters' house, or at his friends,' like Ernesto Montaner, who lent him his room at the Central Hotel in Old Havana, where he also met with old friends from the UIR like Pepe Jesús Ginjaume and with the journalists from *Bohemia* magazine, Bernardo Viera Trejo and Agustín Alles.

From Mexico to the Sierra Maestra

In reality, Castro continued to pursue the possibility of insurrection, and the bulk of his negotiations were directed toward creating in Cuba a network of support for his next adventure. His plan, communicated to very few people, consisted in going into exile in Mexico and organizing from there an expedition similar to the one that the journalist Sergio Carbó had launched twenty years earlier against Machado, in the coastal town of Gibara. The difference would be that the earlier attempt had not been coordinated with a general uprising, whereas Castro had in mind a multi-pronged revolt and perhaps even a massive general strike. In search of collaborators for this task, he had made contact with student leaders at the University of Havana and the University of Oriente. He found a sympathetic echo among the latter, especially in a brave young man named Frank País. Frank, a teacher, Protestant, a kind of hybrid revolutionary and anti-Communist militant, promised to help Castro if he fulfilled the promise of disembarking in Cuba. José Antonio Echeverría, the popular leader of the Federation of University of Havana Students, Catholic and anti-Communist, was the most reticent. Among his closest collaborators were several students who detested Castro. One was Joe Westbrook, the others Faure Chomón, Jorge Valls and Fructuoso Rodríguez. They still saw him as a gangster. He was not even much liked by his two old compatriots in the UR, now close to

Manzanita, as Echeverría was called: Juan Pedro Carbó Serviá and Jose Machado (Machadito). It was Castro's good luck that with the exception of Chomón and Valls, the rest of the audacious revolutionaries of *el Directorio* (the directorate) had been assassinated by Batista's police. Some, by the way, had been denounced by a Communist of obscure psychological motivation named Marcos "Marquitos" Rodríguez.

Once in Mexico, Castro quickly started preparing the "invasion," and he announced the name of his party: *Movimiento 26 de Julio*, the 26th of July Movement. He felt he had already gotten all the men and women of action available from the Orthodox Party — among them Martha Frayde, a dynamic and combative doctor — and incorporated them into his group, and now he wanted to put some distance between his group and the rest of the opposition. This was the moment to make official his rupture with the Orthodox Party, even if he tried to maintain good relations with its leadership. He met a former general from the Spanish Civil War, Alberto Bayo, better known for his defeat at Baleares than for his victories, but someone who, nonetheless, had some combat experience and could train the soldiers whom Fidel was recruiting, along with his ex-compatriots from Moncada, who secretly begin to regroup in Mexico to prepare the expedition.

However, the most important relationship would be with a doctor, an adventurer who arrived in the aftermath of the failure in Guatemala. This was Ernesto Guevara. From their first meeting, the Argentine fell under the Cuban's spell. Fidel talked for hours, as always, and explained his dreams for changing the country. Guevara quickly realized he was not dealing with a deep intellectual but an audacious man of action who, from his point of view, combined the perfect elements to achieve the right outcome. He was a leftist bourgeois, radical and anti-imperialist, with a nearly Marxist interpretation of world events. He had no respect for the market economy or the Yankees, whom he detested, while he quietly admired the Russian Revolution. His diagnosis for the world was chaotic and disorderly, but it coincided with the Third World analysis of Guevara. In addition, he was ready to resort to violence, as much as necessary, because he had no bourgeois scruples. His brother Raúl, on the other hand, shared with Guevara a more structured (if sketchy) Marxist vision and even had a curious contact at the

Soviet Union's embassy in Mexico: the agent Nikolai Leonov, who very soon came into contact with the three.

Guevara started to think that destiny had presented him with a character who was superior to Colonel Jacobo Arbenz. Fidel was a true leader, who could be forgiven for the superficiality of his analysis or the tiring loquacity he employed to convince his interlocutor of the most diverse theories. So, the Argentine revolutionary, ascetic and ironic, a bit disheartened by the lack of cultivation among the Cubans he had met, accepted Castro's leadership and agreed to accompany him on the adventure. He humbly joined the team. After all, maybe it would be possible to carry out a Communist revolution in Latin America. He could not lead it, himself. All he could do would be to subtly lead Castro, and contribute to giving the group a coherent ideological orientation. That would be very difficult to carry out because any effort at manipulation would have to be conducted from a position of subordination. Lucky for him, he could count on Raúl's complicity, as an expert in the difficult art of handling his brother while appearing to be submissive, agreeable and obedient.

The same amnesty that gave Fidel Castro his freedom allowed Carlos Prío to return to Cuba — with the will to strengthen the electoral cause. If Batista could not be ousted by force, they would have to settle for the ballot box. Prío's objective, and that of all the democratic opposition, was to have Batista accept the legitimacy of elections in November of 1954 and call another election, this time free and with guarantees in every aspect. Castro and the students had formed an organization for the armed struggle called *Directorio Revolucionario*, Revolutionary Directorate, open to anyone who wished to participate, even if they were not university students. They and the other Insurrectionalists were tenaciously opposed; Batista would have to be removed from power by force. He who lived by the sword would have to die by the sword.

In any case, the electoral cause was revived when an old and honorable colonel of the Independence War, don Cosme de la Torriente, took the initiative. At the age of 83, he dared to ask Batista to engage in a "civic dialogue", to bury the hatchet and start negotiations. But his effort was in vain: it ran up against Batista's stubbornness; Batista who did not perceive how the various sectors of Cuban society had inexorably closed ranks against him. And it also ran counter to the groundwork done by Castro, who was bent on winning, arms in hand. The civic dialogue, then, drowned between the monologues of those who were excluded: the ones who had taken power by force and felt secure, and the insurgents who planned to take it away from them by the same violent means.

That double intransigence did not seem to be reflected in the social arena. The economy was doing well, the flood of tourists was increasing, and development was on the upswing in cities like Santa Clara and Holguin. Skyscrapers were going up in Havana; but none of that had any bearing on the society's feelings for the government. Indeed, the largest share of Batista's detractors were in the middle and upper classes, while what feeble support he could muster was located at the lower social levels.

A strange form of this division could be observed between Catholics and practitioners of the Afro-Cuban religions. The Catholic church, which since the 1940s had developed an extensive secular structure committed to social action, used its entire array of organizations to confront Batista's government: the JOC (Juventud Obrera Católica, Young Catholic Workers), the JEC (Juventud Estudiantil Católica, the Catholic Student Youth), the JAC (Juventud de Acción Católica, the Catholic Action Youth), and the ACU (Agrupación Católica Universitaria, the Organization of University Catholics). These institutions were predominantly "electoralist", and they participated actively and openly in the civic and political confrontation with the dictatorship. Some of their young Catholics became well-known and respected: Angel del Cerro, José Ignacio Rasco and Andrés Valdespino — but some of the leaders later joined the armed struggle when it was evident that an end would come only by force. While this was the position of most militant Catholics, the *santeros*, *abakuas* and other believers in AfroCuban rites did not seem to feel uncomfortable with General Batista. After all, most of the army's rank and file were blacks who found the military to be a way to escape extreme poverty, and Batista was seen as a *mestizo* anyway, a man of mixed race and humble origins who had been able to climb to the highest position in the country.

The "civic dialogue" failed. Fidel saw this as an open door to insurrection, and he was not alone in reaching that conclusion. A group of
professional soldiers, all of them trained in North American academies,
tried unsuccessfully to stage a coup d'etat under the leadership of Colonel Ramón Barquín. They were known as "The Pure." In those days, the
anti-government actions and the bombings had multiplied, and some of
the bombs were placed in public places, an even graver crime. The chief
of the army intelligence services, Colonel Blanco Rico, was killed by
two students, Rolando Cubelas and Juan Pedro Carbó Serviá, while
leaving a Havana nightclub; a woman also was injured in that episode.
The police responded to those events with more crimes and torture. A
group of Authentic Party members led by Reynol García tried to take
over the Goicuria garrison in the province of Matanzas; several assailants died in the attempt or were executed after being captured. After
the failed attack there was an exponential increase in official repression. As the English expression goes, politics made strange bedfellows:
in the Dominican Republic, Prío's Authentic Party members had established a strange complicity with Trujillo and were preparing an expedition led by Eufemio Fernández, one of the people who, years before, had
tried to topple the same Trujillo with the invasion prepared from Cayo
Confite.

After several run-ins with the Mexican police, Fidel finally managed to pull together some arms and a few dozen men to set sail for
Cuba. The last push came with $100,000 given by Prío, $15,000 of
which were set aside to buy a boat, the *Granma*, an old, 20-meter recreational yacht bough from a "North American". They set out on the night
of November 24, 1956.

Castro had already declared that soon they would become either
heroes or martyrs. "Soon" was not a slip, but a sign of his conviction. He
was certain that upon his arrival, there would be an uprising all across
the nation. A few weeks before setting out, he had signed the Pact of
Mexico with José Antonio Echevarría — which almost failed, because
Fidel insisted that Communists be included, a condition Echevarría did
not accept — and he received a visit from Frank País, who had in mind
taking up arms in Santiago de Cuba. The prospect of a long guerrilla
war was not to Castro's liking. His intention was to disembark at

Niquero, advance toward Manzanillo (which should already be in rebel hands), and triumph in a short period. To wage ongoing guerrilla warfare was not in his equation. He did not have the necessary infrastructure to furnish weapons and ammunition for such a campaign. A great optimist, he was looking for this operation to last a few days or weeks, at most.

On the 30th of November, Frank País showed that he was serious when he committed to taking the city of Santiago de Cuba. With some 300 young men, all of them from the upper and middle classes of the city (a fact that later worried the government), he occupied some public buildings and set fire to others, and he machine-gunned the garrisons before the police, overcome by panic, could figure out how to quell the insurrection. Santiago's youth supported and admired him; Fernando Bernal, Fernando Vecino, Jorge Sotús were with him. All of them later took to the hills: the Sierra Maestra Mountains.

His revolutionary onslaught lasted just two days and, miraculously, caused few deaths; but the example was not replicated as Fidel had expected, and the labor leaders close to Castro were not successful in their attempt to call a general strike. Echevarría's Directorate showed no signs of life — for which Fidel would later blame Jose Antonio — so that on December 2, when the *Granma* carried Fidel and another 80 expeditionaries to the southern shores of Oriente (not very far from where Martí had disembarked 60 years earlier), Batista's government had recuperated from the close call it had suffered a few days earlier in the province's capital.

The disembarkation could almost be classified as a shipwreck. They arrived at an inopportune place — the beach not suitable for such tasks — and they were immediately spotted by an old frigate, which opened fire. They quickly gathered what supplies they could and headed for the mountain range of Sierra Maestra. Now they had no game plan. There were no guides or maps. Then began a series of clumsy improvisations, comparable only to those conducted by the highly-divided upper ranks of the adversary. Batista himself, in his palace in Havana, asked for a map of the zone; he was brought one of the kind that are given away at gas stations — not exactly a military chart. But then, he wasn't Marshal Erwin Rommel. He had never been in combat and had no tactical formation. But none of this kept him from deciding the initial strategy: to send army units after the expeditionaries, following their tracks from the point where they disembarked, up into the mountains. One bureaucrat suggested the opposite: drive them from the mountains down to the sea, to herd them into one place with no exit. It was logical. Pushing them further into the mountains would send them to a natural hideout. Pushing them to the sea would mean driving them into a trap.

The Opposition Gets Tough

Batista smiled; he liked cat-and-mouse games. For him, it was a political episode. He knew that at that the invaders were only a few dozen young and inexperienced men, led by "an Orthodox gangster known for his craziness," as described by one of his assistants. Some of the expeditionaries had been captured and it was perfectly well known what scarce armaments the insurgents carried. What risk did Batista's government run if the expeditionaries managed to reach the Sierra Maestra and stay hidden for a while, in those remote and inhospitable places? It could even be beneficial. That "live" guerrilla, in the Sierra Maestra, far from the urban centers, served him well — it divided the opposition and justified his staunch position in postponing the anticipated elections. How could anyone expect him to engage in a political negotiation with the opposition when the country was in a state of war? Even more: Castro's guerrilla threat fit the bill for two other reasons, as well. Now Batista could suspend the constitutional guarantees as he liked, evoking an exceptional emergency; and it also allowed him to approve special budgets for the war, without submitting to the scrutiny of the General Comptroller of the Republic. Castro, then, also gave him the means to steal. Batista and many of the military men in the inner circles found that useful, indeed.

This attitude of neglectful complacency lasted a few months; there was little combat and minimal persecution. That was sufficient to allow the survivors of the *Granma* to avoid capture. Some 20 of them regrouped and acclimatized themselves, created a supply network and expanded their ranks with new fighters. Meanwhile, an important correspondent for *The New York Times*, Herbert Matthews, turned Castro into front-page news in the United States with a series of articles in which he introduced the Cuban leader as a reformist democrat without totalitarian intentions. That phenomenon, with the mere survival of Castro and his group and the simple fact that the army had not destroyed them, had a galvanizing effect on the opposition. First, it shifted the equilibrium of force in favor of the insurrectionalists. Second, it destroyed the old political dictum that assured that "a revolution could be fought with or without the army, but never against the army." Fidel Castro and his improbable guerrillas showed that a revolution could be made *against* the army, especially against Batista's, which (even if it included a few valuable and well-trained officers) was little more than an empty repressive machinery. It was led by dishonest chiefs, capable of such low conduct as selling their offensive plans to the enemy or covering up deaths in their own ranks so they could keep on receiving salaries for soldiers who had died.

After the consolidation of the guerrilla front in the Sierra Maestra, the insurrectionalist opposition became bolder, establishing a climate of competition among the anti-Batista groups who were worried by the prominence Fidel Castro was acquiring. This was the time when the Revolutionary Directorate and the Authentic Party groups combined efforts and launched an attack against the Presidential Palace, with the goal of executing Batista. The military expert in charge of the event was a young Spaniard, veteran of the Civil War and ex-member of the resistance in France — his tank was the first to enter Paris after the liberation. He name was Carlos Gutiérrez Menoyo and he was exiled in Cuba with his family a little after the end of World War II. Gutiérrez Menoyo, like other exiled Spaniards, had ties with Prío's followers and it was through those connections that he obtained funds for weapons. Second-in-command was Faure Chomón, one of the Directorate leaders. Also participating in the attack was José Antonio Echeverría, whose mission it was to take over a popular radio station and to spread word of the demise of the tyrant, and to call for a people's uprising.

The attack failed and 35 revolutionaries died — among them Carlos Gutiérrez Menoyo and José Antonio Echeverría — while only five soldiers fell. The government, irritated and fearful, took the dangerous step of finishing off the electoral option. That night, a group of policemen kidnapped and assassinated Pelayo Cuervo Navarro, President of the prestigious Orthodox Party, with whom it would have been possible to work toward a peaceful and honorable solution to the country's conflicts. In a sense, Batista had stepped over the line. For surviving members of the Directorate, the failed experience of the attack on the palace led them to an inevitable conclusion. The most effective armed opposition, and to some extent the most secure, was not clandestine confrontation in the cities, always within reach of the repressive apparatus, but guerrilla combat carried out in the mountains, just as Fidel was doing. And those who would later form the guerrilla front of the Directorate were Eloy, the younger brother of Carlos Gutiérrez Menoyo (a brave young man of barely 22), Faure Chomón and Rolando Cubelas. Cubelas, a medical student, went on to become one of the most famous guerrilla chiefs in the Escambray Mountains in central Cuba.

When Fidel found out about the attack on the palace, he reacted angrily and classified the action as dangerous and reckless act. In reality, he realized that if the *Directorio* had been successful, the most probable scenario was that the Authentic and Orthodox parties would have dominated the political scene once again, relegating the 26th of July Movement to second place. For him, it was obvious that Batista's death in those circumstances would have meant, if not his own political death, at least a notable dimming of his lucky star. And the Communists thought more or less the same, but with even greater concern: the Communist Party was keenly aware that those who had assaulted the palace were fundamentally anti-Communist, so that the dictatorship would have been replaced by people who were in fact their not-so-hidden enemies.

After the attack, there was a striking increase in clandestine operations in the cities, but now they were masterminded by people using a new code name: *el llano*, the plains — to distinguish them from those who fought in the mountains — and they organized themselves to aid and supply the guerrillas. The urban conspirators no longer formed groups to head the fight but to support the insurrection, which was bey now unquestionably led by the man in the Sierra Maestra. That's how the Civic Resistance surfaced, a vast group of professionals in all fields, led by Raúl Chibás (an educator and the younger brother of Eddy) and later the engineers Manuel Ray and Enrique Oltusky. The Civic Resistance grew rapidly and efficiently in every province, recruiting personalities like the young lawyer from Camagüey, Carlos Varona Duquestrada and the filmmaker and publicist from Havana, Emilio Guede, the propaganda chief. They all shared a clear passion for democracy and a vocation for public service. They were generally anti-Communists and they were upset when they started to hear that a Marxist faction was growing in the Sierra Maestra, outstanding members of which included an Argentine named Guevara, now known as *el Che*, and even Raúl, Fidel's own younger brother.

This was about the time when the friction more or less openly began between the Communist and the democratic revolutionaries. An indignant Frank País, who led the 26th of July Movement in Oriente and the second leading figure in the group, discovered that a Communist named Antonio Clergé was distributing Marxist propaganda among the soldiers. He ordered for him to be eliminated. The execution did not take place, because a lawyer intervened. That was Lucas Morán Arce, an honest and even-tempered man who had close ties to Frank País; in the name of political harmony, he begged that the order be rescinded. País agreed but he explained his reasons for issuing the order in the first place: he was deeply concerned about the increasing filtration of Communists in the 26th of July Movement. He believed that the best way to avoid a major conflict later on would be to stem the tide immediately and provoke a confrontation between the two factions. Ironically, months later, when Morán met the guerrillas and found out the extent to which the Communists (linked to Raúl) had penetrated the movement, and was horrified to see how easily Raúl was executing suspected collaborators of Batista's army (a paranoid attitude that Morán suggested was Stalinist) it is he who became the victim — he was summarily tried and sent back to Santiago de Cuba in the expectation that he would be assassinated by Batista's police. That, happily, did not come to pass, because the regime unexpectedly fell.

After Frank País died, the man who succeeded him, Rene Ramos Latour (called "Daniel", in clandestine circles), maintained an energetic dialogue with *el Che* on communism. Guevara, who made no secret of his inclinations, wrote an explicit letter, displaying a certain intellectual swagger, in which he says: "I belong, because of my ideological training, to those who believe the solution to the world's problems lies behind the so-called Iron Curtain; and I see this movement as one of the many that have been provoked, by bourgeois zeal, to liberate themselves from the economic chains of imperialism. I always considered Fidel an authentic leader of the bourgeois left, although indeed his personal qualities of extraordinary brilliance place him well above his class." Ramos Latour answered him in no uncertain terms. "This is not the moment to discuss where the salvation of the world lies. I only want to state our opinion, which of course is completely different from yours. . . We want a strong America, master of its own destiny, an American that proudly confronts the United States, Russian, China or whatever power tries anything against our economic or political independence. On the other hand, those who have 'ideological training' think that the solution to our problems lies in liberating ourselves from the noxious Yankee dominance in exchange for the less noxious Soviet dominance." Shortly after he sent that letter, Ramos Latour was assigned to a suicidal guerrilla mission, and indeed, he died in combat.

In the Sierra Maestra, however, future political and economic projects were taking shape that were far from being Communist projects. Felipe Pazos, an Keynesian economist well within the CEPAL spirit of the era, but absolutely a democrat in his political dispositions, was the principal architect of the supposed platform of the 26th of July Movement.

Given the evidence that the electoral strategy and the political solution to the conflict were quite unlikely to succeed, the Cuban Communist Party (which naturally was no stranger to the conflict) opted to play the "Fidel" card, and started making contacts and preparing to place some of its leaders in Sierra Maestra. Meanwhile, it gives orders to other mid-sector operatives to create guerrilla units in the Escambray zone, independent of the ones already maintained by the Directorate and by the Authentics organization, another opposition group emanating out of Prío's followers. Even more clearly than Fidel's militants in the Sierra Maestra, the guerrillas in Escambray demonstrated what a false threat were Batista's forces. Here were just a few hundred men, divided and poorly-armed (Gutierrez Menoyo had split from the Directorate and created the Second National Front of Escambray), operating, basically, in a mountainous territory of barely 100 square kilometers, interrupted by towns and well-traveled hunting grounds, where there is always a telephone or an accessible road somewhere nearby. But the army did not come after them, or chased them half-heartedly — partly because they did not know how to pursue them more effectively, but more because they were growing more demoralized.

Batista and the Norteamericanos

One of the reasons why they were discouraged was the evident loss of North American support. Washington, which had accepted Batista in the same spirit with which Roosevelt had accepted Somoza ("he's a son-of-a-bitch, but he's *our* son-of-a-bitch"), was starting to revise its positions. Even while American society didn't have a clear idea of what was happening in Cuba, thanks to the press the powerful image of a bunch of bearded young idealists, led by a charismatic lawyer and fighting against a deplorable tyrant, had started to take hold.

To that simplification were added detailed descriptions of excesses committed by Batista's police, one of them committed in the presence of the American ambassador, Earl Smith. He was stunned to see the police in Santiago de Cuba violently clubbing a group of women, dressed in black and demonstrating in a public street. They had been trying to reach the ambassador to give him a letter, begging his government to stop supporting the Batista dictatorship.

That episode came on top of the effective lobbying activity carried out by exiles in the United States. They were led by Ernesto Betancourt, an able economist and strategist with a fine instinct for political intrigue, with the cooperation of other notable exiles like Victor de Yurre and Manuel Urrutia (a judge who had to go into exile after acquitting several *Granma* expeditionaries). These efforts achieved a spectacular favor for the opposition movement: a weapons embargo. The Eisenhower administration would not sell arms to Batista, and it would not even deliver the ones that had been paid. Obviously, Batista could buy them in another country, but this was a tremendous psychological blow: Batista, in the eyes of society, had fallen from grace with the North Americans. This whetted the conspiratorial appetite of the high military ranks and demoralized Batista's politicians even more. All of his generation perfectly remembered what had happened to Machado when he lost the support of the White House.

In this climate of crumbling authority, in September of 1957, several units of the Marines at the port of Cienfuegos staged an uprising in a plot coordinated by Emilio Aragones. He was a representative of the 26th of July Movement, and an ex-classmate of Castro's in the Belen school. Javier Pazos, a 26th of July chief in Havana, participated in the conspiracy, along with Julio Camacho and Justo Carrillo, a social democratic economist with an "Autentico" pedigree who led a small and imaginative opposition group named the *Montecristi*. The plan, which involved several mid-ranking officers, was partially successful and the city was taken by the insurgents during several hours. However, but it did not convert into an insurrection by the higher naval units — a cruise ship and a couple of smaller ships — with which they had planned to bomb the military installations in Havana.

Shortly, an armored detachment sent from Santa Clara and a bombardment by the air force (armed with old but efficient B-26 planes from World War II) was able to defeat the insurgents in the middle of a blood bath that, as happened so often with Batista forces, was cruelly prolonged for several days, causing a great number of victims. How many? The U.S. ambassador estimated it at 300. Perhaps it was more like 51, but it was, without a doubt, one of the bloodiest episodes in the fight against Batista.

The next challenge to the dictatorship came not in the form of a military conspiracy but a general strike. It was launched on the 26th of July under the leadership of the movement's coordinator in Havana, Faustino Pérez, an expeditionary from the *Granma* who had been stationed to promote the struggle in the capital. Seconding him were David Salvador, a labor leader with the highest rank in the group, Manuel Ray, an engineer, Aldo Vera, an unremitting terrorist of the 26th, Nicasio "Nicky" Silverio and Pedro Luis Boitel, student leader. The strike was a complete failure, and was accompanied by numerous terrorist explosions.

The more observant members of the opposition became convinced that the fight against Batista had no real support at the class level. People were not rebelling against Batista out of their sense of working man's solidarity, nor because they saw the dictator as the representative of the oligarchy. And worse: the Confederation of Cuban Workers, the very powerful CTC, had an agreement with Batista based on a type of *quid pro quo*: the government agreed not to harm the interests of the workers, and the organized union — at least the official one — would not interfere in the political conflict. Batista always presented himself as a man of the left, and he used to talk proudly of his presence in the city of Manzanillo in 1953 (he was just a humble water vendor for the railroads, at the time) when the Communist Party was founded. He did not feel any special hostility against the unions did not perceive them as adversaries; he always presented as his greatest achievement the sugar laws of 1939, which were a great advance in the interests of the workers.

After his victory in April, Batista decided, in May, at last to launch an offensive against Castro's guerrillas in Sierra Maestra. He lamented not having done it earlier, when they disembarked, because now he was confronting an enemy who knew the territory much better than his military chiefs did. That was a lesson that had served the dictator well, some time earlier, when he was quick to annihilate an expedition of Prío guerrillas who had arrived aboard the ship *Corinthia*. Could he wipe out Castro's men, almost 18 months after they had begun operating in the Sierra? He would soon find that he could not. Despite the fact Castro only had a few hundred gunmen and half a dozen real war weapons, with the help of a few well set-up ambushes, thorough knowledge of the territory and a constant flow of information received from the peasants, the bearded ones gained their victory.

A decisive contribution to that rebel triumph against the "big offensive" was a new and recent addition, who arrived in the Sierra Maestra from Costa Rica with the blessing of Jose Figueres. Huber Matos was a teacher born in Manzanillo, he was well linked to the Orthodox Party, and he had landed on an improvised airstrip in the mountains in a plane piloted by Pedro Luis Díaz Lanz. He brought with him a shipment of arms and ammunition that distinctly improved the capacity of the insurgents. Huber Matos quickly demonstrated that he was a formidable organizer and a military leader who could lead the troops on attacks against the enemy. Fidel took note and quickly gave him the rank of *comandante*.

After defeating Batista's offensive, Castro had to initiate a more delicate battle: to control the guerrillas of the Directorate at Escambray. To that end, he planned to send detachments of invaders who would travel to the other end of the island, and along the way — through the central Cuban mountains — would politically neutralize those potential adversaries, and if possible, recruit them for the 26th of July movement. With that purpose in mind, he used two of his most trusted *comandantes*: Ernesto "Che" Guevara and Camilo Cienfuegos. The two, with several dozen men for companions, initiated a long walk in which they avoided confrontations with the army (and bribed some of the corrupt Batista officials who were more interested in making money than in fighting). Finally, both detachments, one traveling along the northern coast, the other along the southern, arrived at their destination, and without having met any real resistance. They astutely complied with their assignment to politically and psychologically subordinate the other rebels, without officially absorbing them into their ranks — although they meet some uncomfortable resistance from the men of Gutiérrez Menoyo, whom they accused of being "sectarians" and "cow-eaters," that is, of not fighting much — something that was surely unfair.

In mid-1958, Batista and his supporters were reasonably worried. The macroeconomic data was generally good: investments continued to flow, inflation was low, and the monetary value was holding up — despite a considerable reductions in the reserves — and the trade balance turned out to be favorable to Cuba. Many new buildings were going up, as well as middle-class neighborhoods. Cubans inaugurated color television. They were the first Latin American citizens to enjoy that technological advance.

Of course there was poverty, inequity, ongoing unemployment and shortages, but since the degree of development is always relative, workers elsewhere looked at Cuba as offering more hope than their own countries. At that time, 12,000 Italians and as many Spaniards had applied for immigration visas at the Cuban consulates. The problem was not in civil society. The problem was political. The biggest periodicals on the island, *Bohemia* magazine, the newspapers *Prensa Libre*, *Avance, Informacion*, the most accredited journalists — Agustín Tamargo, Humberto Medrano, Agustín Alles, Salvador Lew, Mario Rivadulla, Pedro Leiva, Luis Conte Agüero, Sergio and Ulises Carbó — denounced the brazen corruption and crimes of the government with as much vehemence as was permitted by the sporadic censorship.

A general clamor was running throughout the country — "Batista, leave!". The Catholic Church added its voice, looking for some compromise that could save the institution of the nation. What became known as "the live forces of the nation" — the trade unions, the professional organizations, the most prominent personalities — joined in. The U.S. embassy also agreed with that sentiment, although quietly. It was dangerous to North American interests for Batista to continue in power, given that the enormous illegitimacy of his government could precipitate his violent fall and the triumph of Castro — a figure over whom the American policy-makers were divided. Some officials classified him as a dangerous Communist and others as an inoffensive reformist in the old populist tradition of Latin America. Whichever the real Fidel Castro really was, he was not a candidate suitable to Washington's interests.

It looked as though Batista might be inclined to leave, but not before he completed his mandate and left the presidency to an ally who would not persecute him and hold him responsible for the crimes and irregularities committed during his administration. That man was Andrés Rivero Agüero, a lawyer of humble origins, a minister in the cabinet and a person in whom Batista had total confidence. He did not have bloodstained hands nor was he perceived as a blatant thief. He could have preferred the opposition, in the person of Carlos Marquez Sterling, an Orthodox electoralist, a man of integrity and a politician who was amenable to going to the ballot box in the midst of the violent climate all over the country. However, Batista, who was never his friend — and who had a tribal outlook on public affairs — did not trust him. He feared Carlos Marquez Sterling and so he closed the door. Perhaps his last door. Perhaps, the last door of the republic.

The elections finally took place on November 3, amid a climate somewhere between terror and apathy. Several small towns were already guerrilla strongholds and Huber Matos's detachment had the army under siege in the outskirts of Santiago de Cuba. Radio Rebelde, the rebel radio station, was ably directed by Carlos Franqui (a former journalist and a former Communist) who had sided with Castro. He was worried by the influence of his old comrades. The station launched harangues and rallying cries that electrified the population. The rebels threatened to punish harshly anyone who voted, denouncing the fraudulent nature of the elections — and thanks to Batista, they were right: voter turnout was very low, and there were all kinds of irregularities to guarantee the victory of the official candidate. Finally, after the routine recount, Andrés Rivero Agüero was proclaimed the winner — albeit without much conviction. In February of 1959 Batista was supposed turn over the reins of power. Many people believed he would not do it; but no one could have predicted what did happen. At that moment, Castro was calculating that he would stay a few more months in the mountains before he would even come close to victory. Expecting a close ending, but not an imminent one, the 26th of July group had signed a political agreement with other opposition forces to form a type of governmental coalition. It was called the Caracas Pact.

But history surprised them. Here is what really happened. In early December, Batista received information that was a deep secret and a deep shock: his military chiefs in Oriente, especially General Eulogio Cantillo, were in discussion with Fidel Castro over the creation of a combined council that would oust him from power and prevent the transfer of power to Andrés Rivero Agüero.

There was treason on both sides: the Secret Services of the U.S. embassy had also contacted the generals and the rebels. Between the end of 1957 and the middle of 1958 the CIA, represented in Santiago de Cuba by vice consul Robert D. Wiecha, had given the 26th of July Movement some $50,000 while maintaining fluid relations with diverse factions of the opposition. On top of the treason of the military and the U.S. double cross, bad news came from the front in Las Villas, the mountainous province where Escambray is located. An armored train packed with soldiers and military supplies, sent to fight the men of Guevara, Cubelas and Gutiérrez Menoyo, had been sold to the enemy by corrupt officials. Almost the entire army was rotten. Apparently, it was kept intact because the principal garrisons were all under the government's control and no large city had changed sides, but it was an empty shell, a sad mask.

In the midst of all this came the straw that broke the camel's back. In the middle of December, a special envoy from President Eisenhower came to the palace and bluntly told Batista that the White House no longer had any confidence in him and that he should pack up and go, after organizing a government of national salvation to avoid the triumph of Castro's rebels. Batista listened carefully, and mouthed a response appropriate for a wounded patriot, answering that Cuba had held elections and that Rivero Agüero had been elected, and that he would hand over power in February. When the troubled American left the room, Batista began to plan his immediate flight. He would escape from the country. He would not wait until February, nor run the risk of having his own soldiers, in cahoots with Castro, arrest him. He was filled with panic and he remembered the nightmare of the days following the fall of Machado, when some of his supporters were lynched by frenetic mobs. He had no intention of being dragged to death by mobs. And why not dump the problem in the hands of the U.S.? Hadn't they betrayed him? Hadn't the most powerful sectors of the economy, almost all of them *Fidelistas*, betrayed him? Whatever came next was their problem.

At the end of December, the first provincial capital, Santa Clara, fell to the rebels. Guevara and Cubelas were the heroes of that glorious event. Earlier, in the Sierra Maestra, two prominent members of the Catholic University Association had joined Castro's guerrillas: a charismatic doctor named Manuel Artime and a young lawyer named Emilio Martinez Venegas, who was known for his bold action and good organization skills. Shortly before, the Jesuit Armando Llorente, an old mentor of Fidel Castro's, had climbed the mountains to talk with his disciple. The church, discretely and unofficially, increased its commitment to the insurrection.

Batista had disappeared, and he planned to take advantage of the night of New Year's Eve to make his get away — when most Cubans could be expected to have something other than politics on their minds. In anticipation, one of his trusted men had flown to the Dominican Republic to negotiate the future (and costly) hospitality of Trujillo. Batista had sent part of his family ahead, to the United States, "for Christmas." He had a couple of planes prepared, and at the last minute, abandoned a New Year's Eve party, just dropping a word in the ear of a few friends and trusted collaborators. He took off from a military airport. The great majority of *Batistianos* in positions of authority he left to their luck, without caring what would happen to them if the enemies took power. He felt he had been betrayed, and he reacted by betraying everyone.

The fortune he had accumulated outside the country apparently reached $200 million. For him, exile would not be difficult; but for many who called themselves *Batistianos*, an epoch of disgrace and untold penury began. Some of his closest men were ruined, as happened to the minister of governance, Santiago Rey Perna, a cultivated and hard-fighting man (who despite everything continued to show a moving loyalty for Batista). Others, less generous or more rancorous, cursed his name.

It is almost impossible for future history to redeem the memory of this ill-fated politician. It was true that he was not clumsy in the administration of the state. It is true that Cuba in the 1950s had reached a level of development that allowed it to look to the future with optimism. But that is only part of the truth. With the coup d'etat of March 10, 1952, Batista opened a Pandora's box. With his flight on January 1, 1959, he left the republic defenseless, without proper institutions and beset by demons whirling about the island.

IV

HERE'S. . . COMMUNISM!

When Castro got word of Batista's escape, he did not rush to Havana to take his place. He sent Camilo Cienfuegos and Che, from Santa Clara — the midway point from the Sierra Maestra — to occupy the most important military installations while he, cautiously, almost reluctantly, took several days to assess and increase his forces in a slow-moving journey across the length of the island. The propaganda had established that he had thousands of followers, but in truth, he had never had any more than a few hundred guerrillas. Everything had been intelligently and deliberately exaggerated. The figure of 20,000 dead under Batista's harsh hand had been made up; the real number was under 1,800, heart attacks included, and counting the victims on both sides. Soon *Bohemia* magazine would compile the exact figure, along with first and last names. Cuba was too small to hide bodies. It wasn't even possible to raise a monument to the "unknown hero" of the revolutionary fight, because everyone knew each other intimately.

In any case, how much support did Castro really have, at this point, in Cuban society? Before the insurrection, Fidel had been a controversial young political leader without any national influence. What support did he now have among Cubans, after the Moncada events and the two years he spent in the Sierra Maestra? On the other hand, Batista was gone, but his army of almost 40,000 men remained practically intact. Castro also did not know the intentions of the United States, even if the most overt signs indicated that (this time) they were going to abstain from meddling. But, more than his enemies, what perhaps worried him most were his "friends": what were Carlos Prío, the Directorate, the Second Escambray Front going to do? Would Prío re-claim the presidency that Batista had snatched away, to finish his term and call for elections? There was, it is true, the Caracas Pact, but the sudden victory left a power vacuum that could have tempted any of those other groups. Castro, while he suspected his own popular backing, began studying the reactions of all the elements of power as he slowly approached Havana.

This kind of pilgrimage had a surprising catalytic effect. At every step, in every town, more emotional Cubans joined him, showing him total political loyalty. In the city of Holguín, a reporter from *Bohemia*, Carlos Castañeda, a former colleague in the Orthodox Party, intercepted Fidel to interview him, and Fidel asked Castañeda a naive and revealing question: "Do you think Miguel Quevedo (the editor) will give me the front page?" The journalist, known in Cuba for an exclusive interview he had done with President Harry Truman, was surprised and confirmed what Castro perceived intuitively but still did not know for sure: "Of course, Fidel, you are the unquestionable leader; he will give you the whole magazine if you want it."

And that's how it was. That's how Cubans were starting to perceive him. When Castro arrived in Havana on January 8, the entire country bowed down before him. There was no longer any other leadership than his. Carlos Prío was a footnote in history. Grau did not exist. He was barely a whisper, weakened by discredit. Nobody remembered the Pact of Caracas and it did not occur to anyone to doubt the legitimacy of the government that would spring from Fidel Castro's decisions. The other revolutionary groups bowed their heads. The Directorate made an attempt to control certain symbolic centers of power — the presidential palace, the university — but after the first struggles, its leaders admitted defeat and gave way to "the unity the homeland demands." In other words, they accepted the leadership of the 26th of July and the man that they started to call the Maximum Leader, *el Máximo*

Líder. Fidel had the support of almost all the public opinion and all the media. He was the absolute master of the country and no one dared to question or even ask where his legitimacy came from, to unilaterally form a government: he was the victorious hero.

What did he have to do then? He took on several tasks, all of them simultaneous and urgent: to create a government that would inspire confidence in the country and transmit an image of seriousness and professionalism; to severely punish the defeated *batistianos*, to keep them from regrouping; consolidate his control over the armed forces and restrain the other insurgent groups. But all of these objectives were just the prerequisites to the preparation of the true and profound social revolution that he had been mapping out secretly in the Sierra Maestra, and of which barely any signs existed. The Cubans still did not know of the letter sent by Fidel to Celia Sánchez in the summer of 1958, wherein he warned and forecast that the future would be a major and prolonged battle against the United States — a hidden *leitmotiv* of his sleepless nights as a revolutionary.

The first cabinet of the Revolution, was, then, first rate, and impeccable from the point of view of democratic credentials. It even leaned toward anticommunism. The designated president was a judge, Manuel Urrutia, little known but with a long record of fighting for liberty. His prime minister was an illustrious legal scholar, a criminologist named José Miró Cardona, one of the best thinkers among the country's jurists. The labor minister was Manuel Fernández, a public accountant, a social democrat of *Guiterista* mold, an honest and austere man who took as deputies Carlos Varona Duquestrada — one of the opposition chiefs in Camagüey — and the *Granma* expeditionary César Gómez. Roberto Agramonte, a sociologist and Chibás heir, was appointed foreign minister. Rufo López Fresquet, a pro-American economist, became the minister of finance, and he brought in Jose M. Illán, another respected economist, one of the few in Cuba familiar with the work of Von Mises and Hayek, and Antonio Jorge, also a good economist, an exemplary democrat but more Keynesian in his thinking. Engineer Manuel Ray, chief of the civic resistance, was put in charge of the ministry of public works, and he took as his right hand another young democrat, the architect Henry Gutiérrez. The list, naturally, is longer —

Humberto Sorí Marín, Armando Hart, Elena Mederos, and other inoffensive names — but the result was the same: the faces of the first government of the revolution gave no reason for social alarm. There was only one discreet exception, in the judicial arena. He was Osvaldo Dorticós Torrado, a good lawyer of bourgeois origins, born in Cienfuegos, very involved with the Communists; but his fellow townspeople only remembered him as a very active figure in the city's Yacht Club. Apparently, he was what was then known as a "club man". He was named minister of the new Ministry of Study of Revolutionary Laws. In reality, he was the "carpenter" of the secret socialist project.

A Shadow Government

In effect, unbeknownst even to his colleagues, Dorticós — an unknown and hard to define character — was the key figure in the cabinet because it was his job to begin to mold the socialist state in collaboration with Fidel, who ran another government in the shadows, one much more radical, and which included Ernesto Guevara, Alfredo Guevara, Raúl Castro, Antonio Núñez Jiménez, the brothers Camilo and Osmany Cienfuegos and Ramiro Valdés, a kind of Cuban Laurenti Beria, born with a natural vocation for the police. That *other* government, the real one (since the official one was merely a temporary episode for Castro), whose genesis and evolution was the great research success of the journalist and historian Tad Szulc, would meet in a house in the outskirts of Havana. There, secretly, they planned the way and the rate at which they would undertake the transformation of Cuba to a Communist state, a project that required absolute discretion because if it word had gotten out, at that moment, the popular reaction might have been totally against it. Even the 26th of July Movement, founded on the platform of the Orthodox Party, would have revolted given that a good part of its leadership — Raúl Chibás, Armando Hart, Marcelo Fernández, Vicente Báez, Carlos Franqui, Faustino Pérez, David Salvador, Huber Matos, among many others — totally repudiated the idea of a totalitarian state.

It is at this point that Castro called the Communists to the secret meetings and laid on the table his most audacious card: the Revolution, in effect, would evolve toward the model developed by the Marxists, but only at the right moment, and in a process directed by Fidel; and the old Communists would have to become subordinates and integrate with him. In exchange for their collaboration, they would have a clear quota of power, but always within the centrally controlled apparatus that would come together under the most unequivocal leadership of the *comandante*. There would be difficult times, Fidel forecast, and conflict with the local bourgeois and the Yankees was practically inevitable.

Almost all of the Marxist leadership were pleasantly surprised by the proposal. On January 1, 1959, the PSP didn't have the slightest idea that it had come to power. The first public demonstration it staged were, indeed, to demand elections. They had practiced "infiltration." That is, they had "infiltrated" the Revolution to try to control it, placing certain Communist chieftains among the fighting insurgents; or at least, they had tried to influence it. But the outcome of this political game was a complete surprise: the most radical sector of the 26th of July, with Fidel, Guevara and Raul at the helm, were the ones "infiltrating" the Communist apparatus and asking for their frank complicity for two key tasks. They, the *fidelistas*, would need help to master the massive organization of Marxist *cadres* within the armed forces, and to urgently create a political police force capable of subduing the enemies when the fight (that would surely erupt) became severe.

Fidel held the power and identified his goal, but he was not in a position to create a structure and he did not trust the *cadres* of his own organization. What he expected from the Communists, however, would be essential in carrying out his plans: the solid Leninist engineering that is required for building and sustaining a totalitarian state. And there was a third contribution that the Communist could make: by creating a more solid bridge with Moscow, given that Raúl's contacts through his friend Leonov were too indirect and weak with the Kremlin, that cultivated with care its associates and its and bureaucratic hierarchies. The PSP, however, had been a loyal pawn of Moscow since its founding in the 1920s, and had many ties with the comrades in charge at the Kremlin. They could vouch for the Revolution before the Soviets and create zones of collaboration, but those links, naturally, would be handled by the *fidelistas*. The Communist leaders, represented by Blas Roca, Carlos Rafael Rodríguez and Aníbal Escalante agreed to the pact. Escalante, who never stopped seeing Castro as a *putchista* adventurer, thought they would be able to not only control power, but control Fidel. The future would prove him wrong. In less than three years, Escalante and a group of Communists would land in jail, accused of factionalism. Theirs was the "micro faction," as it was then derogatorily called. Fidel had recruited them to obey, not to rule.

Was He Pushed, or Did He Jump?

Why did Fidel Castro take the Marxist-Leninist route? For its intellectual coherence and rigor, and because that political framework turns out to be perfectly suitable for ruling as head of an autocratic government (into which he planned to transform Cuba, and if possible, Latin America and the entire world). He saw himself as a mix of Martí and Bolívar, but "Leninized."

The "intellectual coherence" is not difficult to explain. When radical revolutionary thought is unfolded to its ultimate consequences, the final point of arrival is an openly Communist society in confrontation with the imperialist designs of the United States. If a person believed — like Fidel — that the poverty some levels of Cuban society was due to exploitation by the voracious entrepreneurs and to the implicit cruelty of the system, it was morally justifiable to erase all vestiges of capitalism, to replace the market with bureaucratic controls established by fair-minded revolutionaries, and to procure at all costs equality for all Cubans. If a person thought — as did Fidel and so many revolutionaries of his time — that foreign investment was an immoral form of looting, what else could you do but confiscate the properties of those foreign vampires and "return" them to the people by converting them into state enterprises? Hadn't revolutionaries of every persuasion spent the last thirty years demanding the nationalization of the banks and of the public services? If a person was convinced — like Fidel — that the national bourgeoisie, the Church, and the other conventional estates of the country formed part of the structure that generated poverty and oppression in the service of the neighboring imperialist powers, wasn't it fair and necessary to make war and destroy them? If a person, finally, was persuaded that the pluralist democratic system, with diverse political parties vying for power, was a permanent source of corruption and divisions, then logically if you have the authority to do so, you must eliminate that system in one sweeping gesture.

Fidel, in reality, didn't betray the radical thinking. All he did was follow the logic of his revolutionary reasoning until he reached the totalitarian outcome. He had mistaken ideas, he subscribed to erroneous diagnoses, and he tried, simply, to follow with logical consistency all these wrong turns. He arrived where he wanted to go by using a biased, manipulative and intellectually weak view of the problems of society. In summary, he fulfilled all the promises that the Marxist revolutionaries (and some non-Marxist) had been making for the last thirty years in Latin America, and that none had dared to carry out. All of this could have been avoided if, early on, in his formative years, he had read the right books or had received the right influences, but since the 1930s Cuba had lived in a populist culture, an absolutely fertile ground for nurturing this kind of craziness. And he, Castro, was the ultimate expression of that lamentable mess.

It is important to understand this, because among the foolish things said about the Cuban Revolution, none is more unfair to Fidel or farther from the truth than often-repeated notion that "the Americans pushed Castro into the hands of the Communists and of the Soviet Union." That belittles Castro and Guevara and a number of clear-minded men who changed the path of the history of Cuba. It even borders on racist thinking, because it is like saying that a poor fellow from the Antilles could never be capable of understanding Marxism and would allow himself to be seduced by it. It is almost like believing that the reality of Communist revolutions can only be properly grasped by those brainy European Communists. Of course that is not the case. Castro voluntarily chose the road to communism, as he has gotten tired of repeating (without much success) — he affirmed it in Madrid, for example, in the 1980s, in front of Spanish television cameras. And by the nature of his decision, during the Cold War, he placed himself squarely in the Soviet camp and in confrontation with the United States.

That event was not even all that peculiar, at the time: in 1957, when Fidel was in the Sierra Maestra, the Communists and their sympathizers throughout the West were living in an era of hope, even euphoria. Sartre, in Paris, was sure that the world would soon follow the example of the USSR. All of the news seemed to point in that direction. Moscow had inaugurated the space race by launching the first *sputnik*. For ten years, the Soviet economy grew at a rate of 10% annually and there was talk of a bipolar world ruled by two great powers. One of those two powers, in the minds of Fidel and some other Cubans, was to blame for all the ills haunting the "compromised republic". And wouldn't that analysis lead one directly, into the arms of the other?

The United States was not very clear on Castro's intentions. Since many streams bring information to the White House, the reports were contradictory. The outgoing ambassador, Earl Smith, somberly warned that Washington would have to confront a fanatical and anti-American Communist. The CIA, more benevolent, thought he was a typical Latin American revolutionary (which wasn't entirely false), but could not establish clearly the ties between Fidel and the old Communist party. Yes, there were Communists in the government, but there were also anti-Communists. All of these advisors agreed, however, that Castro was a picturesque and dangerous character who would give the Department of State many headaches, and that given the rapid fame he had acquired throughout South America, it would be best to try to appease him.

So they sent to Havana a new and experienced ambassador, Philip Bonsal, with instructions try to get as close as he could to the flamboyant government, and to ignore the rhetorical attacks made by the hotheaded leader in his marathon speeches — just the verbal expressions of a young man giddy with victory. In any case, what could little, and dependent, Cuba do to the United States? Where would they sell their sugar if the United States stopped buying it? Where would they get the petroleum or the thousands of raw materials with which Cubans kept the country functioning? Eighty per cent of the commercial transactions in Cuba were with the United States. With the exception of Venezuela, Cuba received the most investments from the United States of any Latin American country. Setting aside a military intervention, no Cuban government that would confront the United States could survive more than a few months due to economic realities.

The USSR, it is true, could try to extend its long arm to the Caribbean, but until that moment the Soviet leaders had subscribed to the strategic vision proposed by Lenin and maintained by Stalin: Communism could not reach Latin America until the United States (with its great concentration of proletarians, and consequently, a class consciousness) made its own revolution. Only, in the Kremlin it was no longer Stalin who ruled but Khrushchev, a peasant of less intellectual refinement, clever and audacious, and convinced that in two decades his country would surpass the United States and be at the helm of the planet. This was a peasant who, obsessed with that objective, would allow himself to be dragged to the Caribbean pit. A revealing view of that debacle is given in *A hell of a gamble*, a book co-written by a Soviet specialist who eloquently narrates how the Cubans beguiled the Russians, and not the other way around — contrary to popular belief.

The Firing Squad

Curiously, the judicial model of the first revolutionary government was furnished by Batista. In 1952, when he staged the military coup, Batista (proclaiming verbatim that "the revolution is a fountain of rights") dissolved the two chambers of the Cuban parliament, assigning the legislative function to the Council of Ministers. He suspended all laws and norms of the Constitution of 1940 that were in contradiction to his *de facto* government, and even reinstituted the death penalty to the statutes dictated a few weeks after his takeover (although he never had any detainee "officially" executed). The government of president Urrutia and Prime Minister Miró Cardona followed this precedent very closely. They even repeated the legitimizing alibi of the deposed dictator: "The revolution is a fountain of rights." Since that definition would serve to justify practically any act, events soon took place that were really repugnant to the sensibilities of people who had been educated to respect the law and the formality that it requires. For example, sentences and laws that did not exist when certain acts took place were applied retroactively, so that those acts were classified as crimes. In any case, Miró was only prime minister for a few weeks. He resigned, in agreement with the president, and in February, Urrutia named Fidel

Castro to head the government.

That disdain for laws and the kind of conduct had been observed from the first days of the revolutionary triumph, when Raúl Castro, after a simulated revolutionary trial, executed a few dozen Batista officials by having them stand in front of a ditch and be shot. They were immediately buried without even waiting for doctors to certify their deaths. Later, in Havana — and in all of the island — public judicial proceedings took place in the presence of the international press and thousands of people who attended watched the trial of soldiers and police officials accused of being "torturers" and "war criminals," charges that were not always proven in a convincing way but that frequently brought the death penalty or very lengthy prison sentences. During this period, when the courts started to use a strange argument to impose sentences, the concept of sentencing "by conviction" arises. If the honored revolutionaries were "convinced" of the guilt of a discredited *batistiano*, even if the evidence was shaky or non-existent, they could issue sentences with the harshest severity.

Why did Castro stop being a good revolutionary, the Robin Hood of the Caribbean, and expose his image to the weary task of appearing before the press and on television as a vengeful bloody criminal who filmed the executions of his enemies and showed them in movie theaters? Because he was convinced that intimidation and fear were important tools in governing. He believed punishment, and learning from the experience of others, were two of the best weapons of power. This is clearly reflected in his personal correspondence, where there are frequent references to Robespierre and his admiration for revolutionary terror.

This harshness, of course, was not always shared by his subordinates and on one occasion at least it provoked an incident that began to alert the citizenry as to what type of leader had assumed power. This occurred in the first months of 1959, when a group of military pilots were taken to trial, accused of "genocide". They could not have been guilty of that, because the bombings and machine-gun shootings that were attributed to them were not intended to eliminate certain people because of their ethnicity or religion — which is what genocide specifically denotes — nor could it be established who had shot at whom or at what, because there was no proof and no records that clearly estab-lished the responsibility of the accused. Given all these doubts, the president of the tribunal, Captain Félix Pena, decided to let them go. Castro was indignant when he heard about this, and he got on televi-sion, and before the acquitted soldiers could be released, he expressed his certainty about their guilt. They were condemned to long prison sentences. An embarrassed Captain Pena blew his brains out. Years later, Castro told a visitor why he kept the pilots in prison: they were the most competent soldiers of Batista's era and the ones who had the closest ties with the North Americans, because of the training they had received. They had not even been convicted "with conviction"; it was all based on a political calculation. Their imprisonment was not a matter of vengeance but a preventive measure.

Aside from the revolutionary trials — which, to the historical shame of the country did not offend too many people, as evidenced by the enormous demonstrations of people who would shout, "*paredón, paredón*" (execution, execution) — the vast majority of Cubans received with open arms some of the populist laws directed at solidifying the massive support for the government. The most applauded were the rent laws, (which cut in half the monthly rent to be paid), the reduced tele-phone rates, and the agrarian reform law, which limited land owner-ship, benefiting peasants who had no land or who were in danger of losing their land. To any knowledgeable person, it was obvious that these laws would have a major impact on national production, in the construction industry as much as in agriculture, but at that time the government and especially Fidel were preoccupied not with economics but politics. To accomplish the task before him, at a time when the mechanisms of control and coercion were not yet in place, he needed the massive support of Cubans and these laws guaranteed him that support.

As is natural in any open society — which Cuba still was in 1959 — a few weeks after the revolutionary government was installed, criticism began in the independent mass media. The government acridly answered it, in the official press. Soon it became evident that any differences were branded as "counterrevolutionary" and those re-sponsible for voicing them were classified as *batistianos* or agents of the

Yankee embassy. Scandalous ruptures soon became public. There had been some previous cases, but the first notable "loss" in the confrontation between the democratic wing of the government and the Communists came when the chief of the revolutionary air force, Commander Pedro Luis Díaz Lanz, after making comments critical of communism, ended up being stripped of his authority by Fidel Castro. This prompted Lanz to defect, in a small yacht, and after arriving in the United States he denounced that the military apparatus was totally infiltrated by members of the Communist Party who were indoctrinating and progressively gaining control all of the levers of power. That was in June of 1959, and the government answered by accusing him of embezzlement and by stating that his attitude resulted precisely from the fact that his dishonesty had been discovered.

In July, barely seven months after the inauguration of his presidency, and for the same reasons, it was President Urrutia's turn. He was forced to leave his post, and naturally, he too was accused of corruption. Since then, the custom has become firmly entrenched: those who break with Castro, or who fall from his grace and good will, are always accused of some crime or of holding morally reprehensible attitudes. No honorable person opposes the Revolution; only heartless people. Urrutia was replaced by Osvaldo Dorticós. He no longer had to construct the socialist state in the shadows: he became the new president and was free to act in the broad light of day.

After these two incidents, what followed was almost a monotonous repetition of a classic script. In October, the country was shaken as never before — and for the same reasons. This time, the one who was detained and hauled before the courts was a *comandante*, Húber Matos, one of the heroes of the Revolution, military chief of the province of Camagüey; and the crime he was accused of is uncommon: treason and sedition, for having resigned from the army. He sent a letter to Fidel Castro, as firm as it was respectful, in which he voiced his discontent with the Communist route adopted by the Revolution. Castro had him arrested by Camilo Cienfuegos — who then, hours later, disappeared in a strange airplane accident — and Matos was brought to Havana in handcuffs along with several officers who had reported to him. He was sentenced to 20 years in prison, after a shameful military trial.

A few days before his detention, the minister of labor and assistant secretaries Carlos Varona and César Gomez had resigned. To any impartial observer, it is apparent that Castro had decided to accelerate the course of the Revolution toward a Communist model and he was only making time to accomplish the dangerous transition successfully.

This is the moment when numerous veterans of the fight against Batista decided to begin to conspire against the government. They felt that Castro had betrayed the Revolution. The war against the previous dictatorship, they said, had intended to rescue democracy and restore the Constitution of 1940; turning the island into a Communist tyranny was not part of the original plan. At least, not theirs.

The Destruction of Civil Society

In November 1959, a confrontation between democratic and Communist revolutionaries took place at the Tenth Congress of the Federation of Cuban Workers. There were 3000 delegates, and less than 300 of them were Communists. Fidel's rallying cry, which he transmitted to the "26th of July" leader David Salvador, was "Unity with the Communists"; he planned to bring them into the governing apparatus at any cost, but the labor leaders rejected that. Fidel was obliged to attend in person, to try to salvage the situation. Reinol González, José de Jesús Planas and Eduardo García-Moure, three young labor leaders who had risen through the Catholic ranks, stood out for their passionate defense of democracy. Roberto Simeón was also staunch in that stance, from an *aprista* position. After gross manipulation, a compromise was reached. This was, however, the only defeat that the government suffered, and even this one was only temporary. But soon, the Communists managed to reverse the situation and take control of the labor apparatus. It took them a little time, but they achieved it. Reinol took the road of conspiracy, and would spend many years suffering in particularly severe prisons. Garcia Moure and Planas were compelled to go into exile in Venezuela after they were forced to seek diplomatic protection in that country's embassy, in Havana. They were joined by Roberto Fontanillas-Roig who, years later, would become the most respected leader of the Cuban exile community in that country.

The offensive against the democratic media, and its subsequent takeover lasted approximately one year. Attacks by the newspaper *Revolución*, the official organ of the 26th July (which had the sad job of hounding and accusing) and by the Communists' *Hoy*, followed trumped up conflicts with the unions, and mobs and threats were used to intimidate critical journalists. The unions forced the enterprises to publish a "*coletilla*," a note at the end of each story, noting that the text deviated from the government's official line. Some of the journalists who had been notoriously anti-Batista fought memorably against the incipient dictatorship: Humberto Medrano, Ulises Carbó, Agustín Tamargo, Sergio Carbó, Miguel Angel Quevedo, Luis Conte Agüero, Jorge Mañach, Pedro Leiva, Andrés Valdespino, Jorge Zayas, Viera Trejo, Aguilar León. Others, more conservative, like José I. Rivero and Gastón Baquero — one of the country's great poets — also raised their voices with determination, sometimes risking their lives, because the home they believed in was practically lost. The newspapers, perhaps without their owners even knowing it (or maybe knowing full well what was happening), assumed the institutional role of serving as the last trench in which the republican ideals were buried. One by one they were demolished by the totalitarian machinery: *Bohemia, Avance, Prensa Libre, Diario de la Marina, Información, El Mundo, Zig-Zag, CMQ*. And after each purge, an obscene vista unfolded: mobs, led by agitators, shouted revolutionary slogans and buried empty coffins symbolizing the confiscated newspapers.

Without newspapers, without Parliament, without political parties, without independent unions, with the labor institutions silenced and entrepreneurs impoverished and terrorized, without any means of public participation, it became easier for Cuban civil society to be erased; it was practically in a shambles already.

The next bastion appropriated by the Communists was the private educational system. The pretext was the need to give all the people the same good education so as not to divide society into different classes, with different visions of reality. And it wasn't a false wish of the government to uniformly mold all Cubans into the same point of view; but there was another, more obvious, political element. No Communist state could afford the luxury of allowing pockets of academic freedom, where independent and critical thinking could flourish. Very soon, children began to learn to read using revolutionary flash cards laden with a crude psychological message: "F for Fidel, Ch for Che," and "M for my mother, who loves me and Moscow." All across the entire island there were dozens of good scholarly institutions, generally affordable to the middle and upper classes. They were not "elite" schools; their fees used to be quite reasonable. Among them, the best secular schools in Havana were Edison, La Luz, Baldor, Ruston and Trelles. Among the religious, the best were considered to be Belén — where Castro had studied — La Salle, Los Maristas, Las Ursulinas, El Sagrado Corazón, Las Dominicas, Los Agustinos o La Progresiva de Cárdenas and Candler College — where Fidel Castro's oldest son studied — these latter ones led by Protestant pastors. The best proof of the quality of the education at these centers could be found at the top of the revolutionary leadership, as much in the 26th of July as in the PSP. Every one of them, without one sad proletarian exception, had been educated in good private religious or lay schools. None was the product of the numerous public schools in the country, even if many of them, especially those at the secondary and college level, offered a notable level of educational excellence.

The confiscation of educational centers and the total control or disappearance of independent publications provoked an open confrontation between the Catholic Church and the government. Traditionally, over the many centuries, the Church had concentrated its greatest efforts in three vital activities: propagating and maintaining religious faith in its temples; educating people, especially children and youth; and disseminating information through various channels. Of these three tasks, the last two were suddenly eliminated by the government, while the first became a condemnable practice. All of a sudden, going to church, baptizing the newborn or proclaiming oneself Catholic began to be seen as synonymous with being obscurantist, backward, and finally counterrevolutionary.

The Church, whose most visible leadership was that of the eminent bishop Monsignor Eduardo Boza Masvidal, protested through pastoral letters read in churches, and there were even some processions on the streets. Catholics were upset with the aggression to which they were being subjected. The protests were answered by violent mobs organized by the government, but the truth is that society, in the whole, did not answer the call of the representatives of its faith, and Castro was able to neutralize (and practically annihilate) this dangerous enemy without too much trouble. In a surprisingly brief period, the Church was silenced, reduced to liturgical practices. Before waging the battle, Castro probably knew that Cuban society, more like the Uruguayan and the Costa Rican societies than the rest of the Latin American countries, was not profoundly religious, and did not feel strongly the authority of the clergy. When the bells started ringing to sound the alarm, the people sat at home in indifference. No one dared to protest when more than 200 priests and nuns were forced to embark on ship bound for Spain, nor when the priests Alfredo Petit, today auxiliary bishop of Havana, and Jaime Ortega Alamino, today Cuba's cardinal, were sent to concentration camps. Even less when Franciscan Miguel Angle Loredo became the victim of a fabricated counterrevolutionary crime he never committed, for which he spent more than a decade in prison: 10 years that the political police had vowed to keep him apart from the youth who flocked to his monastery in search of spiritual guidance.

Predictably, the Cuban democrats did not sit still while Fidel led the nation at full speed toward a Communist model. And another easy forecast: the first and most serious conspiracies were organized by those who had fought against the previous dictatorship. Two exceptions are worth mentioning: already in 1959 a small guerrilla band disembarked in Cuba, led by a Batista supporter named Armentino Feria, a former Communist and a veteran of the Spanish Civil War in the International Brigades. He was an extraordinarily courageous man, but his group was immediately annihilated. Many years later, his daughter, Áurea Feria, would be incarcerated for defending human rights. Shortly after, a conspiracy organized by Batista supporters from Dominican Republic, with the clear involvement of Trujillo, was denounced in Cuba by Gutiérrez Menoyo's men, who supposedly had agreed to cooperate with the invaders, but in reality, were setting a trap. Dozens of people — some of them innocent — ended up in prison. Despite all of this, Batista supporters were no remedy to the opposition. The largest anti-Castro movements arose from the ranks of the revolutionaries with Catholic affiliation, the Authentic Party members Prío and Tony Varona and the democratic wing of the 26th of July Movement. Below, we will go over the main organizations and the people who achieved the most prominence, but we can barely hint at the entire list of anti-Communist organizations that arose in those first years of the Revolution and the hundreds of men and women who tried to prevent the establishment of communism in Cuba.

The Anti-Communist Insurrection

The first anti-Communist focus that originated among the Catholics may have been the Christian Democratic Movement founded by Jose Ignacio Rasco in 1959. His purpose was to wage a political battle, but that objective very quickly gave way to clandestine combat. Shortly afterward, another opposition group was formed around the Catholic University Association, an elitist sector of Jesuit inclination, motivated by a profound social conscience and some experience in working with peasants. Its principal leaders were the doctor Manuel Artime, a lieutenant in the Sierra Maestra, the lawyer Emilio Martínez Venegas (also an ex-combatant alongside Fidel Castro), the young psychiatrist Lino Fernández and the engineer Rogelio González Corso.

Two somewhat younger figures soon began to stand out — especially after a much talked-about incident that involved the placing of flowers before Martí's statue, after a similar ceremony held by Anastas Mikoyan, the great Soviet apparatchik visiting Cuba. They were the combative University of Havana students Alberto Müller and Manuel Salvat, whose roots and sympathies lay in the Schools of Law and Social Sciences. Out of that Catholic milieu would come two conspiratorial groups, intimately linked: the Movement of Revolutionary Recovery (Movimento de Recuperacíon Revolucionaria, MRR) and — again as in the 1930s and 1950s — the Revolutionary Student Directorate (Directorio Revolucionario Estudiantil, DRE). The MRR, however, extended its ties to places outside the Catholic militancy and incorporated into its leadership two personalities who had been prominent in the Sierra Maestra: the captains of the rebel army, Higinio "Nino" Díaz and Jorge Sotús, a feared man of action who had been the right hand of Frank País.

In this anti-Castro phase, the Authentics no longer answered to Prío but to three leaders. One was Tony Varona, their former premier, who along with his old colleagues from the fight against Machado — plus some new faces like that of student leader Alfredo Carrión Obeso — had created an anti-Castro movement called Revolutionary Rescue (Rescate Revolutionario). Another was the polemical Aureliano Sánchez Arango, an unreconstructed conspirator, again at the vanguard of Triple A, and as in Varona's case, surrounded by good people, but politically and generationally closer to the Cuban history of the 1930s and 1940s than of the 1960s that were dawning. And along with them, with barely any structure or membership, was Justo Carrillo, an intelligent economist who possessed an overflowing imagination for political intrigue. As the leader of a small party — the Montecristi Movement (Movimiento Montecristi) — he had the enormous advantage and mobility of being almost a one-man-show.

The third source of anti-Castroism, the one that came directly from the ranks of the Revolution's leadership, was the most well-supplied and diverse. It was soon headed by Manuel Ray, a former leader of Civic Resistance in the struggle against Batista and later ex-minister of Public Works. At this stage he was founder of the Revolutionary Movement of the People (Movimiento Revolucionario del Pueblo, MRP) along with, among others, Reinol González, a union activist of Catholic origins, and Hector Carballo, a very young student leader from Las Villas; Pedro Luis Boitel, a university student leader of the 26th of July, and David Salvador, secretary general of the Revolutionary CTC, the creator of a vast clandestine opposition labor party called "the 30th of November Movement" in remembrance of the Frank País uprising on that date in 1956. Various union activists joined the "30th of November" in positions of significant responsibility, and the ex-captain of the rebel army, Hiram González, an expert in sabotage and spectacular prison break-outs joined, too. The "30th" came to count on active cells in almost all the big enterprises of the country, but it immediately became a target of the intelligence services.

All of these groups were known to the United States from the very moment of their inception, although the ties with the "30th" were the weakest and of the MRR the strongest. It wasn't that the U.S. embassy invented them artificially, but the opposition to Castro perceived Washington as a natural ally against Communism. Everyone who participated in this felt, perhaps naively, proud of that natural cooperation — like the French Resistance, the *maquis* who, confronting the Nazis, were always aided by the intelligence services of the United States or England.

And this collaboration was not even new; it had begun in the government of Carlos Prío, from 1948, when the Cold War erupted and the United States decided to strengthen its ties to democrat anti-Communists everywhere, and especially in Latin America. Around those years, precisely in Havana, in an event that notably highlighted Raúl Roa (who was later and for many years a Castro minister), the Congress for the Freedom of Culture was founded with money channeled by the CIA, and a good number of intellectuals and politicians of what was then the democratic left, many of them ex-Communists, began to refute all the Soviet propagandistic initiatives camouflaged behind the abovementioned "congress for peace" or "youth congress" sponsored behind the Iron Curtain. This is the time when the Inter-American Regional Organization (ORIT), with the discreet help of the CIA, was battling the World Federation of Workers, whose strings were fairly obviously pulled by Moscow.

Among the younger Cubans, moreover, anti-Americanism had been weakened enormously, concentrating this sentiment in the political groups of the Marxist neighborhood. Practically all the strains between Havana and Washington had been resolved in favor of Cuba. In 1925, the Americans finally acknowledged Cuban's sovereignty over the Isle of Pines, in litigation since 1898 when they cunningly tried to take possession of it; in 1934 the U.S. had repealed the Platt Amendment; the sugar produced on the island enjoyed a preferential price regime; the North Americans did not support Batista's 1952 coup d'etat (which surprised and upset them), and later they declared an embargo of weapons to the dictator. The United States was, in addition, the country that had defeated the Nazis and had confronted the Communists in Korea.

The American companies based in Cuba paid better salaries and offered better work conditions. The image, then, of the great neighbor to the north, contrary to later rewritings of history, was very positive to the majority of the island's population in the decade of the 1950s. It was generally seen as a heroic country with a beneficial influence.

The Opposition and Washington

However, despite the affinity of principles and interests between the Cuban democratic opposition and American society, the relations between the two entities were totally asymmetrical. For the United States, the Cuban democrats were not allies who deserved to be helped for moral and political reasons, they were not colleagues nor compatriots under siege, and no one in Washington thought to compare them with the French underground resistance. They were at best a simple tool to remove from power an enemy in the service of the USSR. The method selected to achieve this purpose was to let loose certain subversive campaigns, planned and financed through the CIA. Thus, in a distant and police-like manner, the United States dealt with the conflict. That's the approach it took in handling Arbenz's Guatemala and that's the approach it took now with the Cubans. While the USSR treated their comrades from the West with the respect merited by colleagues in the same ideological camp, and related to them in the political arena, Washington only established humiliating and semi-clandestine links to Cubans, who answered to fictitious names through intelligence officials and sold their loyalty and collaboration for money or combat supplies that were only available to those willing to subordinate themselves to Washington's plans. In effect, the CIA, very professionally but with the bureaucratic attitude of one who is "just doing his job" — which was certainly the case — contributed money, training, weapons and materials for sabotage, but along with all of those elements it also gave the orders, made the plans and picked its favorites, divesting the country, in a way, of what should have been the struggle of an independent society to gain its freedoms.

When did the United States seriously try to oust Castro? It's possible — no one knows for certain — that in March of 1960 a CIA saboteur blew up the Belgian ship La Coubre in the Bay of Havana to prevent military supplies from being delivered to Castro's army. One thing is certain: the explosion coincided with the exact moment in which the Eisenhower Administration, which had maintained contacts with the opposition since the middle of 1959, finally decided to remove the Cuban government by force. At that instant the White House, firmly convinced that the growing relations of political and military complicity between Moscow and Havana, under counsel from the National Security Council and the CIA, decided to implement a regime of economic pressures and to support the Cuban-national subversives. The plan included restrictions on the purchase of sugar, stepped up training for and encouragement of acts of sabotage, propaganda, psychological warfare, and the formation of rural guerrilla groups. It very soon crystallized in the creation of the Democratic Revolutionary Front, whose principal leaders were Manuel Artime (MRR), Jose Ignacio Rasco (MDC), Tony Varona (Rescate), Justo Carrillo (Montecristi) and Aureliano Sánchez Arango (Triple A). The movement brought together the Catholic ranks and the opposition groups originally from the Authentic Party. Those who were not in the coalition, at least provisionally, were the anti-Communists originally from the 26th of July. And those who were specifically and deliberately excluded were the Batistianos. No one wanted to give Castro such an easy excuse to discredit his adversaries.

This collaboration between the CIA and the opposition movement quickly translated into a considerable increase in terrorism. Refined explosives like C-3 and C-4 now appeared in Cuba. The bombs, however, were seldom placed in public places — as happened in Batista's time — where innocent lives could be lost, even if some intentional fires did provoke some deaths. Around this time, short wave radio transmissions began from a station called Radio Swan, and there was a feverish bustle of conspirators in all the provinces and at every level of the government. Voluntarily, or egged-on by the CIA, several important figures in the diplomatic corps defected. Among them the most significant was that of José Miró Cardona, who was named ambassador in Spain after his resignation as prime minister. Meanwhile, some leaders of the Revolution, already disaffected with Castroism (like *comandante* Humberto Sorí Marín, former Minister of Agriculture), traveled clandestinely to the United States to meet with other opposition leaders with the idea of planning a general insurrection. The first guerrilla rebels start training under the direction of the CIA. Originally, Eisenhower's plan was not to invade Cuba, but to give Castro the same medicine he had given Batista.

Castro, naturally, was not sitting on his hands. He received thousands of tons of weapons from the Socialist camp, which he distributed to his people, and he sent a few hundred soldiers and trusted officers to receive military training in the academies of the Communist world. It had been a year since he created the popular militias, and only a few months earlier, he had organized — neighborhood by neighborhood — Committees for the Defense of the Revolution (*Comités de Defensa de la Revolución*, CDR).

The Communists, with the help of several experts brought from the USSR, Germany and Czechoslovakia, developed an increasingly efficient and implacable political police. The method most often used was infiltration. The political-military intelligence service, led by Ramiro Valdés with Soviet guidance, had literally thousands of men and women incessantly searching for information and penetrating the opposition groups. And this work was not limited to Cuba: in exile — there were over 300,000 exiles — the FBI estimates that the Cuban authorities had at least 5,000 informants. Some worked out of conviction, others for money, and a third group did it to protect their families who were threatened inside Cuba. Many became double agents. The island's prisons started to fill and the execution squads were working overtime. This was, certainly, a fight to the death.

But where the confrontation started to become more virulent was, paradoxically, where the CIA and the Democratic Revolutionary Front had less influence: in the mountains of Escambray, the old fiefdom of the Directorate and the Second Front, the place where the greatest concentration of guerrilla power in all of Cuba's history was spontaneously taking place. As many as 3000 men were organized in columns, led by former officers of the rebel army with the prestige of having fought against Batista. Soon their names were revealed by the clandestine radio transmissions. They were captain Porfirio Ramírez, President of the

Federation of Students of Las Villas, *comandante* Plinio Prieto, captain Sinesio Walsh, and officers Tomás San Gil, Osvaldo Ramírez, Julio Emilio Carretero, Rafael Gerada and Margarito Lanza (Tondike). There were many more, and among them one of the most notorious was *comandante* Evelio Duque, who displayed uncommon leadership skills. At a certain moment, that placed him at the helm of all the rebels.

But Castro is not Batista, and he knows that the worse mistake a government can commit is to permit a rebel force to exist, unpunished. So he banned the use of the word "guerrilla" in reference to these enemies, and he formed new military units to begin to dispute the idea that the rebels were political adversaries. He called his new forces the "anti-outlaw battalions." He then launched one offensive after another, using tens of thousands of soldiers to search the dense mountains step by step and rock by rock until he located and destroyed the guerrillas, executing them immediately. At the same time, any suspicious or indifferent peasant was deported to the other extreme of the island, to Pinar del Río, to a town created to lodge these new vanquished people called "*reconcentrados*." The town was named Sandino. Years later, when Raúl Castro narrated these events — at this time they were barely reported in the press — he would reveal that the struggle lasted from 1960 to 1966, and that it cost the armed forces nothing less than 6,000 deaths, among them several officers of high rank who fought bravely. Practically all of the guerrilla chiefs died in combat or were executed. Evelio Duque was one of the few who managed to escape to exile.

In the year 1960, elections were held in the United States, and Cuba, little by little, was turning into a campaign issue between Republicans and Democrats. The press reported daily about the growing relations between the Cubans and the Soviets, and American society was beginning to worry about the close ties between Nikita Khrushchev and Fidel Castro. On the other hand, the CIA was communicating to the White House that the subversive struggle was not going well because, among other reasons, the rebels were scarcely receiving any American weapons or supplies. The Escambray war was bloody, but the rebels were not winning. The clandestine groups engaged in sabotage and distributed propaganda, but they were not capable of seriously impacting the state security forces.

In October of that year, 1960, the government of Havana confiscated almost all of the national and foreign companies of importance; and there had been no response from the people. Two reasons may explain the apathy: on the one hand, there was the lethal efficiency of the political police, but on the other hand, Cubans were entirely convinced that Washington would never permit the establishment of a Communist nation allied to the USSR just 90 miles from its territory. Therefore, for anti-Castro Cubans, the most sensible move was to try to salvage whatever movable goods they could — money, jewelry —emigrate to the United States, and wait until the Marines solved the problem for them.

Before that juncture, Eisenhower gave the order to significantly expand the training camps for the exiled Cubans. The idea was that they should build up an invasion force capable of landing on the island, capturing some important city, and adding its population to their ranks, then defeat Castro's army in the military arena (counting on the fact that this invasion would be able to rely on some aid from the United States and on the diplomatic support of other countries). In other words, they went from a scenario in which Castro would fall from power due to internal pressures to another in which the determinant factors were foreign.

To those ends, it was convenient, as the CIA recommended, to expand the opposition spectrum, a measure that was reflected in the creation of a new opposition organization called the Revolutionary Democratic Council (Consejo Revolucionario Democrático) led by José Miró Cardona, the former prime minister from the early days of the Revolution. The engineer Manuel Ray and his Revolutionary Movement of the People joined in, and of course, the organizations of anti-Communist Catholics and the Authentics who already had a presence in the sacrificed Revolutionary Democratic Front. The message, then, was transparent. The government of the United States was determined to finish off communism on the island, while sustaining the revolutionary spirit that encouraged the struggle against Batista.

And to prove it, in the first rows of the opposition mentored by Washington were Miró Cardona and Manolo Ray. And along with them were other respected figures from the previous fight: Tony Varona, Manuel Artime, José Ignacio Rasco, Alberto Müller and Aureliano Sánchez Arango. This latter, disgusted with the way in which the CIA handled its anti-Castro activities (something that later on would prompt him to resign from the council), predicted with a clear vision that the planned expedition would be a costly error.

The Bay of Pigs

Finally, the U.S. elections took place in December of 1960 and young John F. Kennedy — a millionaire, an ex-Massachusetts senator, hero of World War II, Pulitzer Prize winner for his historical essays and a fervent anti-Communist — was elected. During his campaign he had addressed the Cuban situation, attacking the lack of decisiveness by Eisenhower and Nixon, the vice president and electoral candidate. "How could the Republican Administration have permitted the establishment of a satellite state of the USSR in Cuba?" he asked rhetorically. Why had nothing been done to stop it? In reality, Kennedy knew that the CIA had been running an operation to topple Castro, but he also knew that Nixon was obliged to keep it quiet, so Kennedy could strike with impunity in the debates or in his political discourses.

The bulk of the Cuban expeditionary force, made up of exiles, was quartered in a remote region of Guatemala, where the recruits received intensive training. The Brigade soon took on the number "2506" as its name, in honor of soldier Carlos Rodríguez Santana who was accidentally killed during training. As military chief, José San Román was selected: a good career officer who, very young, had served in the Cuban armed forces during Batista's government but who had ended up turning against it, and for a short period he had served in the rebel army after the triumph of the Revolution. The second in command was Eneido Oliva, of a similar biography to San Román's, who later in the fight came to be an excellent military man and over the years rose to become a general in the U.S. Armed Forces. The political chief was Manuel Artime, the MRR leader, and along with him in a position of great responsibility was Emilio Martinez Venegas. The latter was supposed to disembark in Cuba at the helm of one of the infiltration groups that preceded the invaders, staging acts of sabotage and distraction maneuvers.

With him were, among others, Benito Clark, José Basulto, Edgar Sopo, Manuel Comellas, Carlos López Oña, Jorge Recarey, and even four tele-graphers, demolitions experts, intelligence agents and the other neces-sities of paramilitary activities. In an independent operation, Alberto, Müller and Juan Manuel Salvat had already been infiltrated into Cuba to prepare an uprising in the Sierra Maestra Mountains, while the doc-tor Lino Fernández was attempting a similar effort in the mountains of Escambray. The morale of the brigadiers was quite high. They were sure they would win the final battle against Castroism.

When John F. Kennedy arrived at the White House at the end of January, 1961, one of the biggest and most hellish problems awaiting him was "the Cuban question." Close to a thousand men — they would eventually be 1,400 — were waiting, practically ready to be launched into Cuba, but the operation was not exempt from risks. Almost every week, the Kremlin issued an ominous warning that reprisals could be expected if anyone attacked Cuba. In addition, from the perspective of the flamboyant new president, it would hardly send a good sign to the world if he inaugurated his mandate with a military conflict in which the United States appeared as the aggressor. Still, at this point it seemed impossible to dismantle the Guatemala camps and end the CIA operation without exposing himself to a greater domestic scandal, one that was summed up in the likely accusation: "The anti-Communist who criticized Eisenhower and Nixon for their apparent passivity in the Cuban situation, upon arriving at the White House, made it his first act to throw away the Republican strategy against Castro."

Placed in this dilemma, and wishing to do well by both of the con-tradictory aspects of the situation, Kennedy made the worst of deci-sions. He gave a green light to the expedition but without directly in-volving the U.S. Armed Forces and without making clear the relation-ship between Washington and the invaders. He then dedicated himself to erasing all traces, where possible, and tried to reduce the dimensions of the military conflagration. First, he tried to reduce the international "noise" and changed the place of disembarkation. It would no longer be near Trinidad, a medium-sized city known to be anti-Castro, with the mountains to its back — a city that could have added massive numbers of recruits to the expeditionaries, but he chose another point miles away from that site, in an almost uninhabited area on the southern coast, flanked by an inhospitable swamp and known by two different names: Girón Beach and Bay of Pigs.

Secondly, he approved having the troops transferred in slow, heavy cargo ships, unarmed and without adequate protection, so as to give the appearance of being an amateur operation mounted entirely by exiles.

Thirdly, he reduced the number of air raids without taking into account the scant fire-power of the bombers, a limitation that would leave three fourths of Castro's aircraft intact. Kennedy feared the outcry of his adversaries, and furthermore, he knew that under his direction the United States was doing something that is not legitimized by international agreements. He did not have a mandate from the United Nations and he had not even sought the support of the Organization of American States. He therefore dreamed, then, that the invaders would magically, in a quick and painless operation, topple Castro without need of overt U.S. intervention.

The CIA, did not agree with the change in plans nor with the shrinking of the Brigade's military capacity, but neither did it present strong objections to the president. Without saying so, the operation chiefs hoped that the White House, forced by circumstances, would end up ordering American troops to be sent in. Optimism reigned: they embraced the fantasy that, after the expeditionaries landed, the morale of the Communists would crumble and the troops would join the adversaries. Isn't that more or les what had happened in Guatemala?

On April 15, a few sporadic bombings of military airports began, and on the 17th the first expeditionaries began to arrive; parachutists were landed behind enemy lines, led by Alejandro del Valle. Curiously, the teams of infiltrators who were supposed to collaborate with the invasion were not alerted. The bulk of the expedition arrived in several slow, old mercantile ships that soon became the perfect targets for the T-33 and the Sea Fury of the Cuban government. Another smaller force, with more than a hundred men under Capt. Nino Díaz, had gotten close to the beaches of Oriente, at the other end of Cuba, with the purpose of diverting the army; but they did not find adequate conditions and they abstained from landing. The arrival of the expeditionaries at Girón

Beach was preceded by a team of frogmen, coordinated by Eduardo Zayas Bazán, and the combat began immediately. Contrary to what the military intelligence believed, there were guards posted in that zone.

Thus, just a few minutes after the disembarkation had begun, Castro knew that the long-announced and long-expected invasion had finally touched Cuban territory. His instinct told him that he could not allow his enemies to consolidate, because the next step would be to install a provisional government, seek recognition from several Latin American countries and legitimize a collective intervention against him. He thus had to attack them without mercy, until he destroyed them. And so he did, in only three days of furious combat, unleashing thousands of militiamen and soldiers on the expeditionaries. After the sinking or the forced the retreat of the supply transport ships, the invaders were left without ammunition, and even though they had fought with valor and efficiency, leaving the enemy Castro forces with five dead for every one of their losses, they now had no defenses against the incessant artillery of the government or against the air attacks; they were forced to surrender en masse, to avoid being totally annihilated.

Only a few were able to escape, and even then, not all were lucky. In a boat that drifted for many days, several expeditionaries died of hunger and thirst, among them Alejandro del Valle, Raúl Menocal and José García Montes. Their story was told by the horrified survivors, Raúl Muxó and Julio Pestonit.

Nevertheless, contrary to what was customary for the Escambray, those who turned themselves in did find their lives were spared. But at least in one case, the captors were merciless — they locked up a large number of prisoners in a hermetically sealed truck to transport them to Havana. When the doors were opened, nine expeditionaries were dead by asphyxiation and another two dozen were on the brink of death. There were more than 100 men piled into this tightly-sealed box, under the harsh tropical sun, remembers Amado Gayol, one of the survivors. The person responsible for this criminal negligence seems to have been Osmany Cienfuegos, Camilo's brother, and the only known case of an officer in the rebel army who invented himself a captain's rank in the Sierra Maestra without having ever moved from his comfortable exile in Mexico during Batista's dictatorship. Perhaps he believed that cruelty in the treatment of prisoners compensated for his nonexistent history in the insurrection.

Suddenly "Camelot", as Kennedy liked to have his dreamy administration called, turned into Serendip, the tragicomic kingdom in which everything happened to the contrary of what was expected. Kennedy had managed to accomplish exactly the opposite of what he wished: the entire world, given the most convincing evidence, now accused him of launching a military operation against a country with which he was not officially at war; and the invasion, on top of that, had failed. And if the American President did not know what to do with a thousand recruits in Guatemala, he now had to confront the enormous shame that — because of his fault, his inexperience, his indecision, and above all, his lack of knowledge about who Castro was — those men were now imprisoned in Cuban jails and some 150 had died in an absurd battle. It was a terribly uncomfortable situation, given that it directly affected the exiled interlocutors of the CIA and of the White House itself, since among the prisoners were the sons and close relatives of the leaders of the Revolutionary Cuban Council and of the most notable politicians and businessmen in Cuba: José Miró Torras, Carlitos Varona, José Andreu, Juan and Jorge Suárez, Rafael Montalvo, Waldo Castroverde, Enrique Llaca, Jorge Alonso, Ernesto Freyre, Julio Mestre, Alfredo Durán, Jorge and Julio Tarafa and another dozen well-known and respected members of the exile community.

By contrast, for Castro the episode at Girón Beach was the most sensational triumph of his political life. The victory gave him the opportunity to clearly declare and unmask the Communist militancy of the Revolution.

He did so on April 15, when the bombings began, burning all the ideological bridges, forcing society to define itself and the Soviets to commit deeply. But there were even more, and more profound, political advantages: the failed invasion gave him the perfect alibi for having the political police summarily arrest thousands of opponents, real or potential. They were piled into sports arenas and public buildings, under military guard, breaking the backbone of practically all of the anti-Castro organizations that existed in the country. And once the prisoners were apprehended and identified, among them the most important leaders of the opposition, they were summarily executed. Thus died the former *comandante* of the rebel army Humberto Sorí Marín, Rogelio González Corso, Antonino Díaz Pou, and the leaders of the Directorate, Virgilio Campanería and Alberto Tapia Ruano, among others.

There was nothing exceptional in this harshness; it became the norm during the days of the invasion. Dynamite was placed in the political prisons and guards had orders to assassinate all of the prisoners, lest the expeditionaries consolidate their positions. Similarly, all of the foreign embassies (in which a few hundred opponents had received asylum), were surrounded by the army, and it was known that soldiers were prepared to attack the diplomatic missions. If the invasion had succeeded, or if the regime had perceived the danger that such a thing would occur, thousands of heads would have rolled before the final events unfolded, remembers Aldo Messulan. If Castro lost power, his end would arrive in the midst of a Wagnerian uproar. Castro constantly said it: he was no Arbenz, and the scene would not resemble Guatemala.

But he won. At the end of April, the smoke cleared, Castro had reason to feel happy and safe. Almost all of the opposition movements had been beheaded, their leaders jailed or dead, the guerrillas resisting in the Escambray were becoming weaker, and Kennedy's government, to whom the failure was attributed, had been left without any means to remove him. Still sustained by the CIA, but disoriented and inactive, the Council remained in Miami led by Miró Cardona and by Tony Varona, who were distressed by the defeat and the imprisonment of their children, and who were enraged by the treason to which they had been subjected. No one would admit it, but it was evident that the Guatemalan phase had come to an end before the Cuban political reality. If the United States insisted on ousting the Cuban government, they would have to do it with their own troops.

At the same time, Moscow had taken note of the developments. Castro's image had acquired a colossal dimension everywhere, but most especially, in the USSR, where he appeared as the leader who had inflicted a humiliating defeat upon the United States, and as a declared Communist, at that. The Kremlin, for the first time in its history, could rely on a trustworthy and fiery ally in Latin America who did not allow the United States to daunt him and who gave the impression that the American president was indecisive and weak and relatively easy to intimidate.

This fact was important because the United States, as a consequence of the Cold War, and to avoid nuclear parity, had developed the strategy of surrounding the USSR with military bases and it had targeted Moscow with planes and atomic missiles located in Turkey. How magnificent it would be, to reproduce the same scenario in Cuba. Then the Americans could live with a sharp knife close to their jugular, exactly like the Soviet people. The Cubans had already hinted at something like this at another moment, but justifying it from a different angle: if the United States knew that Cuba had nuclear arms capable of destroying the American nation, or at least of causing it extreme damage, the U.S. would abstain from trying to topple Castro's government. No one plays with fire. Especially with nuclear fire.

After the Bay of Pigs fiasco, as the American press dubbed the incident, Kennedy confronted two different problems in relation to Cuba. One was a moral, humanitarian matter: how to rescue the 1,400 men imprisoned in Cuban jails. The other was a strategic matter: it was evident that, stimulated by the failure of the invasion, the Soviets were increasing their military and political ties to Cuba, something that made the Pentagon analysts very nervous. To the first question, fortunately, Kennedy shortly found a solution: Castro was willing to grant the men amnesty and return them to the United States in exchange for large amounts of tractors, medicines and food. It wasn't so much a kindly gesture on his part, but a calculated political measure to humiliate his Yankee and Cuban adversaries with an operation in which the defeated soldiers, as if they were objects, were traded for baby food jars and boxes of penicillin. Castro also thought that to maintain those prisoners in Cuban jails would nurture the obligation and commitments of the United States to the opposition. Thus it would more profitable, at the right time, to ship them to Miami, where they would go on to ruminate in their frustrations, and from where it would be very difficult to repeat the adventure. The delicate operations to effect the exchange were judicious and laboriously planned and implemented by some of the prisoners' family members, and they did not end until many months later when Castro felt it was convenient.

From the Missile Crisis to Kennedy's Death

Kennedy now had to address the second problem — the growing Soviet presence on the island — in a different way. He could no longer insist on invasions by exiles or a redevelopment of the clandestine struggle in Cuba. Those options had been exhausted at the Bay of Pigs. If he persisted in wanting Castro out — something that became an obsession for the Kennedy brothers (Bobby, the Attorney General, had also made it his priority) — the only available option, high in risk and high in cost, was to launch the U.S. Armed Forces into a direct combat. Naturally, anti-Castro Cubans would be part of that invasion but they would act as part of the American troops. The CIA communicated this idea to the leaders of the Democratic Revolutionary Council in the summer of 1962. Around that time, a high official of the DRC traveled to Miami and held secret conversations with Miró Cardona and Tony Varona: the White House was studying the possibility of invading Cuba, and in that case, it was indispensable to assess the likelihood of recruiting young exiles who would go along with the American troops. This time there would be no treason. The United States would never abandon its men in the middle of battle. But while this was going on in the United States, some Cubans, newly arrived in exile, were giving proof and testimony of what they described as a Russian presence in Cuba that was much larger than had been detected so far by American intelligence. In effect, 40,000 Soviet soldiers and technicians were working feverishly on the island to strengthen Castro's defenses, building military bases with launch ramps capable of launching enormous nuclear missiles against the United States. It was, then, as if two trains were traveling toward each other, on the same track. At some point, a collision was inevitable.

It occurred on October of 1962. In the first days of that month, the aerial espionage services gave Kennedy irrefutable proof that nuclear rockets were being installed in Cuba, and were capable of destroying the United States after just a few minutes' flight. Faced with this evidence, Kennedy gave orders to put the U.S. Armed Forces on alert and to accelerate immediately the recruitment of exiles in so-called Cuban Units. They were quickly gathered in Miami, to be sent to Fort Knox in Kentucky. The most probable option would be to order the preventive destruction of military installations on the island and to dispatch American troops immediately.

The tension mounted by the hour and provocations increased. The few hundred Cubans already at the Kentucky camps, as José de la Hoz remembers, were taken immediately to a firing range to teach them how to shoot, and a priest asked them who were Catholic and wanted confession — since it would not be long before they went into action. On the island, all of the Cuban army was also clearing for combat action.

Castro did not sanction spy planes flying over *his* territory, and in the middle of the crisis one of them, a U-2, was shot down by a rocket, apparently fired by a Soviet-controlled base. War seemed imminent. The White House offered the Kremlin two options: either the Russians would withdraw their missiles from Cuba or there would be a military confrontation. Cuba was blockaded by the U.S. Navy. Castro, always bellicose and indomitable, urged Khrushchev not to give in. In a coded telegram, one of the most irresponsible texts in history, Castro asked him to attack the United States first, and never mind what happened to Cuba — since the Cuban patriots were ready to die for the dignified cause of socialism. At the last minute, Khrushchev gave the order to withdraw the missiles. World War III would not be caused by any action of his.

And World War III is what it would have been. What the Americans did not know was, first, that some missiles were already ready to be fired, and second (and much more frightening) was that at that moment Cuba had nuclear arms (in the hands of the Russians) that could be used at the discretion of officers in lesser units. If American troops had disembarked in Cuba, a simple colonel from the Soviet infantry detached to the island would have been able to give orders to attack with those "small" atomic weapons, wiping off the map any secondary regiment; and that probably would have unleashed a complete nuclear response against the USSR.

The Missile Crisis — as the press baptized it — gave a political victory to Kennedy, who had demonstrated a firmness never before seen. The defeated Khrushchev received, however, a secret consolation prize to appease the humiliated Soviet military. The United States pulled out of Turkey the "obsolete" Jupiter missiles aimed at Russia by NATO (North Atlantic Treaty Organization). This was the *quid pro quo* agreed upon with Moscow.

Castro, however, felt profoundly humiliated by the Kennedy-Khrushchev agreement, which had been negotiated behind his back — even though he enjoyed a notable advantage in the deal: the United States committed itself to not invading Cuba, as long as the USSR would refrain from using the island to place offensive weapons that could endanger U.S. security. In other words, with the withdrawal of the missiles Castro had accomplished the same objective he had aimed when he asked that they be installed in the first place: to prevent an invasion by the U.S.. In December of that same year, a few weeks after the most dangerous dispute in history was settled, almost all the prisoners from the Bay of Pigs were given amnesty and finally sent to the United States. In this way, Castro liberated Kennedy from a commitment that he could only have kept by destroying the government that was holding them in prison. It was a clever move by Castro and was played at the right moment. The invaders were in prison less than two years. Only a few were not freed — the government made them pay for pending political causes.

But Kennedy was not a cold statesman; he was a more visceral and emotional man than the public knew. As soon as the ex-prisoners of Brigade 2506 landed in Miami, the President participated in a public event with his wife, Jackie, and received the Cuban flag from the hands of one of the Brigade chiefs, promising that someday he would return it to a free Cuba, liberated from communism. And he did not say those words in a rote way, to flatter the Cubans, but because he was convinced that he had to end the Cuban dictatorship — even if he was obliged to refrain from any plan that involved a direct invasion.

How could that objective be accomplished? He immediately authorized the creation of Cuban-exile commandoes to infiltrate Cuba and gather intelligence toward attacking government objectives, to keep alive the flame of hope. The commandos had to appear to be independent, but they would be aided by the CIA.

But the most important of all the secret measures was the plan to assassinate Fidel Castro. That would be an audacious act, but it seemed the most direct way to end communism, given that all the experts agreed that Cuba's tyranny was personal and dependent on the limitless authority of the Maximum Leader. With Castro dead, the prognosis was that the Revolution would collapse. And who could undertake such a task? The answer Kennedy came up with was not the smartest, nor was it morally acceptable, coming from the leader of a democratic state: the Mafia. The Mafia (which was persecuted in the United States for committing horrendous crimes) was going to be discreetly engaged so that in Cuba it would provide a bloody service to the American nation. This was totally absurd, but it wasn't the first time such a thing had occurred: during World War II, the American government had asked Lucky Luciano to cooperate in helping the Allied forces to land in Sicily. Surely, someone remembered that precedent, when Bobby Kennedy began to move in that dangerous direction.

Only, in this case the pact with the Mafia may be at the root of the assassination of President Kennedy. As is known, in November of 1963, Kennedy was shot by a sniper named Lee Harvey Oswald, who was a member of a pro-Cuba committee, an organization of Castro-supporters founded at the beginning of the previous decade by Che Guevara himself, at the time of his visit to the United States. Oswald, who appeared to have suffered serious mental breakdowns, had lived in the USSR, where he said he had moved for reasons of ideological affinity, and he had married a Russian woman. Shortly before Kennedy's death, he had visited the Cuban embassy in Mexico, and finally, in front of dozens of journalists and photographers, when he was being transferred to prison, a well-known criminal, Jack Ruby, killed him.

What really happened? There are a thousand hypotheses and the case has never been closed. However, according to his closest associates, President Johnson, Kennedy's successor, lived and died convinced that the hands of Castro and the Mafia — combined — were responsible for the crime. How? The famous journalist Jack Anderson, the most widely-read syndicated columnist, undertook an investigation (that he later broadcast on American television) reconstructing the events in this way: Fidel Castro discovers that the Mafia plans to execute him, on instructions from Kennedy. In keeping with his psychology of "an eye for an eye, a tooth for a tooth", he decides to respond in kind, and for that he can count on Oswald, the strange psychopath who is among his well-known sympathizers. The Mafia, on the other hand, is a convincing threat. The Cuban secret services start to kill Mafiosos, with impunity and without the slightest possibility of having the hit returned, because the American gangsters don't even know whom to attack. They, the Mafiosos, are prepared to fight against other Mafiosos, or to kill certain people by contract, but they can't fight against unknown enemies who possess better weapons, are better trained, and have a sanctuary to which to escape from danger. The FBI, restrained by legalities, finds it difficult to defeat the Mafia, but the leadership of Cuba's intelligence is relatively easy. And what would the Mafia have to do, in order to eliminate such a threat? Kill Oswald and erase Havana's fingerprints in the Kennedy assassination.

Is this theory true? Who knows; at least it has a logical structure. A few days before Kennedy's death, Castro, who was visiting the Brazilian ambassador in Havana, enigmatically declared that the weapons that were aimed at him could soon be turned against those who were aiming them. That was Johnson's and Anderson's theory. There are others, in which the villains were Cuban exiles or CIA agents or petroleum magnates, or all of them together. However, this theory contains at least four indisputable facts: the only thing we know for sure is that Oswald killed Kennedy and that he was in contact with Castro agents, that Ruby killed Oswald, and that Ruby was not an idealist perturbed by ideological delirium, but that a Mafioso who managed a dive bar. And if the theory is right, why didn't Robert Kennedy, who continued as Attorney General for a while, explore this to the end? Because it would have made public their shameful and criminal complicity with the Mafia in the attempt to assassinate a head of state, Communist and an enemy of the United States as he was, and perhaps that would have been the end of Bobby's political career and the beginning of a prolonged legal battle and a dishonor for his dead brother.

But in the end, it really is all the same. The truth is that with Kennedy's death, the removal of Castro stopped being an obsession for the White House, and little by little, the active measures aimed at destroying the Cuban dictatorship began to be extinguished, as soon as the fatal shots rang out in Dallas. Lyndon Johnson, Kennedy's successor, did not feel personally humiliated by the Bay of Pigs, nor did he suffer from a particular aversion to Castro, nor did he have friends among the exiles; he sidelined the Cuban issue and began to combat his own enemy in Vietnam. Any public recognition of a link between Castro and Kennedy's death, given the indignation this would have provoked in American society, inevitably would have led to invading Cuba and risking a war with the USSR. Johnson was terrified of that eventuality, according to his conversations with Senator Richard Russell and the confidences he shared with Joseph Califano (his secretary of Health, Education and Welfare), later revealed to veteran journalist Henry Raymont. The most prudent course, then, was to bury the evidence in Kennedy's assassination as soon as possible — a purpose for which the seldom-believed Warren Commission was created — and to learn to live with Fidel Castro, who had turned out to be a dangerous adversary and difficult to remove from power.

There remained, however, as relics of the previous era and as consequences of the Cold War, a "Cuban policy" based on the three long-term objectives written into the general strategy of dealing with Communism:

1. ongoing economic pressures (embargo),
2. political and diplomatic isolation of Cuba, and
3. constant propaganda and negative information about life on the island.

But no one again thought of invasions or serious subversive efforts. Time, they supposed, would take care of that which American politicians and anti-Castro Cubans could not. With the demise of Kennedy, there were no more significant dangers to mar the happy horizon for Castro, who had cleared the way to glory.

On the next page photo caption: The manipulation of history. Three official photos of the revolution. In the first, Castro is accompanied by Carlos Franqui — center — and by Enrique Mendoza. In the second, Franqui has fallen from grace. In the third, it is Mendoza who has been eliminated from history.

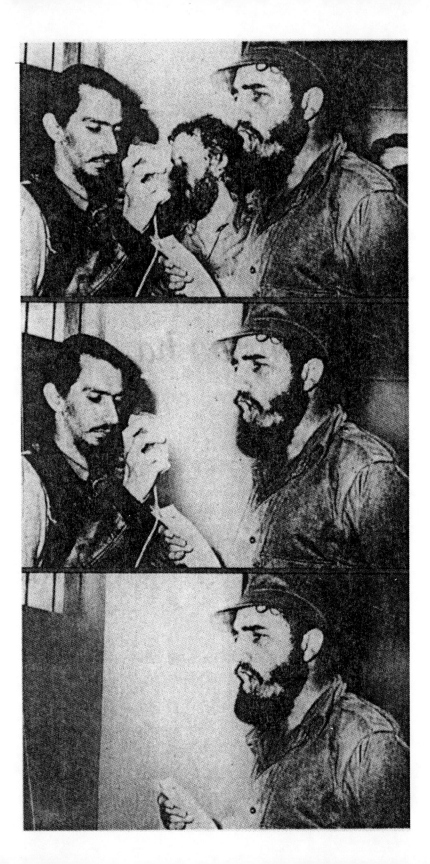

V

THE ENDS, THE MEANS,
THE ACHIEVEMENTS

W hy was all this done? Why carry out the Revolution, such a huge, bloody effort? Fidel Castro and his inner circle would respond with two closely related points — to change Cuba, and to change the world. And to them, "change" meant ending injustice in societies where some people had accumulated wealth and others had been dispossessed of that wealth.

Changing Cuba meant creating an egalitarian society in which everyone had a high level of prosperity and development, by taking property away from those who owned it to provide for those who did not; inequity seemed to be rejected in a visceral manner. To those who were pro-Castro, who were immersed in an outdated concept of the economy, wealth was a static element, something kept inside a treasure chest, an unvarying amount of resources that had to be distributed "appropriately." The same argument later applied to international affairs. Aside from the pleasure the subversive adventure generated — that intense physical thrill of fighting for a sacred cause and being the heroic protagonists of a great feat — the injustices had to brought to an end, the unfair reality in which certain countries owned everything and consumed everything while others hardly attained the minimum levels of survival. Castro and his inner circle felt that the prosperous nations had not created their wealth through their own work and ingenuity, but had taken it away from the weaker nations. Development was a zero-sum game.

That was the *visión.* Castro and the men he trusted lived in a cruel, unjust world that expressed its moral misery in terms of inequities that served to explain the welfare of some and the misery of others. Such a stance was paradoxical, since all Fidel and Raúl had to do was analyze the life story of their industrious father, Angel Castro, a hard-working immigrant like many other Galicians, to confirm that wealth is not something that is taken away from someone but is made, created, for the benefit of many. And had their sagacity allowed them to transfer that assessment to the international level, they would have easily seen that the richest nations on the planet were not necessarily character-ized by the creation of exploitative empires (look at Switzerland, Den-mark, Germany and Sweden), while some of the largest and longest-lasting empires in history — Portugal, Turkey, Spain — never achieved a high degree of development. In any event, Castroism, prey to such ob-vious intellectual misjudgment that encumbered the governing team from the start, derived its *misión* from such flawed diagnostics. The mis-sion they assigned themselves, or that History (with a dramatic capital H) had in store for them, was to correct such inequalities. How? First, by transferring the assets from the "few" hands currently holding them to a beneficent State, managed by fair-minded revolutionaries who would multiply that wealth for the benefit of all. The state-as-enterprise would be a panacea. It would quickly industrialize the coun-try by means of the relatively simple procedure of importing turn-key factories from the Socialist nations. A piece of cake. If the revolutionar-ies had managed to overthrow Batista in one shot, they could apply similar efficiency to manufacturing automobiles or exporting helicop-ters. They believed that. They were sure of it. In 1962 in Punta del Este, Uruguay, Che Guevara candidly explained, in all seriousness, to the stunned audience at an international conference, that in barely a decade Cuba would have caught up with the United States and would be one of the top world economies.

In reality, it was a problem of lack of training, more than anything else. Virtually all the revolutionary leaders were university graduates,

but their academic degrees did not stop them from being perfectly ignorant, both in government and in economic affairs. They had no real-
world experience. Fidel Castro had his law degree, but had basically
never practiced his profession. Raúl Castro had barely passed a few
subjects in Social Sciences. Che was a recently graduated medical doctor who had served during a short period in a leper hospital. Carlos
Rafael Rodríguez had studied law and Marxist economics, but had
been nothing more than a devoted *apparatchik*, modestly subsidized by
the Socialist Popular Party, preoccupied with the party's internal battles, although he had once been a minister at large in Batista's cabinet in
the 1940s. Antonio Núñez Jiménez was a geographer and an amateur
speleologist. Alfredo Guevara had studied philosophy and literature,
but Fidel and Raúl valued him more for his distinguished style and his
personal refinement, expressed in manners rather than in ideas, that
dazzled the rustic brothers. None of these men, to be honest, had the
slightest idea of how to create or destroy wealth, beyond the foolish
notions they had picked up from the popularized Marxist-derivative
discourse of the times. According to Bernardo Martínez Niebla, former
provincial party leader, Fidel Castro, for instance, had taken short
courses in the late 1940s at the headquarters of the Socialist Popular
Party at 609 Carlos III Street. In three magical and speedy lessons, well-
suited to his furious impatience, they gave him the Marxist story of surplus value and other superficialities marvelously useful to urgently
"understand" society's conflicts, albeit in a meticulously flawed fashion.

The other problem with these revolutionaries was their absolute
lack of management experience and, in the cases of Fidel and Raúl, even
work experience. To them, life had boiled down to violence or political
debates over free-flowing coffee and under the dense cloud of smoke
expelled by Cuban cigars. They were revolutionaries of the political
kind, who had never submitted their hypotheses to serious academic
analysis — much less compared them to empirical behavior. They
talked incessantly, nonstop, without the slightest measure or aware-
ness of their own ignorance. They knew nothing about work, savings,
investments; yet they were certain of what it would take to transform
Cuba into a leading nation. They had no idea how to put together a
payroll, a budget, or a short-, mid- or long-term development plan.

They had never even taken responsibility for their own finances. Up to the moment when they reached power, they had lived on money from their parents, or on the resources of the revolution. They had never, ever, taken a glance at the real world of production, or even considered the written explanations of the advantages of capitalism and its superiority over socialism in terms of efficiency in creating and assigning wealth. Obstructed by heavy ideological earflaps, none of them had ever heard of the Austrian School —already consistently mentioned in Havana by the renowned entrepreneur Goar Mestre — of Marshall, Von Mises, Hayek nor any other persuasive advocate of marketing. Blinded by the sparkle of Marxism, though they seemed intent on developing the country, they had not even taken the trouble to peek into the phenomenon of Ludwig Erhard's Germany, in which the liberal Christian Democrat of the Fribourg School performed the miracle of recovery and development that was taking place precisely in the 1950s — right before the closed eyes of the headstrong Cuban revolutionaries. Didn't they know what was happening in West Germany, in contrast to its Communist counterpart . . . even while they dreamt of a radical socialism? By simply examining that experience — or that of Japan — they could have taken far more rational paths if they really wanted to achieve swift prosperity for the Cubans. But such moderate and tiresome avenues lacked revolutionary glamour. These were bourgeois formulas that held little appeal for men of action, as they called themselves in those days of heightened testosterone.

Was it really impossible in Cuba, at that point in time, to understand the concept of development in any other terms than what the Marxists proposed? Of course not. It was all a matter of pondering the causes of poverty, with an open mind. During precisely those same years, in which Castro attempted his "great leap forward" under a Third-World approach, Singapore (which had attained its independence in 1963) pursued similar objectives, but opting for a market economy, private property, and close collaboration with the First World. Lee Kwan Yew, another revolutionary willing to jump start the development process, wisely chose the Japanese model instead of opting for the Chinese or Russian model. Nearly forty years later, the Asian enclave — itself hardly a paragon of democratic virtues, to be sure — even after having started out behind Cuba, has totally eradicated poverty, has a *per capita* gross national product thirty times that of Cuba, and has attained the level of prosperity of the United States with less inequality.

The objectives described by Che Guevara thus were not impossible, only the path chosen to achieve them was one that in fact led elsewhere. The problem had to do with knowledge and information. Castro and his court had absurd ideas that led the nation to complete disaster and pushed Cuba from third place in the level of development in all Latin America (surpassed only by Argentina and Uruguay), all the way down to the most miserable level of the Continent, except for Haiti and Nicaragua, impoverished by the Sandinistas.

It could be said — Castro himself has mentioned it — that the Asian examples are not comparable with Cuba due to cultural differences; but then we could still look at an even more similar case. In 1959, after twenty years of experimenting with state economy, nationalism and autarchy, Franco's Spain began to open up to a market approach and globalization — not a common term, at the time — and embarked on a vigorous transformation of its economic model. In that year, Spain was poorer than Cuba, and thousands of Galicians, Asturians and Canarians were looking for ways to emigrate to the Caribbean island (not only for economic reasons, but because of the cultural affinity between both countries). Where does this comparison lead us? While Cuba became radically poorer, Spain undertook an ascending path toward the First World. Today, it has one of the highest levels of quality of life on the entire planet, and has become a golden dream of sorts for millions of Cubans who would be ready to move to the peninsula if only they had the privilege of obtaining a visa.

Of course, if the Cuban revolutionaries had not been so intellectually lazy, they could have done things differently. Yet, they were psychologically incapable of performing such a task, since in their view the immense complexity of economic development was dependent on just three moral categories: the victims, the victimizers and the saviors. The victims were the poor, those who had been brutally deprived of something that supposedly belonged to them and was now in the possession of others. These others were the victimizers, the capitalists, the rich, selfish property owners, incapable of identifying with their poorer countrymen. The saviors of the victims were, of course, the revolutionaries.

They were the wise ones. They knew what should be produced, and how, when and where. And they knew what proportion would go to every Cuban, in order to make the distribution equitable. And since they held such unquestionable truths and the corresponding moral fury provoked by injustice, they were willing to crush the victimizers and their foreign "masters," especially the Yankees who kept the poor countries in abject poverty. That was why it was necessary to fight them at every turn, at every moment. Every battle — no matter how remote or foreign the enemy might be — was justified. This was an ideological battle against evil.

It is essential to emphasize this intellectual flaw, this poor analysis by the revolutionaries, because it is this simplistic and Manichean way of understanding human beings and the conflicts they faced that prompted the huge abuses they would commit and the absolute tolerance they would grant to their own mistakes. Why hesitate to deprive thousands of people of their possessions, if the fact that they are the owners proves their responsibility for the poverty of the "have-nots"? Why not jail or execute hundreds or thousands of people, when they are but evil victimizers, despicable "worms" morally deformed by selfishness? Why worry about making thousands of mistakes in the administration of public affairs, generating more problems than solutions, adding to the poverty and injustice, if the revolutionary saviors are motivated by pure, honest intentions? Every person should be judged by his acts — except the revolutionary saviors. These are to be judged by their intentions.

"Worms," Homosexuals and the New Man

In the first few years of the Revolution, the economic system that until then had sustained the Cuban nation, and the complex entrepreneurial grid that had evolved over the centuries, were destroyed. First came the confiscations of 1959 and 1960, when all properties belonging to the *Batistianos* were "recovered" in favor of the state. Next on the list were all enterprises having any hint of ideological coloration. In that category were, essentially, the media and the private schools, so that the civil society that preceded the revolutionary era could not articulate its own defense. Later, in October 1960, the great segment of industrial and commercial property, national and foreign, was confiscated, by decree, in just 24 hours. Suddenly the Cuban state, which had practically no management experience, was called to administer 50% of the GNP. And a few years later, in 1968, after a *revolutionary offensive*, the entire entrepreneurial matrix remaining in the country — some 50,000 minute enterprises, nearly all family-owned — also passed into state hands, since Fidel Castro — against the tepid opposition of Carlos Rafael Rodríguez — was convinced that it was the role of government to mend umbrellas, repair shoes and maintain refrigerators, so as to prevent, at all costs, any Cuban from escaping government control and managing his own affairs. To own property was a path to power, and Fidel Castro was determined that nobody on the island would have power except himself. Cuba thus became a more communist state than the USSR.

These confiscations prompted the mass exodus of the entrepreneurial class and of many professionals who saw their lives shrinking. The country was palpably drained of what today is known as *human capital*, and with each emigrant who fled, the strong work ethic that had characterized Cuban society was weakened and replaced by the passive attitude of those who expected the state, since it had taken charge of their lives, to resolve all their problems. To them, it was no longer possible to dream about improving personal or family conditions through their own initiative. The Party decided where they could work, how much they could earn, and how they were to spend the money.

And that was but a fraction of the limitations imposed on society. The Party, besides rationing food to control how much and what the Cubans were to eat, also established the ethical and inter-personal rules that would govern public life. It was the communists who decided which ideas were just and which were despicable; which books should be read and which should be burned; which music conformed to patriotism and which denoted a pro-Yankee and servile attitude (like those rocking Beatles, created by the perverse imperialism). Nothing escaped the Party's implacable eye: which clothes and which hairstyles showed nationalist roots, and which, on the contrary, exhibited personalities rotted by cosmopolitanism. In fact, the Party knew and decided which persons were acceptable to visit and which should be avoided, in order to escape being tinged with guilt by associating or maintaining ties with politically undesirable persons. People found that they had to avoid running into old acquaintances who might be perceived as being opposed to the government, and even certain relatives became inconvenient, for the only relationship acceptable to the revolutionaries was a relationship with an impeccable comrade.

A revolutionary was expected to repudiate his parents, his children or his siblings if they fell into disgrace or opted to go to exile. Abandoning Cuba was considered a sordid form of treason to the fatherland. Such attitudes could not even be attributed to the political immaturity of the early days, for as recent as July 1999, when several basketball players decided to defect in Puerto Rico after an international tournament, the father of one of them — Ruperto Herrera, president of that sport's federation in Cuba — declared them traitors to the nation where they were born and proclaimed the immense shame he felt by the defection of his son, whose only aim was to continue playing basketball in a country where citizens were treated as human beings and not as objects owned by the political power.

Worse yet, it was the Party's prerogative to establish which students could receive a higher education and which were doomed to become common laborers or low-level employees for life. College education had ceased to be a right, within the reach of any talented high-school graduate, and had become a privilege based on the political credo. Castro's slogan was constantly repeated: "The university is for the revolutionaries." When it was discovered that Antonio Guedes, one of the leaders of the University Student Federation at the Clinical Hospital, was an observant Catholic, he was expelled from the university. To be a believer in the 1980s was incompatible with an academic education. This is merely one example among thousands of similar stories. Ana María Sabournin's case was even more disturbing. She was expelled from the university after a tumultuous student meeting, in which people (shouting at the top of their lungs) informed her that her husband was a homosexual. It was known that a homosexual could not be a university student — those who were found to have such inclinations were publicly expelled in dishonor — but her rejection was even more brutal. The rule now applied to the spouse of a homosexual as well. The regime's homophobia, which in the 1960s had crushed thousands of Cubans regardless of their intellectual hierarchy (Lezama Lima, José Mario, Virgilio Piñera, Reynaldo Arenas, Ana María Simo) was still alive in the 1970s and 1980s. There was no let up. The university was only for heterosexual revolutionaries, who had better be careful in choosing their spouses. And the same held true in every segment of the state. Leadership positions went to the "good revolutionaries" — even if they lacked intellectual merit or a suitable preparation for the job. Che Guevara, who had no relevant experience, became the head of the National Bank; a basketball coach, José Llanusa, became the minister of education. The only required merit was to be a revolutionary, loyal to Castro; the big crime, the unredeemable flaw, was not be one.

And what were the revolutionaries like? They were pretty interesting. First of all, they had no ideas of their own. They subscribed to Fidel's ideas across the board, and went as far as summing up that parasitic symbiosis in a deplorable refrain that they repeated at Revolution Square or posted at the doors of their houses: "If Fidel is a Communist/ Put me on his list." Castro monopolized the function of thinking. One could not be a revolutionary and disagree with the official line, and the official line covered all of history. To be a revolutionary meant to believe what Castro thought of the past: that the republic was a sewer, a Yankee colony; that the revolutionaries had emerged from the best *mambisa* tradition of the 19th century to save the Cubans from their unhappy contemporary abjection. You had to believe that the Cuban revolution had invented decency and dignity among the inhabitants of that land so ill-treated by Washington.

Castro was not only the master of the present, but of the past as well. He owned the past, and anyone advocating a conflicting interpretation was a dangerous, a "revisionist", "divisive". This was a serious sin. The Cubans could only survive as a historical entity if they held a univocal, concerted vision capable of protecting them like a magical amulet from the "gringos". The stubborn strategists of the Pentagon were patiently waiting, in hiding, for the Cubans to become divided, so that they could take over the island. That had been their intention during almost two centuries.

Pure historicism, a follower of Popper would say. The argument was too weak and relied on the presumed existence of a permanent conspiracy within the U.S. power structure which, neurotically, from generation to generation, transmitted the imperialist desire to domi-nate Cuba. Any intelligent person, even moderately well-informed, was bound to reject such a notion. Plus, why would a Marxist, convinced of the dialectical mechanisms that move the wheels of history, believe that Jefferson's temptation to annex Cuba — at a time when it was shock-ingly easy for Louisiana, Florida or entire countries in Europe to change hands due to wars or simply through marriages — could remained un-changed in the second half of the 20th century? But, alarming as it was to find that being a proper revolutionary required understanding the past through Castro's arbitrary prism, what was even more upsetting was the obligation to share his view of the future. No one could specu-late that events that had not yet occurred might turn out some other way, for that would lead to social ostracism or, in extreme cases, to jail. All projections as to what might lie ahead were designed by the Party, in accordance with the faithful interpretation of what Fidel had in store in his untidy mind. A revolutionary was expected to believe in the radi-ant destiny of communism and in the unquestionable triumph of the good Marxist forces against the evil demons of capitalism. And if any-one in a classroom or in a workers' rally or an official meeting dared to shyly express an opinion that the economic, scientific and technologi-cal symptoms pointed in a different direction, and that it seemed that communism showed huge contradictions and weaknesses that did not predict a splendid future, that person was immediately stigmatized and excluded from the group. Castro was also master of tomorrow.

And this is where the New Man makes his triumphant entrance. The New Man subscribes to Castro's worldview, adding certain atti-tudes and behavior that can only be considered angelic. The New Man is a man full of hope, disinterested, obedient, who has surrendered his mind to Fidel and the Party to be equipped with ideas, beliefs and judg-ments that match up minutely with the Party line, because he lacks the faculty of thinking with his own brain. He is a character who has also donated his arms to the revolution, who will work seven days a week — oh, those marvelous Red Sundays! — and will march with the militia on Saturdays without expecting any additional reward for his tireless labor. All he expects is moral compensation, as proclaimed by Che Guevara, because material incentives are just nauseating remnants of a capitalist past that will never come back. The New Man is, undoubtedly, a saint.

The Anatomy of Terror

What happens to human beings who can't feel like heroes, revolutionaries or new men because they are too exhausted by the task of living and raising a family under increasingly precarious conditions? What happens to sensible people who simply can't endure so much foolishness and decide to silently flee the madhouse, claiming absolutely nothing except the clothes they are wearing and surrendering even their wedding rings to the implacable political police? Those people, in "normal" times, are punished in various ways for their disillusionment. They are fired from their jobs as if they have committed some horrible crime, their possessions are inventoried, and they are not allowed to dispose of anything they owned — it all becomes the property of the people. Or they are sent to forced labor in "agricultural" tasks — to cut sugar cane, to harvest tobacco — in the countryside, where they must remain for months and even years "earning the right" to emigrate. Yet that is only what happens in "normal" and happy times.

In "abnormal" circumstances — when the government feels threatened or when Castro has suffered what he interprets as public humiliation in the eyes of people who ostensibly rejected his leadership — at such times, beatings, insults, and spitting at the potential emigrants becomes legal. That was the case in the early 1980s, when the Mariel exodus took place. In just 72 hours, in a phenomenon unprecedented in the history of human desperation, 11,000 people sought refuge in the Peruvian embassy in Havana; it happened again in the 1990s, when the "boat people" crisis took place. It happened to television repairman Rafael Muiñas, one case in hundreds — and others were fatally worse. After humbly and quietly expressing his desire to leave the country because he was tired of the unsuccessful attempts at the

Frankenstein-like genetic engineering of the New Man, Muiñas was forced to kneel on the sidewalk in front of his workplace with a poster hanging from his neck saying, "I'm a traitor." Then he was forced to crawl on his knees, while a mob yelled at him, beating him and spitting on him. Years later, as he recalled the story, his eyes would redden with feelings of outrage and bitterness.

Muiñas, like thousands of other Cubans, was the object of an "act of repudiation." What is that? A person or a family is brutally mobbed by a crowd organized by the Communist Party and the Security forces, giving the impression that the people are so outraged that they take justice into their own hands against the "social degenerates." It's not the police nor the army, but "the revolutionary people" who "spontaneously" come out to settle things with those who try to be different, dare have a different opinion or try to flee the country because they can no longer tolerate the contradictions. How is the "act of repudiation" carried out? The police select the victim — a dissident, a nonconformist journalist, an intellectual who expresses a critical view, or a simple worker who opts not to go on living in that marvelous paradise. They call together the Communist Party thugs, and they explain to them the extent of the operation.

If the victim is well-known, even the leaders may be called upon to perform. The act of repudiation against the Arcos brothers, Sebastián and Gustavo — the prestigious human rights defenders and heroes of the *26 of July* — was personally led by Roberto Robaina when he was the Secretary General of the Union of Communist Youth. An act of repudiation can be limited to yelling and insults, as it was done for weeks against the Catholic leader Dagoberto Valdés and his family, or the mob can be incited to enter the house of the repudiated person and destroy the few pieces of furniture he owns. Even more severe treatments may be applied. María Elena Cruz Varela, the great poet who received the National Literature Prize, was forcibly hauled out of her house, dragged to the middle of the street, thrown to her knees, and forced to eat her own manuscripts while the mob yelled, "Let her mouth bleed, damn it, let it bleed!" And then she was accused of public disorder and sentenced to two years in prison. After the international protest gained noticeable proportions, an old woman who was a Party member and had not even taken part in the mob, met with the media blaming herself for what had happened and explaining that she just couldn't accept in silence the "María Elena Cruz Varela's provocations and her counter-revolutionary writings." It was merely the voice of the police rewriting history.

Why carry out these uncivilized "acts of repudiation" when the government, which controls the lawmakers, the courts and the media, could discreetly arrest the victim, conduct a brief trial under trumped charges and sentence him or her to whatever time the police decide? Because that is not what the acts of repudiation are about. Their aim is not only to punish a person gone astray, but to convey an intense intimidating message to the population. The arrest, trial and imprisonment of dissidents and a brief report of the incident published in *Granma* does not carry the same profound dissuasive effect. When neighbors watch the mob arrive and brutally beat the defenseless victim, with the absolute impunity of the para-police force, it is another story. And this is not even a Cuban invention. In the sad jargon of Cuban repression experts it is known as the "control techniques of *Kristall nacht*," an allusion to what Hitler did in the 1930s against the Jews, using his ferocious *black shirts.* On a specified date, the Nazi mobs would go to the houses or shops of thousands of Jews and destroy their property, before the eyes of the entire terror-stricken, paralyzed society. The Jews were the direct victims, but the real aim was far broader — to show every German, Jewish or not, who owned the streets and to demonstrate that the group in power was beyond the law. The immediate purpose was, of course, to humiliate the Jews, but also to frighten everyone else.

These acts of repudiation are not the only technique that Castro learned from Nazism. The Cuban political police, whose structure and training is based on the East German *Stasi*, took from the Nazis a repressive element that did not exist in the other Communist countries — the Committees for the Defense of the Revolution. The CDR (in its Spanish acronym) is the basic unit of repression in Cuba. It is an espionage network managed by the Ministry of the Interior, with thousands of units throughout the island. There is one on every block, and if you don't want to be considered a dangerous outcast, it's best to sign up and participate actively. Besides keeping alive the "ideological purity" of the revolution by indoctrinating citizens (who are forced to study and accept the official government views in every aspect of existence), the CDRs' mission is to monitor the lives of all the citizens. Who is living in a given house, who are their visitors, what are their religious beliefs, what letters do they receive and where from, how do they express themselves about the revolution and its leaders, do they have relatives who oppose the revolution or live in exile, or are they exemplary revolutionaries? It may also be convenient to know who sleeps with whom, or what are the sexual preferences of the neighbors, their social customs, what they eat — especially if it is "illegal," as is the case of seafood or meat — which can be known by the scraps in the garbage bags. One never knows what use the intelligence forces can give to such "sensitive" information.

Nobody knows for sure who, within the CDR, are direct informants. Yet every Cuban knows that the CDR spies on everyone, and is, in turn, spied upon. Novelist Eliseo Alberto was recruited by the intelligence forces to spy on his own father, the poet Eliseo Diego. And he did it, as he tells it in *Informing Against Myself*, a heartrending book published in Spain. Mutual distrust is one of the consistent elements of totalitarian societies, and the first thing families teach the children is to distrust and to pretend, for the child's chances of not running afoul of the repressive machinery will depend on his skills in those two behaviors. At the same time, that family training, the development of cynicism and lying as means of protection, helps convince the child that the system is invincible and that it would be futile to try to oppose it. There is no sense in fighting. Survival is achieved by faking it. There is no point in running risks by defending dangerous principles. Sacrificing oneself for others — in a community of informers — would be idiocy. It's sad, but the same situation has been experienced in societies that have lived under communism: characters educated in duplicity and lying tend to manifest themselves in a lack of shared sympathy and indifference, the behavior of those who don't believe in anything or anybody — exactly the opposite of the Marxist project of building a world ruled by fraternal bonds.

How is this repressive machinery structured? Every CDR regularly reports to a zone committee, which in turns reports to a municipal, then a provincial, and finally a national committee. From the zone committee, all the information is gathered by the professional police officers, who feed the insatiable computers of the Ministry of the Interior. No one can escape its magnifying glass. Everyone has a political dossier. Even the most harmless citizen has an assigned officer in charge of monitoring his file, simply because you never know where an enemy of the fatherland may be hiding. And the term "everyone" includes minors, for the cumulative dossier begins the moment when the child is registered in school. On that registration form, notes indicate whether the parents are under suspicion of serving the imperialists or are brave soldiers in the revolutionary struggle. The term "everyone" does not even exclude illustrious visitors, like the Colombian writer Gabriel García Márquez, who tells about the overflowing folder containing notes on every contact and every bit of information about his multiple stays on the island, as well as transcripts of his telephone conversations. This was revealed by a young man named Antonio "Tony" Valle Vallejo, a defector who had been part of García Márquez's intellectual circle in Cuba, where García Márquez circulated in a carefree and irresponsible way — unaware that his hosts spied on him and followed him closely, minute by minute.

These CDRs were the organizations that, in the 1960s, compiled lists of youths to be taken to forced-labor camps where rough military treatment was to reeducate and convert them from "antisocial" beings into radiant New Men. These terrible agricultural work camps — euphemistically called Military Units of Production Aid (UMAP in its Spanish acronym) were fenced in barbed wire and managed by a whack of the rifle-butt. 50,000 Cubans were condemned, accused by anonymous spies of being or of resembling homosexuals, Catholics, Protestants, or — those subjected to the harshest punishments—Jehovah's Witnesses and Seven-Day Adventists. This phenomenon was explored by filmmakers Néstor Almendros, Orlando Jiménez Leal and Jorge Ulla in the documentary films *Improper Conduct* and *Nobody Listened.*

The "crimes" could even be less apparent — wearing "suspicious" clothes, reading "weird" books, or not showing respect toward the symbols of the Revolution, as in the case of the composer/singer Pablo Milanés, who was interned in those rural prisons because the CDR members on his block decided that in some oblique way his songs concealed "counterrevolution, homosexuality, or both." Many of those youths, like the writer José Antonio Zarraluqui, never knew why they had been taken to the UMAP camps, but they will never forget the things that were done to them — from a Jehovah's Witness who was buried up to his neck until he learned that it was better to renounce his religious beliefs than endure the stings of the fire ants on his face, to a homosexual who was kicked in the back until his spine was fractured, for refusing to shave his gloriously colored hair.

This repressive organization, the CDR, is more Nazi-Fascist than Leninist. It was founded on two hypotheses, which regrettably history has confirmed. The first hypothesis is that in a totalitarian state, the ties of complicity are strengthened if all the participants are equally guilty, having stained their hands in "the enemy's" blood. Everyone has to throw stones. Everyone has to repress each other, and this shared dirty work turns into an obscure moral vehicle. It is not possible to be a Cuban revolutionary and stay out of immoral tasks. You can't be a revolutionary by supporting the regime's efforts in education or health care, while rejecting the repressive aspects. Such ethical finesse is not allowed. One must be a revolutionary in all circumstances and with all the consequences: one must exult the obsessive vigilance, the denunciations, the "*actos de repudios*", the execution squads, and the growing ranks of political prisoners. That's the way revolutions are, and perhaps it is this fatal tension that explains the high number of suicides in the Revolution's hierarchy. In Cuba, none less than President Osvaldo Dorticós has taken his own life, as well as Haydee Santamaría, the tragic heroine of the Moncada attack and a sister-in-law of Raúl Castro, plus so many others whose names now represent the problems of conscience that sometimes arise out of cooperating with the executioners. When the very competent scientist trained in Cuba — Mayda Donate, a Communist Party member — escaped to exile in the 1990s, she brought documentation that corroborated the facts previously provided by the sociologist Norma Rojas. The rate of suicides in Cuba is among the highest in the world — three times the average for Latin America — but among women, it is even worse. In no society on this planet are so many women killed as in Cuba.

And the second hypothesis of those who analyze dictatorships is that the permanent vigilance of organizations like the CDR inhibits, in effect, one of the tendencies that would be most dangerous for any totalitarian state: the spontaneous creation of independent institutions and organizations in the heart of civil society.

One of the most important functions of a totalitarian state is to break down society, to keep people from coming together for any purpose that isn't defined by the government. While open societies are characterized by the free presence of institutions created by people who feel an urge to participate and have an influence on issues of shared concern (institutions that other citizens can join, if they wish to), by contrast, closed societies as a rule offer just a few very narrowly defined avenues for social expression, all of which are under tight supervision. Under the strict control of the ruling apparatus, everyone is assigned an obligatory role for participating in what the Constitution calls "mass organizations", and citizens are forced to participate under the threat of becoming outcasts or being punished. Totalitarian states create stable-like societies and with each one of its organizations, which are nothing more than barns where people congregate according to age, gender or profession, to hear the instructions imparted by the center of power.

And what is that center of power? Fidel Castro, obviously, but he has a whole apparatus at his disposal and service: the Communist Party and its various regional and national tribunals, including the Central Committee, as well as a shadowy Parliament, the National Assembly of the Popular Power, whose function is to meet for 72 hours, twice a year, to unanimously approve the measures taken by the public administration through decrees or simple administrative memorandums.

According to this model, the children are first "*pioneros*," (literally, pioneers), then they are enrolled in student associations created to control secondary education and college and to start selecting those who will go on to the Communist Youth organization. Later, if they are not "revolutionary" enough to enter the university, they are picked up by the Federation of University Students; the ladies join the Federation of Cuban Women and everybody, through the workplace, becomes part of the only and obligatory union that defends. . . not the interests of the workers, but those of the Party; in some sectors, there are special organizations, since artists and intellectuals, for example, tend to be isolated creators; these, too, are carefully supervised by the state, of course. There are other institutions, but there's no value in mentioning them separately, because the role of these structures is not to facilitate citizen participation nor to stimulate their particular initiatives, but to serve as a conduit to transmit orders emanating from the top.

Death to the Intelligentsia

The first inkling the world (including the Left) had of the absolute lack of space allowed for independent thinking in Cuba was what came to be known as "the Padilla case". There were many others, but they went, painfully, unnoticed. Everything started in 1967, with a piece of literary criticism which *El Caimán Barbudo* (*The Bearded Cayman*), a Communist Youth publication, asked the poet Heberto Padilla to write. Padilla, a young but already notable Cuban writer, had recently returned from the USSR. He had figured out that if the future of Cuba was what he had seen in Moscow, then the most appropriate course would be to flee that miserable destiny. He was asked to write a piece on *Pasión de Urbino*, a failed novel by Lisandro Otero, who was then and is to this day the regime's official writer (as his embarrassing memoir, published in 1999, shows). Padilla attacked the book, contrasting Otero with Guillermo Cabrera Infante, a famous Cuban novelist who liked to experiment with language, and who after a period of revolutionary militancy had taken exile in London. In his critique, in addition to outlining the weaknesses of Otero's book, Padilla took the opportunity to criticize Party bureaucrats.

The year after that incident, a year in which articles and public letters had already started to accuse Padilla of aligning himself with the counter-revolutionaries, an independent jury convened by the UNEAC (Union of Cuban Writers and Artists) and including foreign critics gave an award to Padilla's excellent collection of poems *Fuera del Juego* (*Out of the Game*). The collection was openly critical of totalitarianism. In that same contest, playwright Anton Arrufat was also honored, for his work *Los siete contra Tebas (Seven Against Tebas)*, in which you could easily read between the lines a rejection of the dictatorship. Alarms went off immediately. In Cuba, no one has license to attack the system. The Revolution did not block the publication of such counterrevolutionary works, but had them appear with a disclaimer in a prologue written by the literary critic José Antonio Portuondo, a meticulous Stalinist of the old PSP.

The incident was highly publicized and Padilla became a noted figure in Havana. In a way, he was the only free Cuban in the country. He said what he wanted to, out loud. He was a critical intellectual and he communicated to visitors everything that everyone else in Cuba was trying to hide: the fact that the Revolution had turned into a nightmare. The poet Belkis Cuza, like many other European intellectuals, visited his house (which he shared with his then wife). The Polish writer K. S. Karol, the Frenchman René Dumont, the German Hans Magnus Enzensberger, the Spaniards Juan Goytisolo and Carlos Barral: all of them visited the island and listened with admiration to Padilla's judgments. He was intelligent and gifted with an extraordinary oral ability. His commentary was bitter. He did not just stick his finger on the wound, he ripped open the wound with the tip of his tongue. The police watched, and took notes. Little by little, he became an *enfant terrible. . .* until one day in 1971. In that year — the unfortunate year of the First National Congress on Education and Culture — Castro decided to tighten the screws on the intellectuals, and Padilla was a perfect scapegoat to impart the necessary lessons. The Congress was scheduled to take place at the end of April, and it was high time to start disciplining the always timid ranks of the intelligentsia. By destroying Padilla, humiliating him, forcing him into line, the tight margins of creation allowed by the Revolution would become clear to the rest of the intellectuals. On March 20, his arrest was ordered.

But Castro had not noticed — or he didn't care — that Padilla has developed extensive international relations; numerous intellectuals in the West were prepared to protest his detention. On April 2, the Pen Club of Mexico sent a dry telegram to the *comandante,* criticizing the arrest of the Cuban poet and urging that he be freed. The letter was signed by people of the caliber of Octavio Paz, Carlos Fuentes, Juan

Rulfo, Gabriel Zaid and Jose Luis Cuevas — in total, some twenty of the most important Mexican creative minds, some of them identified with Marxism. A week later, *Le Monde* in Paris, from a leftist perspective as always, ran a letter expressing the same sentiment. The signatories were, among others, Jean-Paul Sartre, Italo Calvino, Alberto Moravia, Simone de Beauvoir, Juan and Luis Goytisolo, Jorge Semprún, Marguerite Duras, Carlos Franqui, and Mario Vargas Llosa. These latter were the most indignant and the ones who began to feel the greatest repugnancy for the Cuban dictatorship.

In Havana, meanwhile, in the torture chambers of State Security apparatus, the political police were diligently at work. They insulted, beat and intimidated Padilla until, as they say in police jargon, he "broke." Padilla agreed to publicly retract his "crimes." Security proposed that he read a humiliating text. Padilla "enriched" it with additional vile statements, and memorized it. The police did not realize what a subtle maneuver this was. The poet arrived at the conclusion that the more cowardly he seemed, and the more abject his declaration, the less credible its contents would be.

On April 27, 1971, the UNEAC met. The meeting was packed with writers. The intellectuals were in a panic. They already knew that, the night before, Padilla had been set free and that he was going to explain what had happened. Nicolás Guillén, the UNEAC's very elderly president, opted to stay at home. Maybe, that was due to some stirring of his conscience. Nicolás was not a bad person. The session was presided over by José Antonio Portuondo. A mixture of fear and curiosity prevailed. Padilla began his lengthy and tiresome speech. It was a perfect genuflection. He described his own degenerate morals, he attacked Guillermo Cabrera Infante, he reconciled with Lisandro Otero, he sang the praises of the generous Revolution, he flattered the boundless cordiality of the fraternal police officers who interrogated him during an unforgettable month of political education, he celebrated Fidel's wisdom.

How much farther can one go? You'd be surprised. Padilla denounced the ideological weaknesses of other writers: Lezama Lima, César López, Belkis — his own wife, Pablo Armando Fernández, Manuel Díaz Martínez, Norberto Fuentes. In the eyes of the public, he had turned into a pathetic and cowardly informer. Not to those in State Security, who knew perfectly well his critical political stance with regard to those writers; they took the poet's accusations as an excuse to launch a sinister warning. Padilla ended his deposition with the ritual clamors of the Castroist tribe: "The homeland or death! We shall triumph!"

The nauseating ceremony had its consequences. In Paris, Plinio Apuleyo Mendoza and Mario Vargas Llosa, editors of the magazine *Libre* (*Free*), wrote another letter, far harsher this time, referring to the trials in Moscow when the Stalinist police extracted the most incredible confessions and self-criticism from detainees. They collected 100 signatures. Susan Sontag, Alain Resnais, Valerio Riva, Juan Marsé, José Angel Valente, José Miguel Ullán, Carlos Monsiváis, and Jose Emilio Pacheco, among many others, lent their names to the overwhelming denunciation.

Padilla's declaration had the effect the poet had intended, and it multiplied. His case was turning into a breaking point for a large proportion of the intellectual left, which until that moment had supported the Revolution. That rupture has lasted until today. Sacrificing his own honor, he dealt a heavy blow to the image of the Revolution abroad.

But none of this mattered much to *el comandante*. For Castro, it was vital to maintain tight control on power and to restrain his wayward intellectuals. On April 30, he closed the Congress and launched a ferocious attack against the foreign intellectuals who had dared to ask his government to allow Cuban intellectuals the freedom to express themselves. He warned that, from that moment on, the standards would be even stricter. "There are books," he said, "of which not a word, not a comma should be published." He ended the text with a definitive phrase: "Within the Revolution, everything; outside the Revolution, nothing." There was not the smallest of spaces allowed for dissidence. The nervous intellectuals applauded. The UNEAC was not a forum for open debates, but an institution by which to receive orders and instructions. The "Padilla case" was only another turn of the screw.

It's not strange to find that a society organized in such a rigid manner — in which "everything that is not prohibited is obligatory", as they say — generates huge numbers of disaffected or disillusioned people, who are executed, sent to jail, live in ostracism in what they call "the exile within", or find themselves obliged to flee the country. Throughout these last 40 years, how many Cubans have been condemned for political crimes that range from real or imagined conspiracies to the sale or purchase of meat, in the black market, to sustain their family? Literally, tens of thousands of people.

And you did not have to be a well-known poet like Padilla to go to prison for intellectual whims. When he was an adolescent, Juan Manuel Cao (today a star reporter for Channel 51 in Miami) suffered two years of confinement because the political police — weapons drawn and yelling "Nobody move!" — confiscated some Beatles records, a book by Jorge Edwards, and a few humorous political verses ("I shit on communism/on Fidel and on Marxism/and on any strange word that ends that way"). Lazaro Lazo, turned in by his brother-in-law, was sentenced to prison for having written to a friend an "irreverent" letter against Castro in which he called the dictator "Comandante Guarapo" — the name of the popular sugarcane juice. During the ensuing house search, they found the manuscript of some old unpublished stories by the writer José Antonio Zarraluqui, wherein Zarraluqui made veiled criticisms of the regime — so he, too, ended up in prison for a good number of years.

How many Cubans have been in this Kafka-esque situation? Probably some 150,000, scattered in more than 100 prisons and "re-education" farms, says Arnoldo Müller, who became an expert on the unfortunate topic of the Cuban Gulag. He was one of its prisoners for an entire decade, during which he alternated between working like a slave and enduring constant surveillance. And how many Cubans have been executed for actively opposing the regime? There are many numbers. The smallest estimate is 5000; the highest is 18000. In any case, the number is painfully high. Pinochet is condemned, justly, for assassinating a little more than 3000 opponents. Castro has killed at least twice that amount.

And when the *comandante* defends himself, saying that in Cuba there has been "not one case of torture or of missing people," he lies without shame, or he disguises the truth until it is unrecognizable. In addition to the many moving denunciations, like Armando Valladares' book *Against All Hope*, year after year Amnesty International, Pax Christi, Of Human Rights, and the Human Rights Commission of the Organization of American States report on the terrible abuse suffered by prisoners in Cuban detention centers. Juan Valdés de Armas, a student sentenced to twelve years, remembers that the student leader Alfredo Carrión Obeso, Francisco Noda, Danny Crespo, Diosdado Aquit, Ernesto Díaz Madruga, Julio Tang, and Eddy Alvarez Molina were assassinated in jail — to name just a few. So many prisoners have received horrific beatings, among them Eloy Gutiérrez Menoyo, Alfredo Izaguirre, Juan Antonio Müller, Emilio Adolfo Rivero Caro, and Miguel Torres — who became a paraplegic. There are also those who endured many years without visits, isolated in *tapiadas*, enclosed cells in which they had to sleep on the floor, on top of their own excrement, with no other company but the rats and cockroaches. This was the fate of the poets Angel Cuadra and Ernesto Díaz Rodríguez, and of Angel de Fana, José Pujals, Nicolás Pérez, Ramón Mestre and the architect Salvador Subirá. And while it may be true that cases of "missing" opponents are exceptions, not the rule, unlike what happened in the military dictatorships of the Southern Hemisphere, this is only due to the fact that in Cuba it is legal to assassinate opponents. In the Argentina of Jorge Rafael Videla or the Chile of Agusto Pinochet, the law did not permit this barbaric treatment. Why stop your opponents, under cover of night and anonymity, shoot them in the head and leave them in a ditch — as happened frequently in South America — when it is perfectly possible to arrest, try and execute them in 24 hours, as has been done in Castro's Cuba an infinite number of times?

If there is a difference in the degree of bestiality prevailing in the conventional dictatorships of Latin America and Castro's — forgetting the lamentable fact that the Cuban regime has gone on for twice as long as that of Pinochet's and four times as long as Argentina's — it is in the treatment of women. The truth is that Castro has not executed women, he has not kidnapped their children, and he has not applied electric shock torture to their genitals. But those self-imposed limits have not stopped his government from treating female political prisoners with prolonged and extraordinary cruelty, unseen in the history of Latin America and absolutely unknown in pre-Castro Cuba, even during the

141

Machado or Batista dictatorships.

Hundreds of Cuban women have survived for years in infectious dungeons, their guards have beaten them until they passed out, they have suffered hunger and malnutrition, or have been prohibited from contact with their families, children included. All of this has been related in detail by testimonies such as that of Dr. Martha Frayde — once a collaborator, friend and ambassador to UNESCO for Castro, and later political prisoner — in books like *Todo lo dieron por Cuba (They Gave Everything for Cuba)* by Mignon Medrano, or the shocking biography of Ana Lázara Rodríguez, *Diary of a Survivor*, a brilliant medical student who went into prison at age 20 and came out, destroyed, at 40.

Raft People and Prostitutes

Another notable characteristic of Cuban society is the spectacle of the *balseros*, those tens of thousands of people who have taken to the seas on rafts and inner tubes, and whose infinite tribulations we hear about almost daily and which we have witnessed thousands of times on the TV news. In the mid-1990s, in just one episode, more than 30,000 raft people were intercepted by the American Coast Guard, ending up temporarily at the U.S. military base in Guantanamo. How many never make it?

According to José Basulto, president of Brothers to the Rescue, a humanitarian organization founded to assist the rafters — the group whose two planes were shot down by the Cuban government, over international waters, killing the four crew members aboard — as confirmed by aerial photos, — the number who die or go missing is estimated at 20 – 40% of those who venture to make the attempt, but the final count is difficult to determine. In towns all along the island's extensive northern coast, many families have lost some of the their younger family members, or in the most tragic cases, all of them. Why do they die? Sometimes, because the Gulf currents are treacherous and divert the fragile vessels out into the Atlantic, where the desperate fugitives die of hunger and thirst. Other times, because the waves overturn the rafts and sharks then devour the crew. And frequently, the Cuban government's marine or aviation forces take it upon themselves to sink the rafts or the boats, as happened with the tragically notorious tug-boat *Trece de Marzo* in July of 1994, when a few miles from Havana some 40 people, mostly women and children, were deliberately drowned by boats from the political police which rushed the small craft and swamped it, despite the cries of the women who held up their children, over their heads, screaming for mercy.

The Cuban government always tries to justify this almost suicidal exodus by alleging that Haitians and Dominicans also try to enter the United States illegally. But in giving this explanation, Havana ignores three fundamental differences when it comes to the Cubans. The first is that the naval units of the Dominican Republic or Haiti have never treated their unfortunate emigrants as enemies. They do not gun them down, they do not sink, and if the people are captured, they are not condemned to several years in prison as happens to the Cuban boat people, victims of a criminal political phrase so typical of totalitarian societies: "illegal exit from the country." The second is something that throughout the history of Cuba, the island always was a destination for European immigrants, and never a place from which the nationals tried to flee. The Cuban exodus is a phenomenon that coincides with the establishment of the Communist system. And the third has to do with the psychological profile of the Cuban raft people: while the Dominicans and Haitians who try to reach Florida or Puerto Rico often are poor, illiterate farmers, the Cubans generally have a high degree of education. Cuba is the only country in the Caribbean from which doctors, engineers, and teachers flee, because it is one of the few societies on the planet in which a good academic training does not translate into a better way of life.

This phenomenon is comparable to prostitution. Communism, or the terrible lack of economic opportunities in general, has turned Cuba into one of the sad destinations of "sexual tourism." Thousands of very young women and men, sometimes adolescents of 13 or 14 years of age and frequently in complicity with their families (who provide their own homes and beds for the sexual commerce), sell their bodies to strangers for small sums of dollars, which are indispensable. Food and necessary supplies are inaccessible to those who only receive the miserable salary paid by the state, equivalent to some $10 a month. The government defends this hurtful spectacle with allegations that border on cynicism. Castro himself has declared that, in effect, there is prostitution — they call the women *jineteras*, an obscure euphemism — but says that this is due to contamination with capitalism, and that in any case, thanks to the Revolution, they are the only educated prostitutes in the Third World.

In terms of placing the responsibility for this on the old regime, it is curious that, in the past, the government would blame capitalism for the existence of prostitution in the pre-Revolutionary epoch, and now, after 40 years of communism, capitalism is blamed again. They cannot admit that the only thing proven by the widespread resurgence of this phenomenon is the absurdity of a system in which, after the Soviet subsidies were removed, lack of opportunity forces everyone — even those people who possess the intellectual abilities to forge a future — to resort to the most degrading of activities in order to maintain a way of life that is even then nothing like the one enjoyed by the ruling elite.

It is not true, then, that this is a consequence of the flow of tourism and of capitalist vices. That is an unacceptable excuse. The Spanish tourist paradise of Mallorca, for example, receives 10 million visitors every year without causing the young men and women of that Mediterranean island to resort to selling their bodies. On the contrary, tourism, combined with an open economy, has created the conditions under which Mallorca has become one of the zones with the highest per capita income and the lowest unemployment index in Spain, and prostitution is almost nonexistent. This is important to understand, Castro's government confronts prostitution, like everything else, by resorting to the repressive police — severe concentration camps for the "re-education" of prostitutes, and penalties that can go as far as execution for the pimps, if minors are involved — instead of accepting that what's wrong is not the tourists nor the "corruption the dollars bring," but the insistence on maintaining, against all common sense, a system that prevents people from creating wealth and achieving even a minimally comfortable way of life.

He could claim that all the difficulties Cuba is experiencing are the result of the demise of the USSR and the disintegration of the island's ties to the European Communist bloc, but that is simply not true.

In Cuba, food rationing began in the 1960s, and since then the ration book, or the "provisions booklet" — that prodigious Orwellian political expression typical of Castroism — has gone hand-in-hand with a shortage of goods and services that affects the entire spectrum of consumerism: from meats to drinking water, from milk to electricity, from shoes to transportation. Sometimes, during a brief period filled with promises and wishful official figures — statistics being the area in which socialism shows the greatest creativity and imagination — the Cubans have managed to stabilize their misery, but only until the arrival of the next recession.

To save the Revolution in the late 1960s and the early 1970s, when inflation became uncontrollable and the shortages were pretty much all-encompassing, under the Che Guevara model, the government resorted to the administrative schema of the USSR. These were more rational and decentralized, and had a certain emphasis on rewarding and encouraging entrepreneurial productivity. That turnaround was called the *institucionalización*, remembers Carmelo Mesa Lago, the great economic historian of revolutionary Cuba. It reached its apex in 1975 at the First Communist Party Congress, with the implementation of Soviet economic development plans. But in the following decade, faced with the country's growing poverty, the *perestroika* process started to take root in the USSR, and Castro was alarmed by the rampant "materialism" of his Cubans — no doubt a curious quality to find in a Marxist. He decreed the "policy of error correction," regressing to the Guevara ethic of moral incentives and closing the farmers' markets that had somewhat alleviated the food shortages. In 1986, after failing in the creation of a Third World syndicate, of sorts, intended to defy the international banks, his government went totally bankrupt. Castro was forced to stop payments on his foreign debt, despite the fact that Cuba was still receiving annual subsidies worth $5 billion. In other words: the Cuban Revolution has been an ongoing failure as a development model, including in the periods of its greatest (relative) apogee. And that makes it even harder to understand the immense sacrifices demanded of the Cuban people and the great efforts made to export this model of organization to other countries in difficulty.

The Conquest of the Third World

If Marxism (as applied in Cuba) produced such lamentable results, why was there such a rush to conquer other nations and territories for the socialist cause? In April of 1959, Castroism began its "international" work, sending its first guerrilla forces to another Latin American country. The expedition was launched against Panama; it ended in complete disaster.

It is important to remember the date, because Castro's government tries to explain this stage in Cuban history with the argument that such interventions in the internal affairs of other countries were his answer to Yankee aggressions during the Cold War. Instead, it is evident that it was in Havana that the conflict began, out of sheer adventurism.

Seventy days later, in June of the Revolution's first year, he targeted the Somoza dictatorship in Nicaragua and the tentative democracy in Venezuela, born in 1958. In that summer of 1959, a group of guerrillas disembarked in Nicaragua while others began to organize an uprising in Venezuela with the aid of Rómulo Betancourt's communist enemies. This fact is also relevant because, in addition to claiming to be justified by the Moscow-Washington conflict, Cuban "internationalism" has been portrayed as a leftist struggle against dictatorships, when the reality is very different. For Castro, there was no difference between Rafael L. Trujillo and Rómulo Betancourt, between Anastasio Somoza and the Peruvian Manuel Prado, or between the Colombian Julio César Turbay Ayala and the Paragüayan Alfredo Stroessner. He attacked legitimately elected governments and dictatorships alike, and he did not at all mind aligning himself with terrorists like the Uruguayan *tupamaros*, in an attempt to destroy one of the few exemplary democracies Latin American had known. Similarly, he was happy to maintain the best of relations with dictatorial regimes like the Argentine military man Jorge Rafael Videla and the drug trafficking dictatorship of Panama's Manuel Noriega, and the beastly tyrannies of Uganda's Idi Amín and Guinea's Francisco Macías, whose personal guard was composed of Cuban soldiers.

In 1966, to make his subversive efforts even more efficient, Castro convened in Havana the Tri-Continental Conference. Thus began his close collaboration with terrorists around the world, including, among others, Palestinians, Irishmen, Basques, North Koreans, Libyans, Argentinians, Nicaraguans, Dominicans, Brazilians, Chileans, Venezuelans and Colombians. Practically all the nations in Latin America sent their sinister representatives, including some unarmed democracies (as was the case of Costa Rica and Jamaica). There were also radical American blacks and violent Puerto Rican *independentistas* who operated on U.S. soil. These radicals find sanctuary in Cuba, and military training, supplies, money and political formation. Cuba is the center of coordination and a instigator. Any terrorist, if he is from the left, can hang out there. Even Ramón Mercader, Trotsky's assassin, went to Cuba and became the inspector general of prisons — after spending twenty years in a Mexican prison, himself. He died on the island and was discretely buried, with the honors of a general. His body was later moved to the USSR.

It is the *desideratum.* Castro was preparing to conquer the Third World, and Cuba was the base from which that grandiose project would be launched. The sky was the limit. There were conspiracies in Yemen and in Zanzibar, where Cubans showed up to stage a coup. "Cuba is not an island, but a nest of machine guns on maneuvers," said Eduardo Palmer, the cinematographer who has produced the most (and the best) documentaries about Castro's long subversive epoch. A Cuban brigade fought in the desert along Algeria against Morocco. With no success, Che Guevara raided black Africa, the Congo, and former Portuguese colonies. He was preparing for his last adventure: he was trying to create another Vietnam, in Bolivia. Vietnam was like a dream, for him (as for many): annoying and bloodying Western democracies, and especially the hated North Americans. Castro and his closest men planned to expend even more young lives destroying the capitalist system, replacing it with the glorious socialism. No well-informed observer was surprised, therefore, when Havana supported the Soviet invasion of Czechoslovakia later in 1968. Castro himself gave an energetic speech praising the action. For Castro, it was much more important to sustain Communist dictatorships than those romantic and insignificant sovereign states.

Che arrived in Bolivia in 1967, endowed with a political strategy designed by him and derived from the Cuban experience. It is known as *foquismo* and it was popularized by the Frenchman, Régis Debray. You can make a Marxist Revolution, *foquismo* argues, even without the socially conscious urban working class that Marx supposed was necessary. Che was closer to Louis-Auguste Blanqui, the French Carbonarist, a contemporary and an enemy of Marx who preferred tactics similar to those of the Argentine. All you need is a bold vanguard, a focal point in rural areas that will create the general conditions for a progressive uprising that will move from the countryside to the cities. That focus will expand until it has built a revolutionary army which, at the right moment, will segregate the great Communist Party uniting the different revolutionary factions. Communism will not make the Revolution. On the contrary; the Revolution will make communism.

That is what happened in Cuba, and Che planned to elevate that anecdote to the level of universal political law. First they would take power by force, and later they would figure out how the party should be organized. Fidel, for unclear reasons, preferred to keep Che far away from Cuba. To keep him from coming back, Castro even publicized a letter that Che had sent him from Africa, in which he explained that he was dedicating his life to the cause of the Revolution, thus sparing the Cuban government from that task. That letter had not been sent in order for Castro to read it at that moment. By publishing it, Castro closed the door to Che's return to the island. The truth is that Castro had gradually lost trust in Che (if he ever had any). He was disturbed by his oral radicalism, the dangerous frankness with which he defended his Marxist convictions, his pro-China whims, and his insolent air of intellectual superiority. Castro worried that the Argentinian would express a certain disdain for the lukewarm way in which the Russians defended the Communist cause, since Guevara harbored a certain trace of anti-Soviet feelings — and for bad reasons: he saw Moscow as a timid power that did not stand up to the Americans with as much vigor as they should.

In any case, nothing in Bolivia went the way Che had expected. The peasants, far from uniting with him, turned him in. The local Communist Party viewed his presence with great distrust and refused to help him. The Bolivian soldiers, aided by the CIA, pursued him. Reinforcements from Cuba never arrived. The terrain was more inhospitable than he expected and it was hard to find food. The Bolivian election, despite everything, was not a foolish strategy but a calculated risk. Che planned a guerrilla movement that would expand to Argentina and Chile. Its ultimate purpose — in twenty years? — was the creation of a great multinational Hispanic-American army that could reproduce Mao's fight in China after World War II. Very soon, his men (and he himself) knew they were lost. His diary reveals a tone of dry melancholy. He shows up as a brave but harsh, disillusioned, cruel man. He had an intuition that he was about to die.

Finally, the end came. A captain of the Bolivian rangers, Gary Prado, tracked him down. Che was wounded and captured. A CIA agent of Cuban descent, Félix Rodríguez, interrogated him. (Rodríguez was a young exile who experienced the defeat at the Bay of Pigs. He was part of the infiltration teams that preceded the invasion, and he was later recruited by American intelligence.) He acted professionally, without hatred, and suggested to the Bolivian military not to kill the Argentinian. Not out of kindness, exactly: he thought that a defeated Che would have a demoralizing influence on the Left. He claims that that strategy worked with the Frenchman Regis Debray, Che's cellmate in Bolivia, who as time went by and gray hairs appeared, ended up harshly criticizing the Argentinian.

The military hierarchy, however, thought differently and ordered his execution. Che died; and immediately his personal legend began to grow — but *el foquismo* was discredited. His deputy, Dariel Alarcón Ramírez, known as "Benigno," an intelligent and daring country man, managed to get away in an escape worthy of the Count of Montecristo. Many years later, exiled in Paris and once again lucid, he met Félix Rodríguez and they embraced. They believed that, in different ways, they were both victims of Castroism. Benigno thought, at first, that Che deserved respect; in the end, he concluded that in reality, fear was the more appropriate response. For many years, he felt obliged to think that even if Che was mistaken, the boldness with which he defended his ideals merited special appreciation. Later, he realized that you cannot separate the means from the ends. The stubborn boldness of Hitler, who took his life rather than give up, or the suicidal heroism of the "brown shirts" who put up a futile defense of Berlin, do not redeem them before history. If courage is not at the service of noble ends, it is nothing more than a fatal consequence of a dangerous hormonal secretion. Che's temerity, his moral coherence, his Robespierrism and his lack of interest in material things do not spare him from the final truth that drove his acts: he killed for the purpose of imposing an inhuman dictatorship.

This defeat did not in any way stop Castro or dissuade him from his international tasks. What he did was to put a greater emphasis on the conventional military apparatus. Cuba, poor and relatively small as it was, would soon have the 9th largest army on the planet. It was a force that at its moment of glory, when the Soviets armed them to the teeth with more than 60,000 tons of equipment and ammunition a year, included 225,000 soldiers and infantry officers, 190,000 reserves, 500,000 militiamen, 1,400 war tanks, and a similar quantity of artillery, two frigates, four submarines, and another 60 ships of various sizes, while the air force reached the figure of 400 combat and transport planes and helicopters — not counting the legions of people in the Ministry of the Interior. That's more than the Brazilian, the Canadian or the Spanish forces. As the troubadour Pedro Tamayo sings, in his dissident's response to Silvio Rodríguez, in Cuba "there are no onions — but there are truckfuls of soldiers."

And upsetting the law of physiology, the instrument, in this case, creates the function, the factory. The development of an enormous armed force, explains political analyst Irving L. Horowitz, generated a more aggressive behavior within Castroism. In 1973, during the Yom Kippur war, the Israelis discovered that on the Syrian front there was an entire brigade of Cuban tanks. They fought skillfully, but the Jewish air force and artillery obliterated them. The Jews are better soldiers.

Two years later, Castro found his opportunity to take revenge. The African empire in Portugal had collapsed and three Angolan insurrectionary forces were vying for power. In January of 1975, these groups had signed a pact to participate jointly in the government that would replace the Portuguese, but none of the three groups planned to comply with it. They began jockeying for position. Battles to take over Luanda and smaller cities quickly ensued. This was a civil war, with foreign powers participating both openly and covertly.

Three are three leftist organizations, trained in Marxism, but participating in different strategic alliances. Over all, the Popular Movement for the Liberation of Angola (MPLA), led by Agostinho Neto, was supported by the Soviets and the Cubans, and maintained strong ties to the Portuguese Communists. The National Union for the Total Independence of Angola (UNITA), under the leadership of Jonas Savimbi, was receiving aid from Communist China, and would also receive support from South Africa. The National Liberation Front of Angola (FNLA), created by Roberto Holden, was the smallest of the three irregular armies, and had the backing of both the CIA and Beijing. Everyone was looking after his own interest. Pretoria feared the establishment of a Communist regime in the region. Moscow, Washington, and Beijing were looking to increase their influence in the southern Atlantic. Havana wanted to procure the glory of a military victory.

Castro felt he was the sharp end of the spear of the Communist cause in the Third World. His country may be small, but it had developed a foreign policy, just like a world power. The Angolan episode is an expression of the purest Caribbean Napoleonism. Castro disguised his intervention in Africa with the excuse that Cuba, certainly, is a country where half the population, one way or another — by way of racial mix — has roots in Africa; but that is only a coarse pretext. He also sent soldiers to Yemen, where they installed and removed governments, but there are hardly any Arabs or Muslims in Cuba. The propagandistic simplification that his troops went to Africa to stop the racist abuse of white South Africans is also not true. South Africa was only a secondary factor and was scarcely significant in the conflict. That soon became clear in Ethiopia, where the Cuban army defeated one group of blacks to the benefit of others.

His true motivation is the pleasure of winning battles and forging a position for himself in history at a level above the mere mortals. He is looking for that glory and that feeling of power that some people experience from deciding the life or death of thousands of people. Castro has built his own war room filled with maps. From Havana, he directs battles. When has a Latin American country sent an entire army to fight in another continent? Bolívar and San Martín fought in the Latin American neighborhood. Castro sees himself as having a larger role in history. Angola is a country blessed with great natural riches, but it is not the treasure that dazzles and mobilizes the *comandante*, even if he does get petroleum and large sums of dollars in exchange for his troops. The deal— if it even exists — is not the priority. That is not his psychology. Neither did he go to Africa because the Russians ordered it. On the contrary: it is Castro who entwines the Soviets in the Angolan knot, tempting them with offers of control over the most well-traveled maritime passages on the planet. Mozambique in the Indian Ocean, plus Angola and Namibia on the other African coast, would have given the USSR the chance to hold the right of passage in the south Atlantic.

Given Lisbon's withdrawal, everyone was fishing in stormy waters. It was a zero-sum game. What one side won, the other would lose. But the one who took the prize was Castro. He moved rapidly, convincing the Russians to send troops under the Communist banner, and announced that he was ready to provide the necessary bodies. The Russians would only provide the administration, the weapons and the ammunition. The East Germans could provide a few officers and a German knack for organization. The Cubans contribute would contribute the cannon fodder. Theirs and the enemies'. Deadly units, ready for combat, began to be transferred. A fishing fleet, a cargo fleet, and every airplane capable of making the journey were tapped for this project — causing serious difficulties in the provision of supplies to the Cuban people, but that did not matter. According to Castro, his compatriots are always happy to make sacrifices to accomplish their revolutionary tasks. Castro has discovered, to the surprise of the Cubans themselves, that his is an anxious country full of sacrificed warriors.

So that was it. Starting with the summer of 1975, at an accelerated pace, Cubans transferred some 70,000 men to Angola — a figure that was later stabilized at 40,000 soldiers and 6,000 civilians — who stayed in that country no more than a scant twelve years, the longest war fought by any army in the American hemisphere, including the United States. From 8,000 to 10,000 men were lost, and at first, they achieved the objective of propping up the MPLA. But that did not mean the definitive defeat of other groups, and especially of UNITA, which has never to this day, 20 years later, given up control of a good chunk of the southern part of its country.

Excesses were committed. General Rafael del Pino, who led the Cuban air forces in Angola and later defected, told of terrible massacres by Cuban soldiers against the civil population. The writer Jorge Davila, a soldier himself who lost a brother in the war, has given brilliant and painful testimony. These were not troops of gallant musketeers defending the noble cause of comrades in danger. They were an army, brutal (as all of them are), which despised the natives, whom they thought were lazy and cowardly. Some of the "heroes" in this absurd foreign conflict, like Rafael del Pino, later were vilified. But a worse fate awaited the hero who was really the star in this war, General Arnaldo Ochoa, as will be shown later. Reluctantly, after reaching peace accords in 1987, and visibly outraged by the "treason" of Gorbachev and the "softness" of the Angolans, the Cubans finally began to pull out of Angola.

The victory in Angola whetted Castro's imperialist appetite. He had now confirmed that the United States was paralyzed by its defeat in Vietnam, while Jimmy Carter prayed like an archangel in the White House. And so, in 1977-1978, Cuba intervened in Ethiopia, an ancient kingdom shaken by revolutionary commotions after the fall of Emperor Haile Selassie in 1974 and the installation of a pro-Soviet regime in 1975. If we analyze what happened there we come to understand the fundamental lack of principles of Castro's "internationalism." Thankfully, there is an excellent book, *Castro: Subversion and Terrorism in Africa*, written by Juan F. Benemelis, a member of the Cuban special services and an Africa expert, now defected.

Let's first look at the actors. Two groups were fighting Ethiopia. Eritrea was a province of Ethiopia, tacked onto a state that where a different language and religion predominated. This artificial linkage was the result of the diplomatic maneuvers of the European empires, those chiefly responsible for carving up the African continent. The Eritreans had long sought independence from Ethiopia and had trained a force of Islamic-Marxist guerrillas, aided by Cuba, Moscow and Libya. Then there was Somalia, a nation once in the grip of England and Italy, which achieved its independence (with great difficulty) in 1960. Somalia is the

most homogeneous country in Africa, an ethnic group that has occupied its own natural territory for centuries. In a distribution organized
by the great European powers, a border zone in the Ogaden desert,
populated by Somalians, had been assigned to Ethiopia, a country also
claiming its sovereignty. In 1969, Somalian general Mohamed Siad Barre
staged a military coup and proclaimed the Democratic Somalian Republic. He placed himself in the Soviet orbit and began to receive military aid from the USSR and Cuba. The Communist allies agreed that
Somalia should take over the territory of Ogaden, and Havana sent cadres to train the Somalians. But that assessment changed radically when
Ethiopian colonel Mengisto Haile Mariam came to power in Addis
Abada, executed all of his adversaries — the Red Terror, historians call
him — enlisted the tutelage of Fidel Castro and asked the Caribbean
dictator for help in defeating both the Somalians and the Eritreans.

Suddenly, there was a change of alliances. Fidel Castro decided to
become the godfather (in the Mafia sense) of the Ethiopians, against his
old comrades. The Somalians and Eritreans, radicals and Marxist sympathizers, were suddenly painted as the despised agents of Yankee imperialism. An extraordinary army of 30,000 Cubans rushed from Angola
to Ethiopia, via Mozambique, along with 2,000 Soviets, 2,500 Yemenis,
Bulgarians and Poles, 120 tanks and several squads of MIGs. Why that
bloody change of alliances? Because after an intense 7-week tour
through the area, Castro — with his uncontrollable obsession with
unifying and his pathological hatred of diversity (as if these whims
were some kind of intolerable sickness) dreamed of creating one great
country "in the horn of Africa" for the glory of the Socialist cause.

Not incidentally, he also wanted to control access to the Persian
Gulf through a radical super-nation that would include South Yemen,
Somalia, Ethiopia, Eritrea and Ogaden. The nationalist quarrels in the
area ruined his ambitious plan. Perhaps weapons would change the
minds of the disobedient revolutionaries of that dusty but important
region of the world. He would impose on them the necessary discipline.

The result was predictable. Thousands of Somalians died in combat and many tens of thousands more were forced to emigrate. It was a
total triumph of the Cuban armed forces against an enemy that had not
been a real adversary. It produced an enormous human catastrophe that

destabilized Somalia so brutally that still, a decade later, and after having received the first humanitarian intervention decreed by the United Nations, the country continues to writhe in chaos.

Naturally, there were a number of casualties among the Cubans, roughly estimated at 1,200 dead, but it was such an overwhelming victory that the United States, even under the weak command of Carter, hastened to create a Rapid Deployment Force, conceived to act in Third World wars. The victory of the Communist Cubans, of course, was only partial and transitory. Eventually, Mengisto, the Ethiopian, fled to Zimbabwe and his regime collapsed in 1991. Eritrea became independent in 1993 while in Angola the MPLA and UNITA, without stopping their war, began to move closer in their political positions in an attempt to reach a peaceful agreement. The sacrifices extracted from the Caribbean people by this African adventure — few bodies were repatriated — were more than a crime. Time would show that it had been an act of indefensible stupidity.

By the end of the 1970s, Fidel Castro felt he was at the height of his power and influence, and certainly, he had reason. He had been elected president of the Non-Aligned Movement (a grotesque idea since all that his military and diplomatic efforts had managed to achieve was to place the Third World under the banners of the USSR and the Socialist camp), and his armies had triumphed in Angola and Ethiopia; there were Cuban troops and advisers in a dozen African countries. The Americans, demoralized and defeated in Vietnam, were incapable of responding and very soon, in 1979, Havana would rack up another two victories.

In March, in the little Caribbean island of Grenada, the New Jewel Movement overthrew Eric Gairy, a politician whose eccentricities bordered on insanity. Their leader was Maurice Bishop, a radical leader who described himself as Marxist. He installed a regime that, as Bishop himself said in Cuba shortly thereafter, took its inspiration from the Cuban Revolution. In July, it was Nicaragua's turn. For 20 years, Castro had been trying to overthrow Anastasio Somoza's dictatorship and the America Department of his Central Committee did an excellent job managing the diverse insurrectional forces. They trained, funded and unified them under the name of the National Sandinista Liberation

Front. In addition to placing all the forces under one umbrella, just by showing his preferences Castro indirectly — especially for Humberto — elected the brothers Daniel and Humberto Ortega as *primus inter pares*, the *comandantes* who would carry the most weight among the nine who made up the Directorate, and he convinced everyone not to openly promote their Communist intentions.

They were to do exactly as he had done to Batista: in the first phase — there would be ways of expunging them from the Revolution later on — they would have to join forces with the democratic bourgeoisie, so as not to frighten Nicaraguan society nor give the United States an excuse to intervene. The Sandinistas accepted the advice. The war against Somoza was revitalized as a result of the assassination of the journalist Pedro Joaquín Chamorro, an anti-Communist democrat who was, in a way, the most prestigious and visible leader of the opposition. Once the Front had been mounted and the offensive launched, Castro looked for other international supporters. Paradoxically, Cuba could send its army to Africa but not to Latin America, because that would be too much of a provocation to Washington. But there are always other means to arrive at an end. In Venezuela, Carlos Andrés Pérez was in power, and he too felt that his was a country with regional responsibilities. He had nothing better to do than to compete with Fidel Castro, collaborating with him in the Nicaraguan adventure; while in Panama, Omar Torrijos was in charge — an able and corrupt populist with whom Cuba maintained the best relations. All the three countries had to do, under Castro's underground leadership, was agree to supply the Sandinistas with weapons, ammunition and soldiers, by psychologically seducing or bribing Costa Rican officials —Costa Rica stands between Nicaragua (to the north) and Panama (to the south). The Sandinistas would only confront a small but feisty National Guard, less than 10,000 active men, an institution that because of the total discredit of *Somocismo* and the continuous negative propaganda had completely lost the backing of the United States.

The Sandinista victory immediately had the effect of re-energizing the subversive and terrorist groups in El Salvador and Guatemala. In a moment of supreme euphoria, it is no surprise that Fidel Castro assured Venezuelan historian Guillermo Morón that in ten years all of the Caribbean would be under Cuban control. He saw himself at the forefront of a great federation of Communist states that would deliver the final blow to the hated American adversary. He would be Saint George slaying the dragon. The world, which had chorused: *"Fidel, seguro/ a los yanquis dales duro"* — "Fidel really hit the Yankees hard" — would remember him as the great conqueror of American imperialism. They would never know how hard he really hit them. The future would be red.

And he wasn't the only one who saw things that way. The truth is that at this stage in history, the planet seemed condemned to take refuge in the Soviet model. It was no coincidence that someone as clear-thinking as Jean-François Revel began to write his pessimist *Why Democracies End*. It was perfectly credible to think that the end had arrived for the historic period that had begun in the 17th century with the English Revolution, later followed by the American in 1776, and later imitated by a few fortunate nations, France among them. Jean-François Revel and other concerned democrats feared that these would turn out to have been illusion-filled centuries that would disappear, given the West's inability to respond to the imperial spasm of the Soviets. Soon the dream of freedom, plurality and a State of Law would be replaced by the asphyxiating control of one party, while the enormous gulag archipelago extended itself throughout civilization. Democracy had been just a wonderful and ephemeral mirage in the political history of the human species.

Paradoxically, this pessimism, fed by the successes of communism, had an unforeseeable result. It contributed to the election of Ronald Reagan to the White House in November, 1980. After Carter's administration — bogged down in inflation and paralyzed by multiple enemies who easily kidnapped dozens of Americans, as in Iran, or installed an openly pro-Castro regime in Managua — a politician came to power on the promise of taking a strong hand with Moscow and its satellites. "We will fight against the currents of evil," Reagan warned, bending an ominous gaze into the cameras with a talent honed in Hollywood. Here was an old pro, who had learned the lines of a good script, and he soon showed that he was serious. How? In several ways, all of them rooted in the old "strategy of competition" designed by the brilliant American diplomat George Kennan in the late 1940s.

First, he turned the enormous economic and scientific capacity of the country to the development of a defense plan called the Strategic Defense Initiative (nicknamed "Star Wars" by those with little imagination), a challenge that became economically devastating for Moscow and that perhaps is one of the causes of the final crisis in the USSR. Secondly, he signed the corresponding executive orders so that the CIA could confront Cuban-Soviet politics in Central America and Africa.

In Latin America, the first beneficiary of this change in policy in Washington was the government of El Salvador. The weapons, advisers and economic aid that flowed in from the United States allowed that country to halt the advances of the Communists and save a shaky democracy that was trying to consolidate itself, amid horrible crimes and military battles and despite the dangerous offensive launched in the capital city by the guerrillas in 1981. Naturally, Castro began to worry. He had to take seriously the new tenant in the White House. He soon learned that an invasion of Cuba, if that were judged necessary to stop the advancement of Communism in the region, had been discussed in the first meeting of Reagan's cabinet. And he would shortly confirm, in 1983, that the threat was real. In October 19 of that year, the Stalinist sector in Grenada, led by Bernard Coard, succumbed to internal quarrels and bloody sectarianism. They staged a military coup and executed Bishop; Reagan immediately took advantage of the circumstance. In barely a week, he launched a military invasion of the small Caribbean island and removed the Communists from power. All of them: those with Bishop and those with Coard, because even though the pretext of the invasion was to protect the lives of Americans on the island — a few dozen medical students — the Pentagon's real purpose was to prevent the island's leaders from completing an airport with a long landing strip. That, according to U.S. intelligence sources, could only be intended for use by Soviet bombers and the new generation of MIG 29s.

For Castro, the Grenada episode was an embarrassing defeat. Firstly, because it was a territory under the direct influence of Havana, in close proximity to Venezuela — his golden dream. And secondly, because the Cuban contingent on the island, a thousand soldiers and construction workers, all of them armed and with military training, had received orders to fight to the last man and the last bullet, to show the

United States the immense cost of trying to invade Cuba. So sure was Castro that his wishes would become reality that Cuban radio, informed of the heroic instructions of the *comandante*, after an emotional rendition of the national anthem, announced that the last of the Cuban combatants had fallen, wrapped in a bloody Cuban flag. Cuba was stunned. Children were taken out of the country's schools to salute the flag in honor of the new martyrs. Even anti-Castro Cubans, moved by the patriotic heroism, shed tears of Cuban solidarity. There were 24 hours of national mourning.

Then the videos arrived, showing what had actually taken place: the Cuban soldiers gave up without offering any resistance. There were few losses, and they were courteously treated by U.S. troops. Shortly thereafter, in an arrangement made by Spanish Prime Minister Felipe González, the Cubans were repatriated to Cuba and every one of them carried in their hands a glorious box of food and first-aid, supplies lovingly donated by the American Red Cross. It was very strange to see them arrive at the Havana airport and to hear them say to Castro: "Mission accomplished, *comandante*." The colonel in charge, Pedro Tortoló Comas, a prudent military man who felt it was immoral to sacrifice a thousand people for political considerations and for a gesture of obscure significance, was demoted and sent to Angola as a rank and file soldier. Unfairly, his name became the subject of perverse jokes about the lack of courage of Cuban soldiers.

Castro and Gorbachev

If Fidel could not teach the Americans a lesson, he did learn his from the Soviets, who did nothing to stop the loss of Grenada. In 1982, his loyal friend Leonid Brezhnev, who had always felt a costly weakness for Castro, had died, and it was now evident that the Kremlin was charting other seas. Very little attention was paid when Castro urgently asked the new premier to maintain an energetic position against the Americans in the case of Grenada. In place of Brezhnev came Yuri Andropov, a refined man, a former KGB chief; and he was profoundly aware of the deficiencies and the real problems his country faced. He did not seem inclined to exacerbate them in order to maintain the fruits of expansionism — an expansionism that even the Soviet strategists were beginning to question. What purpose did it serve to conquer Angola, Ethiopia or Nicaragua, only to tack them onto the already strained Soviet budget? The USSR was beginning to realize it was a metropolis — the only one in history — looted by its colonies. Had it been wise to try to take over that hornet's nest that was Afghanistan, at the cost of thousands of men and who knows how many rubles? And how much had the Cuban adventure cost? The subsidy to Cuba already cost billions every year, while the economic picture in the USSR was quickly deteriorating, in terms of both financial strength and production. It was well-known, for example, that the life expectancy of the average Soviet citizen had been decreasing. The country was on its way to joining the Third World as a consequence of the enormous economic blunders.

In 1984, Andropov died; he was succeeded by Konstantin Chernenko. Fidel Castro went to the burial wearing an astrakhan hat that underlined the worry on his wrinkled brow. It was February, a daunting month in Moscow. The same day the foreign correspondents announced the successor, an old and obscure man, they warned that he was very ill. And they were not wrong: in March of 1985, a year later, almost to the day, Chernenko died.

His designated heir was young — at the age of 50-something, he was almost a child in the Communist hierarchy — and his name was Mikhail Gorbachev. He was firmly determined to put order to the growing chaos from which his country suffered. Gorbachev was more of a technician than an ideologue; he was a protégé of Andropov, but under the influence of Alexander Yakolev. The latter was a World War II hero who was wounded in combat, and a former ambassador to Canada (where he was sent because of the unconventional things he used to say). Yakovlev had developed the theory that the cause of the Soviet Union's relative failure was its inability to look squarely at the problems that affected its society. The USSR, to save itself and surpass the West, needed *glasnost*, freedom of expression, something that could only be achieved under *perestroika*, a reform of the state that would have to be far-reaching enough to eliminate the Leninist violence in the relations between society and the Party. Gorbachev believed this. He was convinced that by taking that path he could position the USSR at the helm of the world. Fidel Castro, whose intuition told him what was happening in Moscow, did not even bother to go to Chernenko's funeral. March is also a cold month in Russia.

With Gorbachev firmly in power, it wasn't long before he began to emit worrisome signs to his always bellicose Cuban ally. In 1986, Soviet troops began to withdraw from Afghanistan and the Kremlin's emissaries warned the Sandinistas and the Angolan government that they should not count on Soviet aid indefinitely. The withdrawal from Afghanistan not only ended a failed military episode but an entire epoch. The new Russian government's priority was economic development and the need to reach certain agreements with Washington in the difficult arena of the arms race. The existence of a pro-Soviet regime in America's backyard, one that was at war with the U.S., did not reflect well on the renovated USSR announced by Gorbachev. On the other hand, at about that time the Nicaraguan contras, armed by the CIA, had acquired great efficiency and appeared to be militarily undefeatable — despite the fact that the Sandinista army was now one of the largest in Latin America. The $10 million Russian subsidy had been multiplied to ten times that of Somoza's National Guard. Confronting the foreign advisers in Nicaragua was (or had been) the best Cuban general, Arnaldo Ochoa, trained in the USSR, a hero of Angola and Ethiopia, a former guerrilla in Venezuela and the protagonist of many exploits of Cuban internationalism (some well-known and others clandestine, like the training of the Argentine guerrillas and terrorists who attacked the La Tablada garrison in 1988 during the weak but democratic Argentina of Raúl Alfonsín).

The Narco Revolution

Despite all that, in 1989, shortly after Gorbachev made a highly publicized visit to Cuba, the Cuban press shook the world with news of several arrests. These included Generals Arnaldo Ochoa and Patricio de la Guardia, chief of the "Special Troops" (the Cuban Rangers); the former general and Transportation Minister Diocles Torralba; Colonel Antonio "Tony" de la Guardia, Patricio's twin brother, a powerful man

who was close to Fidel Castro and who had played a role in the majority of the most delicate clandestine operations. Along with them lesser-
known officers of the Interior Ministry were also arrested. What had
happened? The story has been meticulously reconstructed in two books
which are fundamental to the understanding of today's Cuba: *End of the
Century in Havana* by Jean-François Fogel and Bertrand Rosenthal, two
French journalists, and *Castro's Final Hour*, by the Argentine-American
Andrés Oppenheimer.

At first, the reports were confusing. The Cubans immediately
warned that the two key figures were Arnaldo Ochoa and Tony de la
Guardia, but it wasn't easy to see how these two characters could be
scripted into the same play. Even though they knew each other and
were friends to some extent, Ochoa was an army man who moved in
military circles, and de la Guardia was more of a Scarlet Pimpernel type,
closer to the Cuban intelligence services. Tony was a courageous, intelligent man, an amateur painter with some intellectual refinement; he
was capable of carrying out actions that bordered on suicide. For example, it has been said (although never confirmed) that he and his brother
placed explosives in the principal chambers of the United Nations during the Missile Crisis in October 1962, planning to detonate them if
Cuba were invaded by the United States. Fidel Castro, like Samson,
was willing to destroy the temple together with the Philistines at the
cost of an international catastrophe.

After the initial hesitation, Cuban authorities formulated a concrete accusation: these military men were involved in drug trafficking
and corruption. There was a scandalous trial in which the prosecutor
was General Juan Escalona, a trusted man of Raúl Castro's who, like his
own boss, had had serious problems with alcoholism in the past. After
a shamelessly manipulated hearing, in which the sessions were interrupted when the accused began to say embarrassing things, almost all
of them — the exception was Patricio — were condemned to death.
Following the old tradition of the gangs — that all members must
bloody their hands equally — the sentence by the Military Tribunal
was ratified by the Council of State and by numerous generals, who
were later prodded to express their agreement with the execution and
their scorn for the accused. Those who did not go along with this, or

who did not do so with enough conviction, were removed from their posts. General Raúl Tomassevich was one of them — a Cuban whose ancestors had been slaves, and who felt genuine affection for Ochoa.

What had really happened? Had they discovered criminals in the heart f the honorable Cuban Revolution and were they simply being punished for their felonies? Not at all. The crime had been discovered, yes, but not by the Cuban intelligence service — who were delinquent — but by the Drug Enforcement Administration, the U.S. DEA, which polices and prosecutes drug trafficking in the international arena. Simply put, the Cuban government had been caught with its hands in cocaine.

The DEA had proof that the Marines, the Air Force, the Interior Ministry, and even the Ministry of Foreign Relations of Cuba were involved in the drug trade. U.S. authorities had infiltrated into the operation a Taiwanese pilot, Hu Chang, who on May 8, 1987, landed at one of the Cuban government's secret installations after a flight from Colombia, carrying a load of cocaine. This definitive proof corroborated the previous experience of two Cuban American drug traffickers, Reynaldo Ruiz and his son Rubén, linked through family ties to a high-ranking Cuban intelligence official stationed in Panama, Miguel Ruiz Poo. Reynaldo and Rubén, forced to cooperate with the DEA in order to reduce their drug trafficking charges, had given the U.S. government all the proof and leads necessary so that Castro could be taken to court for his links to drug trafficking and money laundering.

Nevertheless, the U.S. government, which had hoped to make the case water-tight, made an unforgivable blunder. It tried to set a trap for the Minister of the Interior, General José Abrantes, and to that end, released from jail Gustavo "Papito" Fernández, a Cuban drug trafficker who had in the past collaborated with the CIA. He was offered a substantial reduction in his sentence if he agreed to set the trap. The plan required the use of a submarine; it included arresting Abrantes in international waters and hauling him before the courts and the press. Gustavo Fernández accepted, naturally, but naturally he gave the slip to those responsible for keeping an eye on him. He escaped to Havana and there he spilled everything he knew: that a scandal was about to break and that Castro would no longer be the heroic figure of the Revolution, but would, in the eyes of the world, be depicted as a vulgar narco-dictator like the Panamanian Manuel Noriega, who had been totally discredited in those times.

All this took place between April and May of 1989. The *comandante* was worried. He knew that, this time, the Americans could destroy his image. He blamed Tony de la Guardia. As always, he used the mother-land as his excuse: Tony had endangered the Revolution with his mix-ture of fearlessness and irresponsibility. Now the United States would be able to invade Cuba, and no one would come to defend her. In his eyes, Tony's crime was not the drug trafficking (Castro knew all about it, since it had been a frequent practice since the early 1970s). Selling drugs in the United States was seen as another way of destabilizing Yankee imperialism, according to Juan Antonio Rodríguez Menier, a major in the intelligence services who defected to the United States. His interview with *El Nuevo Herald* came out shortly before the scandal. That was not the problem. Tony's crime was indiscretion. And indis-cretion, in this very serious case, amounted to treason against the motherland. But for Castro there was another element that was just as: his counterintelligence services, led by the tireless General Colomé "Furry" Ibarra, had brought forth compromising tape-recordings of conversations between the twins, Tony and Patricio de la Guardia, and Diocles Torralba and Arnaldo Ochoa. The men made fun of Castro and his brother Raúl, they told jokes, they expressed favorable views on Gorbachev and *perestroika*, and they complained of the stubborn Stalin-ist orthodoxy of the government.

So, behind his back, Fidel Castro was the laughing stock of the Cuban leadership. The *comandante* knew it, and he was incensed. In fact, he was so out of touch with reality that he had asked the Center for Biotechnology and Genetics, then led by Manuel Limonta, to "design" a little household cow so that every Cuban could have in his house a dwarf animal that would provide a gallon of milk every day. And he wasn't joking: the *comandante* had appeared before a meeting of scien-tists with a plan for the equipment needed to feed a domestic cow. Cas-tro was reinventing the cow. In the midst of this climate of generalized ridicule, the Maximum Leader discovered that Ochoa and the de la Guardia brothers were also making a fool of him. How they laughed!

Why weren't they afraid? They were no longer true revolutionaries. They had turned into dangerously disaffected men who were on the verge of a conspiracy. This was something truly dangerous, because Ochoa was about to take charge of the Western Army, including Havana, where Patricio de la Guardia's troops were quartered. While there may not have been any conspiracy in place at that moment, there potentially could be one, given the relaxed principle of authority founded on the reverence to the *caudillo*. And Castro is one of those people who is convinced that "only the paranoid survive."

Given all this, the *comandante* made a clean break. He made a drastic decision: he would kill three birds with the same shot. He would arrest Ochoa, the de la Guardias, and other lower ranking officers — there must always be a chain of command — and he would have them tried, publicly. What would he achieve this way? First and foremost, he would be defending his own image. It would be useless to deny that there had been drug trafficking, so he admitted that, definitely, yes, there was some trafficking but he had not been aware of it. What better proof of his own innocence than to execute his most valuable general and his favorite James Bond? In the second place, he would be teaching a lesson to the Ministry of the Interior and to the state bureaucrats. Anyone who manifested sympathies for *perestroika* would now know what he could expect. Anybody who deviated by one millimeter from the official line was exposing himself to the worst. Thirdly, he was eliminating the risk of placing his government within reach of an ill-advised attempt by the military. There remained only two loose ends: how to get the accused to cooperate, and how to make the world believe it?

The first was not so difficult. Security forces would apply a well-known softening technique. For hours and hours, day after day, without letting the prisoners sleep, under the blinding light of the special dungeons, they will convince them that they have acted with negligence and temerity, and they have put the motherland at risk. Didn't they remember the example of Che, who prior to his Bolivian adventure, to protect the Revolution, had written his famous letter? Now, the hated *gringos* could invade Cuba. They had a good excuse, and the world would not lift a finger to stop them — because drug traffickers have no public friends. But there was still a chance to avoid this: if they admitted their total and exclusive responsibility, if they exonerated the government, the reputation of the Revolution would not be questioned and their lives would be spared. The government did not necessarily have to execute them. There were precedents for mercy. Didn't they spare the life of Rolando Cubelas, despite his complicity with the CIA in a plan to kill the *comandante*? If they collaborated, the Revolution could be generous.

The accused cooperated. Sometimes they would deviate from the script, and the trial would be stopped; they would review the testimony and start again. "It was like the bad takes in the filming of a movie," says Orlando Jiménez-Leal, who made the electrifying docudrama, *8-A*, about the case. But, in the end, they were betrayed and were condemned to death. The Minister of the Interior, Jose Abrantes, did not agree with that, and he dared to object. He told Castro, "You knew perfectly well what they were doing; and not even all of them were doing it, Ochoa never had anything to do with those operations". Castro had him arrested and jailed. Shortly after, he died in prison of a mysterious heart attack. He was about 50 years old and in good physical condition. His cellmates and his relatives are convinced that he was killed.

To give credibility to the pantomime, Castro needed credible testimony. Who better than his good friend Gabriel García Márquez, the prestigious Nobel Laureate for Literature? No one would think he praised the Cuban government for money, since the Colombian was known to be wealthy and had no reason to sell himself. He also would not support Castro's version for ideological reasons, given that Gabo — as his friends called him — was not Communist. He had abandoned his Marxist illusions at the border between the two Germanies, as early as the 1950s. He had even had a good personal friendship with Tony de la Guardia, and exhibited one of his paintings on a wall in his house (although, according to Tony's family, he did nothing to stop his execution). García Márquez watched the trial from a secret window and viewed the spectacle, side by side with Castro. This was not the first time he had witnessed a political trial in Cuba. When he was a young journalist, in 1959, he traveled to Havana along with Plinio Apuleyo y

Mendoza, his compatriot and friend, another great writer, and both of them were horrified by the trial of the *Batistiano* war criminals. Thirty years later, something had happened to García Márquez's sensibilities — he had lost the capacity to be outraged by injustice. Once, he asked Castro why he did not make changes toward democracy — changes that García Márquez would have liked — and the barbaric answer he received only made him smile. *"Porque no me sale de los cojones,"* the *comandante* answered — "Because I don't feel like it" would be too polite a translation.

García Márquez's well-deserved fame and success, for reasons that he probably can't explain himself, has turned him into a sort of Caribbean God who is above good and evil. Life, time or something else has anesthetized him to human conduct. He can deal with a guerrilla torturer, a drug trafficker or an annoying bore who flatters him to no end, all without feeling disgust. It doesn't occur to him to judge human beings, as it doesn't occur to him to judge the characters in his novels. He lacks, or has given up, a reasonably-structured scale of values. The mechanisms of his ethical judgment have become atrophied. Fidel fascinates him, awakens his indomitable anthropological curiosity. He talks so much. He tells so many stories. He is so crazy. And so García Márquez likes to help him and do him favors. Why? García Márquez is a helpful guy. He enjoys being useful to the powerful, though he can do the same for the less fortunate. He is also generous. He has secured the freedom of political prisoners (Reinol González) and has negotiated difficult immigration permits (Norberto Fuentes). But his enjoyment doesn't seem to be derived from the moral rewards of his acts, nor even the gratitude his services merit —he doesn't expect gratitude — but from the pleasure of showing the immense personal power he has won through his well-earned prestige as a novelist. And what greater joy than to be able to solve an important problem for one of the most powerful men in the world? Here is a writer lost in the labyrinth of his own complex psychology.

In any case, why did the Cuban government get involved in this criminal behavior? First, because no one will ever be able to accuse Castro of respecting bourgeois law. That is not in his nature. Laws are for other people. If the final cause he defends is just, then any means are acceptable. The $62 million the Argentine armed rebels received as ransom for a rich agricultural entrepreneur found its way to Cuban banks. Castro did not see any harm in that. The kidnappings, like the drug traffic, are only expressions of a fight against imperialism. The Panamanian diplomat José Blandón, a Noriega representative, told how Castro (in his presence) mediated a dispute between his president and the Medellín Cartel for $200 million in drug proceeds. The Colombians ended up giving in. That is only one example. Cuban agents have held up banks in Mexico and Lebanon — there is a credible account of these and other misdeeds by Jorge Masetti, a protagonist of many of those "revolutionary actions," which include the kidnapping of millionaires in Ecuador and Panama for ransom. In Cuba, counterfeits are made of dollars, Treasury Bonds, Wifredo Lam paintings, Moet & Chandon champagne, Levi's and Winston cigarettes. Living and working for the government in Cuba, as the covert head of all these operations, was Robert Vesco, a well-known American crook, who today is imprisoned on the island for trying to lie to Castro in a medicine-related deal (a wild and crazy guy, that American).

Contact between the Cuban Revolution and drug trafficking began in the Colombian jungle. The first reliable testimonies came in the 1970s. The guerrillas needed weapons and the Cubans needed money. Inside the Cuban Ministry of the Interior, an office had been created, the MC, with the purpose of violating the American embargo. It was a secret structure that included dozens of front companies located in diverse parts of the world, but especially in Panama, under Torrijos and Noriega. Tony de la Guardia was the star of the group. The MC, which was serviced by its contacts with the radical left all over America, didn't hesitate to start doing business with the Colombian guerrillas. The Cuban ambassador in Colombia, Fernando Ravelo, was an intimate friend of Pablo Escobar Gaviria and other notorious drug traffickers. The guerrillas' money came from the drug trade, and what developed is known in contemporary business jargon as synergy. The two groups united in an almost natural way to maximize their benefits. First, Cuba was paid $1000 for every kilo of cocaine that the planes dumped over its waters. Boats picked up the drugs and the packages were transferred to the United States. Later, the drug traffickers used military landing strips. The relations became closer and closer. . . until the day it all blew up.

With Ochoa and Tony de la Guardia dead, Castro believed he had deactivated the drug trafficking scandal. He knew that no one believe him, but he wasn't worried. He had his alibi, and he would not move one inch from that position. His purpose was to establish an official truth, his, and to distribute it *urbi et orbe* to comfort his sympathizers, to give peace of mind to those who were indifferent, and to annoy his enemies. That is what he has always done: interpret reality, imprint it with his version, and later order the informers to repeat it without any hint of doubt. But he now he faced a harder task: to keep the strong winds that were raging throughout the Communist world from also razing the Cuban Revolution. It was evident that the Ministry of the Interior — the fiefdom of Abrantes and Tony de la Guardia — was full of reformists who were pleased with what they saw in the East. So he ordered his brother Raúl, the defense minister, to intervene and purge that ministry, substituting the corrupt or the *perestroikos* with Army officers who had proven to be loyal. Fidel himself, who boasts of having the gift of being able to tell when people are lying, personally interrogated hundreds of officers from the political police, and had a good number of them retired. He even jailed a few, including the generals Pascual Martínez Gil and Luis Barreiro Caramés. It was the biggest purge that the apparatus had known since its creation.

Post-Communism

Was it a paranoiac spasm, or was the regime really in danger? Both. Shortly after the Ochoa case, the Berlin Wall came down, and while they were at it, the wrecking balls took down all of communism in the East. The USSR disappeared as a trusted ally — soon, it disappeared entirely — and the Cuban government was advised that its economic aid would be substantially reduced. A Western journalist who was with Castro when he witnessed, on television, the events in Romania — when the multitudes took to the streets, harangued by a Protestant pastor from the Hungarian minority — remembers the *comandante's* enraged screams. "Ceausescu is a faggot; if they did that to me, I'd take the tanks out on the streets and I kill them all." He said it loud enough for his subordinates to hear. The message was very clear: what was happening in Europe would not occur in Cuba.

Why not? Basically, because he didn't want it to, and he had enough authority to prevent it. However, he quickly supplied a rationalization: it was because, the Cuban Revolution, by its very origins, was different. The Russians didn't impose the Revolution. They came as guests, not as hosts. Martí was swept away and Marxism-Martianism was the new theoretical basis. Ricardo Alarcón, president of the National Assembly of the People, without the least intellectual scruples, was one of the first to subscribe to this asinine fallacy. At one time, he was seen as an intelligent and critical-minded man; but he later became a pathetic, spineless parrot. Armandito Hart went stuttering after him. That was more predictable. Eusebio Leal, by contrast, had the good sense to keep his mouth shut; Miguel Barnet, too. It's one thing to defend the Revolution in the abstract, but it's worse to make concrete, foolish statements. Even if the Socialist references were lost, the theoreticians defending Castroism were capable of digging through Martí's thinking until they found half a dozen phrases to which they could tie the rhetorical justification for a one-party dictatorship. At the height of the manipulation, they even proposed the following axiom: "Martí only created one political party, not two or three; so the multi-party system is not something that belongs to Cuba's historic tradition." We could also claim that since Lincoln only belonged to the Republican Party, and not to the Democratic one, the United States should renounce the bipartisan system and convert *en masse* to the party of Lincoln. No one dared to say — they would have gone to prison -- that all of Cuba's problems had emerged precisely because one group had curtailed the political liberties of the others by imposing a single party.

The years between 1989 and 1992 were a time of fear and uncertainty for the *comandante*. But Castro, when he fears, flees forward; therefore, he hardened his stance and announced the beginning of a deadly catastrophe in which everyone would fall, defending the last bastion of communism. There would be no going back, no transition to any other model. All the transitions there were going to be had already been done, and forever, in 1959. All he talked about was holocausts and death. He made fashionable the tragic Spanish legend of *Numacia*, in which all of the habitants died before the city would surrender, and he coined the corresponding attitude: *numantinismo*. He decreed a "special period" — a time of exceptional shortages — and he went about stashing huge caches of rusty weapons all over the country in anticipation of the Yankee invasion, the uprising of the opposition, or the arrival of some unspecified enemy whose identity was obscure. In Europe, the Communists could surrender without a fight, but that was not the Cuban way. The island would become a moral reserve of scientific socialism preserved in all its purity. Some day, when humanity came back to its senses, then the world could find in Cuba an ideological hotbed capable of revitalizing Marxism on Earth. Cuba was the Jurassic Park of communism, the last bastion, the revolutionary sperm bank, call it what you will; as long as Castro did not have to accept the demise of the ideas he had ardently defended since his youth.

He was still nourishing some secret hopes, however, based on his old ties to the KGB. His best source continued to be General Leonov, his old friend from Mexico, his translator on all his trips to the USSR. He knew that the Soviet Right was not totally finished, and he awaited an uprising that would turn back the course of history. It simply could not be true that the glorious October Revolution would disappear from the face of the earth.

In the spring, Castro met in Mexico with Salinas de Gortari, Carlos Andrés Pérez, César Gaviria and Felipe González. The four leaders offered to lend a hand to help Cuba handle the loss of its massive aid from the Soviet Union, and to contribute to the transition to another model, as was inevitable. These were intelligent men, with experience and education. They talked, persuaded, reasoned. Castro listened silently. Suddenly, he opened his mouth and started to talk. It was capitalism that was going to disappear; it would blow up after a financial crisis worse than that of 1929. The New York Stock Exchange was a time bomb. The West was condemned to a social explosion and the redeeming revolution would provoke the eruption. The four leaders watched him, in shock. Was he crazy? Communism, he asserted, would return in a renewed form, and very soon. He knew something. He had something in mind. And in indeed, on August 1991, part of the Red

Army, led by hard-line Communists, instigated an uprising in Moscow. In Havana, champagne bottles were uncorked. Communism had returned. Or, so they thought.

But the cheering didn't last long. Boris Yeltsin, then President of the Republic of Russia, managed in a few hours to halt the uprising, and the democratic forces (or whatever those forces were) uprooted the insurgents with canon fire. On December 25 — was there another heavenly star traveling the firmament? — Mikhail Gorbachev resigned. The USSR ceased to exist. The Communist Party of the Soviet Union already had been dissolved by decree. Without one tear being shed. Without one poem from the opportunist Yevtushenko. This was not a party of 20 million fanatics. They were 20 million fakes.

Now Castro's dilemma consisted in how to pay the bills without Soviet financing and without opening the door to private property and a market economy. He came up with three ways: tourism, the export of biotechnology — he had happily forgotten about the dwarf cow — and money sent in by émigrés. To exploit the latter, he would have to legitimize the possession of dollars. If exile "A" wanted to help his mother "B" who is still in Cuba, he would have to be allowed to send dollars; it would no longer be a crime. He adopted such a measure a bit later, in 1993, when the noose was tied around his neck; meanwhile, he moved more discreetly. Castro knew that throughout the Caribbean basin, remittances from émigrés are the largest source of foreign currency for those weak economies. He calculated that the 2 million exiles could end up sending the island between $500 million to $1 billion a year; and he was right. That is more than the sugar harvest is worth.

Quietly, those wretched people who had been sentenced for having dollars were released from jail. What had previously been prohibited now merited applause. Euphoric, Castro now promised that in two years the country would have solved its food shortages. This was in 1991, during the IVth Communist Party Congress. The congress, despite many peoples' illusions, was not being held to announce changes but to apply the brakes. Castro was traveling to the past. But people were hungry, and he had to promise food. He therefore claimed to be launching a plan that would resolve this issue.

In Havana, people were saying that everything had been resolved, in Cuba; you only had to expect three little problems: breakfast, lunch and dinner. And those three problems would end up provoking a serious epidemic of malnutrition, with neuritis affecting thousands of people. Many ended up blind, after it attacked their optical nerves, and others would suffer from pain in their limbs for the rest of their lives. Hunger had damaged the membrane that covers certain nerves.

But there was a problem even more severe than these illnesses, and that was talking about them, admitting that they existed, and correctly attributing them to the food shortages. The Minister of Health did that, and he was fired. Such arguments cannot be given to the Enemy to use against the Revolution. Years later, another researcher, Dr. Dessy Mendoza, would go to prison for warning that there was a dengue fever epidemic in Santiago de Cuba. Denouncing the mosquitoes, according to Castro, is a way of cooperating with the CIA. In Cuba, communism has even eradicated bad mosquitoes. There cannot be any of those. Thousands of Cubans, because they did not heed Mendoza's warning, suffered from the illness.

To develop tourism and biotechnology, Castro proposed a strategy of joint ventures. If someone wants to make money in Cuba, he can now partner with the government to jointly exploit the docile and educated native worker. Castro guaranteed total peace in the labor force. The foreign partner would have to supply the capital and know-how. The capital, in strong currencies, would be used to import raw materials and to pay the government for the labor. The government would be not only a partner but an employment agency. And a profitable one: a foreign hotelier, for example, pays $500 a month per worker, and the government pays that worker some 300 pesos. Since the exchange rate is twenty pesos to one dollar — and at some points it has even been one hundred to one — the government pockets $485 and pays the employee $15. In other words, the government confiscates 95% of the worker's salary. Inside the country, workers trying to organize a clandestine union have warned that, "When the government changes in Cuba, investors will have to return to us what has been stolen."

There is clearly resentment in Cuba toward foreigners, especially among males. In 1993, when there were street disturbances in Havana, the Deauville Hotel, managed by Spaniards, was angrily pelted with rocks. This is the result of an explosive mix of political anger and humiliation. It is very easy to understand. Many women prefer relationships with foreigners rather than with Cubans. It doesn't matter the age, the appearance or the personality of the visitor. It can be a fat old man, ugly and idiotic. A foreigner has hard currency and can purchase goods in special stores and medicine in certain well-stocked pharmacies. The other stores, those who take pesos, don't even have aspirin. A foreigner doesn't have to stand in endless lines. He can visit restaurants, hotels and party halls. A foreigner is a good provider and a door from which to escape from this hell. He has a marvelous passport, a magic carpet enabling him to fly to other lands. He embodies all the features of power. An ordinary Cuban, on the other hand, is a poor man with no future, riding a bicycle all day in the heat of the sun. Enrique Patterson, an Afro-Cuban essayist, has made this astute observation: "As long as slavery lasted, black women instinctively preferred white men to guarantee themselves support and a better personal life. Castro has managed now to make all Cubans, including whites, feel like the black male slaves of the last century."

Cuba now has four classes of people. At the top are the foreigners, who can do everything, who are treated obsequiously by the government; then there are the *pinchos,* the members of the ruling hierarchy. They have access to dollars, maintain more or less unrestricted contacts with foreigners and enjoy all kinds of privileges. Then come the Cubans who receive dollars from family members abroad, or who earn them — like the prostitutes, known as *jineteras* — by selling their bodies. They can't go where they want to, but at least they can visit the State stores and purchase goods with dollars. They can support their families. (On average, the merchandise the government sells them is marked up three times over cost. The State, an entrepreneur who enjoys a total monopoly on commercial transactions, takes advantage of its privileged situation and exploits its citizens without compassion. It squeezes them. That's how monopolies are. This ruinous commerce, which one has no choice but to engage in, is one of the main sources of income for a government incapable of producing wealth.) The fourth category is the saddest and by far the largest: 75% of the population receive no gifts from abroad and have no means of acquiring dollars on the internal market, because they have nothing to sell — and even if they had something, they would not find any opportunity to do so. This immense legion of Cubans subsists in its own homeland like third-class citizens always vulnerable to arrest on suspicion alone, and they are denied access to all of the pleasant recreational places in the country like the resort, Varadero. These Cubans spend their lives ruminating on the bitter knowledge that they are discriminated against. The Cuba of this last period of Castroism has been conceived for the use and the delight of foreign capitalists.

Capitalists, however, are not flocking in with the numbers and the resources that Castro was banking on. Hordes of young tourists come to buy cheap sex, but investors are in short supply. Despite what the *comandante* believes about the market economy, the truth is that the system of free enterprise is based on the existence of a lawful state, with clear rules, reliable courts, and the possibility of making long-range plans. And none of that exists in Cuba.

Castro himself has said that any reform to the economy that they are forced to undertake will be temporary. When they recover, they will return to their orthodox ways. That "temporary" attitude is reflected in the joint venture contracts signed with foreigners. The government always establishes partnerships for short periods. The Spanish economist Carlos Solchaga, at the urging of Felipe González, traveled to Havana and explained to Castro and his henchmen that this is short-sighted, and he proposed recommendations that would help Cuba come out of this predicament. He was wasting his time. Solchaga later admitted as much, with all honesty, in an article published in *Encuentro*, the magazine published in Madrid by the novelist Jesús Díaz. For Castro, the economic changes were and are nothing more than a temporary concession to a system and to people who provoke in him an almost uncontrollable disgust. He is willing to use a few band-aids, but he refuses to consider any real surgery. He wants it to be clear that the future will continue to be Communist. But that is not what the investors believe. On the contrary: in Cuba, the general understanding is that this is the end of the regime, and everyone is watching to see what will happen "when things change." Fidel seems to be the only person in the world convinced that Cuba will continue being a Communist State, century after century.

Rumor has it, moreover, that Castro is ill. He apparently suffered, some time ago, two "small" cerebral hemorrhages. It has been reported in the press that he nearly fainted in the presence of Spanish Ambassador José Antonio San Gil (one of the best European diplomats to have worked in Havana). Castro couldn't even reach out his hand to him. Disoriented, Castro was looking at the ambassador but could not see him. He had to be helped to a seat because he was in danger of falling over. Something similar happened in the presence of Violeta Chamorro, the President of Nicaragua, during one of the Ibero-American summits. He passed out. Two of his bodyguards took him away to the bathroom to take care of him. There is no doubt that he was ill. His sudden weight loss, his pallor, and his concave chest signaled lung cancer, in the opinion of Dr. Andrés Cao, an excellent clinician. But he quickly added: "The difficulties with motor skills, however, signal cerebral episodes driven, perhaps, by high blood pressure." It is difficult to establish a diagnosis. Journalist Pablo Alfonso learned that Castro was examined by a cardiologist in Switzerland. Nothing unusual: a former smoker, now seventy-some years of age, may be close to death. In any case, all this news inhibited the investors even more. Betting on the health of *el comandante* is like playing roulette. It might be a good idea to "position oneself" in Cuba before the change, but there is no way of knowing how and when that change might come, and given that Castro, far from facilitating development is dedicated to obstructing it, the most prudent thing to do is to wait and see. As they say in the financial enclaves, no beast is more cowardly than a million dollars.

Dissidents and Civil Society

This climate of uncertainty was fueled, in addition, by the opposition's work inside Cuba. In the early 1980s, in prison — under the guidance of Ricardo Bofill, a social sciences professor who was originally Marxist but who split with the government after the 1970s (when he was first jailed for ten long years), the Cuban Committee for Human Rights was created. It followed the model of the opposition movements among Eastern European dissidents, especially people like Vaclav Havel and Andrei Sakharov. It was a peaceful movement that did not

try to overthrow the government by force, but fought for the fundamental rights of the people. Prisoners from the revolutionary ranks who
had been condemned for denouncing the authoritarian nature of the
government joined the movement — and that was the most opposition
possible, given the realities. Bofill managed to recruit figures like Gustavo and Sebastián Arcos, and Sebastián's children Sebastián and María
Rosa, and María Juana Cazabón, Adolfo Rivero Caro, Yanes Pelletier,
Reinaldo Bragado (a talented writer), Elizardo Sánchez Santa Cruz (a
professor who later formed her own group with a social-democratic
twist), and Oscar Peña, a history teacher, an idealist and fighter who
ran afoul of communism precisely by trying to comply honestly with
the instructions of the party. Once their sentences were completed,
these people continued trying to organize a civil resistance and managed to enlist hundreds of sympathizers and collaborators all over the
country and abroad.

Following the Bofill and Arcos example, and enthusiastic about
what was happening in Eastern Europe, dissident organizations inside
Cuba began to multiply; but they were always persecuted, controlled
and infiltrated by the political police. Alternative Criteria, a liberal-
leaning organization, was founded by José Luis Pujol, his daughter
Thais, and Roberto Luque Escalona, and it was later led by María Elena
Cruz Varela. For the first time, the name Osvaldo Alfonso Valdés appeared in the press; he would later preside over the Liberal Democratic
Party of Cuba and gain recognition among the international liberal
thinkers, along with Fernando Sánchez's Democratic Solidarity Party.
María Elena initiated the publishing of an open letter from the Union of
Cuban Writers and Artists (UNEAC), demanding civil liberties and
free elections. A dozen intellectuals had the courage to sign it, and a
few others would follow later. From the outside, this may look like a
small thing, but in the context of the closed Cuban society this was a
daring challenge. Among those with the courage to sign it were the
prominent Cuban intellectuals Manuel Díaz Martínez, Raúl Rivero,
Roberto Luque Escalona (a magnificent writer, who without leaving
Cuba dared to publish abroad a fierce essay against Castroism), Fernando Velázquez (an art critic and narrator who actually drafted the
letter — and for that, went to jail for several years), Bernardo Márquez,

Víctor Serpa, José Lorenzo Fuentes, Jorge Pomar. This took place during a visit to Cuba by Hattie Babbitt, who shortly thereafter became the U.S. Ambassador to the OAS. She interviewed the dissidents and smuggled out the letter. Her husband, Bruce, former governor of Arizona, was accompanying her; he soon joined the Cabinet of his friend, Bill Clinton. After that visit, no one would be able to lie to them about the Cuban issue.

The government responded with a letter of its own, reiterating its most unadorned Stalinism. It was produced by Carlos Aldana, then* the chief ideologue of Castroism. He was a competent official in the most slippery of professions: he was the great intellectual repressor. He knew how to attack his enemies until he destroyed them, even while simultaneously showing signs of a certain political openness (according to Lissette Bustamante, a dissident journalist who is exiled today and with whom Aldana was on fairly friendly terms). Aldana came from the Department of Revolutionary Orientation, an Orwellian organism whose purpose is to define reality. Abel Prieto, a short-story writer and the political commissar of the small Cuban intellectual world, did not believe one comma in the texts he recited, but he was put in charge of collecting 400 signatures. Rogelio Quintana, a sculptor who had been his friend at university when both were rebels, laughed: "Abelito is the inquisitor? No way." Sometimes Abel faked the signatures. Some of the signatories excused themselves, in private, heads lowered: "I had to do it; you know how these things are." Cowardice is the only thing that is not rationed in totalitarian regimes.

At the university, a sense of protest was also boiling. Professor Félix Bonne Carcassés, from the engineering school, drafted a document along the same lines as Maria Elena's. It was signed by several professors, among them Georgina González Corbo, Dani González, Miguel Morales, Rafael González Dalmau. There were dozens of them, and

---

*Aldana dreamed of taking Castro's place, and he had figured out how to do it: turn the *comandante* into something like the Queen Mother and assign him the job of symbolically representing the motherland, while governing in his stead. That fantasy came from his poetic bent — he used to compose verse, and not badly. A few months later he was removed from his post and accused of corruption; it is said that what fueled his downfall was the publication of the speeches he had drafted as self-proclaimed heir apparent. But at the moment we are discussing, when the international press has the news of the "Letter of the Ten," he was still the country's ideologue.

they all were summarily expelled. Acts of repudiation were staged against some of them. Gossip and lies about their private lives were used, in an effort to discredit them. The discord extended to the other end of the country. In Oriente, physics professor Robier Rodríguez was jailed for more or less the same reasons.

Curiously, repression is harsher in the provinces than in Havana. And for good reason: in the provinces, there are no foreign correspondents nor diplomatic missions. The government can act with total impunity. Political prisoners at the eastern end of the country almost never have an opportunity to let their afflictions be known.

Castro's response to the challenge from the intelligentsia was very harsh. The government wants Cubans to know that opposing the government comes at a high personal price. Every dissident was assigned one or two police officers who "babysit" them, meaning they visit, "counsel," intimidate or detain, according to the instructions of the Minister of the Interior. The police officer, the same one, may pat one's back or slap one's face. He is authorized to do everything. But the resistance continues. Imaginative new ecologically-minded organizations have cropped up — Harmony is one of the most often mentioned — and the political groups have started to sound out the world abroad. René Vázquez Díaz, a social democrat of Cuban origin who was raised in Sweden and who is close to Pierre Schori, an ex-sympathizer of Castroism, visited in the name of his party and of his adopted country and made contacts, aiming to strengthen civil society with apparently innocent activities. The political police, who wasted no time after giving him a nasty interrogation, banned him from entering the country.

What has been going on out there, in the world behind the straw curtain straw? For some 30 years, the doors and windows had been closed. René Gómez Manzano, one of the country's most respected jurists, organized an independent association of lawyers. He called it Agramontista, in memory of Ignacio Agramonte, a 19th century Cuban man of letters and military man. Some of the professors and doctors have attempted to get together. The names of some dissidents become known: Samuel Martínez Lara, Omar del Pozo, Luis Pita Santos, Roberto Bahamonde. The latter, a fearless engineer surrounded by an enthusiastic family willing to make sacrifices, tried to gain sufficient popularity to win an elected office and he ended up a recluse in a psychiatric hospital. The evidence of his craziness is that he believed that a dissident could challenge the government at the voting booth.

This was not the first time the government used psychiatric hospitals and electroshock treatments to deal with the opposition. An entire ward at Ameijeiras Hospital — the "Carbó Servía" — is set aside for this repressive task. Mederos is the name of the person who usually applies the electroshock treatment to dissidents. The list of victims is long, and includes the cinematographers Marcos Miranda and Nicolás Guillén Landrián, the journalist Amaro Gómez Boix, the engineer Andrés Solares, and the historian Juan Peñate. The scholars Charles J. Brown and Armando Lago have written a valuable book (*The Politics of Psychiatry in Revolutionary Cuba*) that documents about twenty such cases.

But the brutal punishment did not dissuade the opposition. At a certain moment, two dozen independent organizations were able to unite and form a council to ask for liberty and democracy. The government assailed them. The work of the political police is to break up society, to prevent the organization of institutions that are outside of their control. Journalists created "press agencies" — a Smith Corona manual typewriter, and with luck, a ream of yellowing paper. The police broke them up them and confiscated the typewriters as if they were machine guns. Through friendly embassies, the news traveled abroad. At least two Spanish diplomats helped the dissidents and the persecuted, with an admirable sense of compassion and affection: Jorge Orueta and Mariano Uriarte. They were responsible diplomats, but also people who would not hide their indignation. In Madrid, their bosses fretted. They discretely but firmly continued alleviating the misery of the dissidents. Bless them.

That embassy has been a great observation outpost. In the 1970s, a commercial attaché, Alberto Recarte, a curious economist who was shocked by what he saw, took notes during his travels through Cuba and later wrote an excellent history of the contemporary Cuban economy. Some independent journalists have taken the risk of using the telephone and dictating their stories. In exile, friendly hands reproduced them: in Puerto Rico, those who have helped include Carlos

Franqui, Angel Padilla and Ariel; in Miami, Juan Granados and Nancy Pérez Crespo; in Switzerland, Alexis Gainza and Carlos Estefanía; in Italy, Laura Gonsalez and Valerio Riva; in France, Jacobo Machover and Eduardo Manet. Journalists Without Borders has made it their cause to defend these persecuted colleagues. International Solidarity embraces them. Roberto Fabricio and Roberto Suárez , through the InterAmerican Press Association (SIP), opened the door to them in the big newspapers of Latin America. The magazine *Desafíos* in Venezuela, managed by Heriberto Fernández and Pedro Pérez Castro, offered them their pages. The official Cuban press was confronted for the first time with the critical views of independent journalism.

The Internet has also become a battleground. On the island, that marvelous technology is vetoed, for Cubans. You cannot have e-mail or a cable antenna without the authorization and control of the police. Everywhere else on the planet, the Internet is a magical and democratic medium of universal participation. But not in Cuba. In Cuba, the Internet is a privilege available only to certain top-ranking revolutionaries and is the tool for a new way of exercising repression.

Guillermo Cortázar, the Spanish delegate who generously embroiled himself in Cuban politics, created a magazine and a foundation in Madrid to give voice to the persecuted. The day he inaugurated the foundation, the Stalinists of Spain — instigated and organized by the Cuban embassy — orchestrated in Madrid the first "act of repudiation" seen outside of Cuba. Annabelle Rodríguez, the daughter of Carlos Rafael and an exile in Spain, was thrown to the ground and hurt in. Insults and eggs flew. But Gortázar did not back down. He is a professor and historian, he comes from the left, and he is not afraid of to fight. Another Spaniard, Mari Paz Martinez Nieto, had done the same, for years, to make her compatriots aware of what was going on. In Cuba, the police threaten, jail, or beat up independent journalists. But the journalists persist. Or others appear. And the names become known: Yndamiro Restano, Raúl Rivero, Tania Quintero, Rafael Solano, Néstor Baguer, Héctor Peraza, Ana Luisa López Baeza, Orlando Fondevila, Olance Nogueras. Their texts are read abroad with admiration. This is a civil society, laboriously beginning to give birth to itself.

There is talk of Christian democracy, of social democracy, of liberalism. There is a clear will to break with the isolation imposed by the government and to become integrated with the contemporary world. The name of Leonel Morejón Almagro, a lawyer/poet who ended up in prison for a long time, has come to light. An engineer with leadership skills, Oswaldo Payá Sardiñas, a devout Catholic, has created the Christian Liberation Movement — but he does not have the support of the ecclesiastical hierarchy. He is respected — who wouldn't respect Oswaldo? — but they find that he places them in a compromising position, even if he doesn't deviate from the strictest legal definitions. He is a civic leader, not an agitator. Vladimiro Roca, the son of Blas Roca, founder of the Communist Party and a principal figure in the Marxist movement in Cuba until Castro's arrival, joined the dissidents under a social democratic banner, alongside Elizardo Sánchez Santa Cruz. They later would part, but not before contributing to the foundation of that political group, a group that has just been recognized by the Socialist Internationale (because of the work abroad of Antonio "Tony' Santiago, an old political leader, among other reasons).

Roca's dissidence is not the exception. This is exactly what happened in Eastern Europe. Arthur Koestler — or was it Ignacio Silone? — once prophesied that the final confrontation would be between Communists and former Communists. And the opposition is often nurtured by former comrades. From prison, Ariel Hidalgo came up with an intelligent Marxist criticism of the Revolution. Later, in exile, he maintained a similar position. He has not evolved much; and that is his right. By contrast, Enrique Patterson, a former Marxist, takes the theme of democracy and runs with it until he finds a liberal opening, a long stretch that's characteristic of an open mind. The opposition within Cuba, poor, beaten down, persecuted, and in rags, even then embraces the entire spectrum of Cuban society. Fortunately, what prevails among the dissidents is the conviction that the only salvation for the country lies in democracy and pluralistic expression. But the truth is that the great masses, the bulk of society, doesn't dare to demand its rights; it waits for freedom to fall from the sky.

The Pope's Visit

The closest Cuba has come to that sort of miracle was during the Pope's visit in January of 1998. It wasn't heaven — but it was close. Fidel received him at the steps of the airplane, and right then and there read him the riot act: the church had a lot of repenting to do. While he was at it, Castro also assailed the events of the Spanish conquest. His Holiness spent four days in the country, traveling from one end to the other. He officiated at several well-attended masses and gave conferences and homilies in which the customary language of the Vatican — deliberately vague, flowery, compassionate — allowed one to sense that the church was betting on freedom and democratic change. The bishop of Santiago de Cuba, Monsignor Pedro Meurice, courageously, unambiguously, defended the right of Cubans to live democratically. The people, full of enthusiasm, chorused a fearful: *"El Papa, libre / nos quiere a todos libres"* ("The Pope, free / wants all of us free"). If anyone was going to be beaten, let it start with His Holiness; he was the one asking for liberty. They, the people, were merely transmitting the request of the Holy Father. His Spanish words filtered through a guttural, baritone Polish, Wojtyla planted his terse message with the expertise of a Madison Avenue advertising man: "Let Cuba open up to the world and let the world open up to Cuba."

And the world opened up to Cuba. The Canadian Premier arrived right away — Jean Chrétien — the first visit of a Canadian prime minister to Cuba — and the same thing happened to him as to the Pope. Right during the welcoming ceremony, Fidel Castro gave a speech reaffirming the bases of his regime: nothing was going to change, because Cubans already enjoyed the best system possible. The democratic sermons of those who defended the vile and exploitative capitalism, thus, were not welcome.

Chrétien, who had arrived with the best intentions of contributing to alleviating the tensions between Washington and Havana and whose government had encouraged private ventures in Cuba, was not very happy. He thought — some people in his cabinet had let him think — that Castro's problem was that he was cornered by Washington. Chrétien thought that what was needed was to open some escape hatches, so that Castro could adapt to the international reality after the dissolution of the Eastern Bloc. Chrétien was stunned to find a man so absolutely convinced of the moral superiority of communism and of the material advantages of a planned economy, despite four decades of failures in Cuba.

Nevertheless, he made a special request: to free the four dissidents who made up the Working Group on Internal Dissidence, who had been imprisoned for writing the famous document "The homeland belongs to all". They were Vladimiro Roca, Marta Beatriz Roque Cabello, Félix Bonne Carcassés and René Gómez Manzano, four ex-Communists with excellent academic backgrounds. The Canadian made this request on the strength of his standing as one who had been friendly to Cuba despite the American pressures, and he represented the nation that had made the most investments on the island and had sent the most tourists. On the other hand, he was not asking for much: it was indefensible to keep people in prison for critically analyzing the country in which they lived. Castro was impatient, and he ignored the request. As an act of defiance in the face of a world that was asking for clemency and rationality, the Cuban Parliament tightened up even more the repressive legislation used to silence journalists and critics. Now one could go to prison not only for disseminating information against the dictatorship; it was enough to gather it. The dissidents were sentenced to five-to-six years in prison.

Chrétien returned to Canada in disgust. Shortly afterward, his country suspended several agreements that could have helped alleviate the island's conditions. He and the politicians who visited Havana in 1998 and 1999 confirmed that the *quid pro quo* proposed by the Pope has not had the least effect: the world had opened to Cuba, but Cuba would remain closed to the world, by decision of Fidel Castro. They also confirmed that Washington's policy of isolation, regardless of whether it was wrong or right, could not be held responsible for Castro's totalitarian obsession. With or without an embargo, Castro's regime would remain, in fundamental ways, within the Communist model adopted by the USSR in ages past. It was naive to believe that extending a hand to Castroism would increase the possibility of establishing a democracy in Cuba.

Why was Castro so enraged by these four Cubans? First the Pope and later the Canadian prime minister asked for their freedom, and neither one got it. Earlier, and equally unsuccessfully, the Socialist Internationale and forty other institutions had made similar requests. Even the King of Spain had the liberation of these detainees a condition for his trip to Cuba, but he received no promises. Robaina, then Foreign Minister, took note and said he would deliver the request, but he could guarantee nothing: "They are Fidel's prisoners," he would excuse himself when asked.

And that was it. Fidel had ordered their detention and only he could liberate them. What crime did these four Cubans commit? None. They had simply answered a challenge issued by the *comandante* himself, leaving him in ridicule. During the Vth Congress of the Communist Party, the *comandante* had mapped out his vision of history and of the present in a document that was intellectually weak. The four dissidents responded, with solid arguments and an ironic tone. Castro simply wanted to give them a lesson.

It was an episode like the Padilla case, three decades later. These fellows thought they had the right to criticize the Revolution, and they deserved severe punishment. The political police would take the job of "breaking" them. That is a goal they almost always achieve. All it takes is to put people in prison for a certain length of time, scare them, and make them issue some kind of retraction before releasing them. Later, confused and discredited, they would be sent into exile, to any country that would take them in, and the incident would be over. But as it happened, these four dissidents remained firm, and Castro, who analyzes everything in life as if it were a personal challenge, "man to man," decided not to give a centimeter; because to grant freedom to these dissidents, without first breaking them, would be a sign of weakness in his regime and would represent a personal defeat. So, at whatever price, he preferred to sacrifice his good political relations with Canada rather than give in. Abroad, the spokeswoman for the Working Group on Internal Dissidence, Chuny Montaner, waged an energetic and effective information campaign and made Castro pay the price by deeply discrediting him.

The Achievements of the Revolution

Despite the confrontations between the government and the opposition — prisoners of conscience, abused journalists and former ad-
juncts all over the country — those foreigners who were invited on official visits to the island found themselves obliged to tour schools, day
care centers, sports facilities, model hospitals, and the modern buildings of the Biotechnological and Genetics Center (where, needless to
say, no one mentioned the dwarf cow envisioned by Fidel Castro). The
government insisted on legitimizing his totalitarian model by exhibit-
ing good results in the field of education, health, sports and science.
With the incurable megalomania that characterizes Castro, in speech
after speech, as if all he needed was an infinite net of words, Castro had
woven a rhetorical alibi with which to shield and justify 40 years of
dictatorship, while the state-controlled media systematically drew contrasts between Cuba and Latin America that were favorable to Cuba, or
between Cuba and the Eastern bloc countries that had abandoned communism. The subliminal message was clear: "Don't try to change, it'll
only be worse."

Castro insisted that Cuba was "a medical power," unequaled in
the world, with more doctors per capita than any other country, and
where all Cubans, without any direct costs, received free medical care
(albeit in hospitals — why not call a spade a spade — in which there
are no medicines, cleansers, not even clean sheets, except for the mod-
ernized hospitals that give service only to the high-ranking officials or
to tourists with dollars). While this proud information is nauseatingly
repeated, Cubans were treated to images of children assassinated by
the police in Brazil, of poverty-stricken people in Haiti, and to some of
the most deplorable sanitary facts of certain Latin American countries.
The average life expectancy of Cubans was equal to the First World, as
was the infant mortality rate — quite a contrast to Haiti, Honduras or
the Dominican Republic. Of course, no one mentioned that it had been
the same before the Revolution, obscuring the fact that throughout the
20th century Cuba, like Argentina, Uruguay and Costa Rica — according to credible annual statistics from the Pan American Union, the

United Nations, the World Health Organization, and FAO — had been part among the developed nations. Nor was it said, obviously, that in countries like Argentina, Mexico, Chile, Uruguay, Costa Rica and Puerto Rico the poorest population also has access to a doctor's care, only that their installations are infinitely better-stocked than the Cubans'. The purpose was to convince Cubans — and the rest of the planet — that, thanks to the Revolution, the poorest sectors of the society had been redeemed from the most abject situation.

Few people realized, however, the extent to which the Cuban healthcare model was based on Castro's Pharaonic ambitions and his sick ego. Why should Cuba wish to have twice as many doctors per capita than Denmark, a rich country that set the world's standards in health care? More than an achievement in Cuban medicine, this is evidence of the idiocy of communist planners and an outrageous waste of the country's scarce resources. Educating a doctor in the West costs approximately $350,000 (divide the immense cost of university installations by the number of medical students, multiplied by the number of years required to earn the degree). With 65,000 doctors in Cuba, the price tag is $22.7 billion. If instead of having a superfluity of doctors, they had half that number — the Danish proportion — and if they were used effectively, there would be a savings of $10 billion. Then the Cubans would be able to furnish every city with abundant potable water, sufficient electricity and telephones, and they even would be able to repair buildings and streets in Havana, which looks like it has been bombed by NATO. In other words, the "medical power" that Castro flexes with such pride, is evidence of the crazy and arbitrary deployment of resources rather than an "achievement", in a society where there are no democratic controls to stop this sort of distortion. Nobel Prize winner James Buchanan has made this observation, with the disgust that is provoked by having to state something that is so obvious.

What does Cuba do with so many doctors? It exports them. There are Cuban doctors in half the countries of the world. In general, they are competent and committed people who, if they could, would choose exile. Some of them do, indeed, but that "defection" — as if they were soldiers fleeing in the middle of the war and not civilians who simply choose to live elsewhere — has a high price. They are punished with five years of complete separation from their families. They can't return to Cuba to visit, and their families can't leave Cuba. The spouse left behind is expelled from his or her workplace, unless he or she signs a letter condemning the "cowardly acts" of the partner.

Castro is rigorous in this issue of medicine. For him, his immense crop of doctors is today his biggest revolutionary symbol, a pillar of his foreign policy and the only element that allows him to make the gestures suitable to a great power. They are *his* doctors. He lends them or rents them out to the highest bidder. It is a professional class that belongs to him, wholesale, and those who are part of it should be perpetually grateful for the opportunity he has given them. That is why, when Hurricane Mitch destroyed half of Central America, he sent brigades of doctors to help the victims. When the war in Kosovo ended, he offered a thousand doctors to help close the wounds, a proposition that didn't even merit an answer from the victorious nations. In 1998, at a moment when Cuba was in more need of resources than anyone else, he even announced the creation of a School of Medicine in the province of Matanzas, to give scholarships to 10,000 Latin Americans. With what purpose? To pose as a great power, in whatever respect he could, to merit international recognition, to be perceived as a moral force in the world, to exert his influence in Central America, Africa and the Caribbean, by offering scholarships to students of that area.

Those who have to deal with Castro in the diplomatic sphere have perceived the overweening vanity of the *comandante* and they always begin their requests or their criticism by recognizing Cuba's extraordinary importance in the field of medicine and public health. Then Castro smiles magnanimously, and sometimes he agrees to fulfill their requests. For reasons that a profound psychoanalysis may discover one day, Castro — who now knows he is not going to conquer the world for the communist cause — associates his dignity as a person and justifies his path through history by the number of appendicitis operations or kidney transplants undertaken by his legions of doctors, and he dreams that *his* scientists will discover and develop some magic potion that will cure cancer or AIDS, so that he can stand shoulder-to-shoulder with the United States, Europe and Japan in the scientific sphere. He has announced that Cuban will soon cure AIDS. And since the researcher who was supposed to produce this miracle — Manuel Limonta — did not achieve it, he was removed at lightning speed. When the *comandante* gives an order to cure AIDS, he simply must be obeyed.

The same thing is happening in education. The Revolution has built many schools, but it did start out with one of the highest educational levels in Latin America. When Castro boasts of having ended illiteracy — 24% of the population — but he hides the fact that in 1958 Cuba had proportionally fewer illiterates than Spain (and that was true since the end of the 19th century), and that the deficit was gradually being addressed. The same could be said of the school indexes. When the Revolution began, they were not satisfactory, but they were very close to Italy's, a fact that must not be overlooked, since development is always an exercise in comparisons and contrasts. In the field of education, in the 1950s, Cuba had problems and difficulties, of course; but there is one curious fact that is very eloquent. At that time, most of Latin America was using mainly textbooks written by Cuban professors and printed in Cuba — Marrero, Baldor, Gran, Marbán, were some of the authors. That could only have been possible if Cuban educators had achieved an exemplary level of quality and professionalism.

The truth, however, is that education in Cuba has reached even the most remote corners of rural life, and the country today has a high proportion of university graduates. But this auspicious achievement — which obscures the fact that the education is ideologically rigid, full of censorship and prohibitions, indoctrinating students more than training them — also raises a question. How is it possible that a society that has so much human capital lives so miserably? How is it possible that so many engineers, economists, doctors and teachers haven't been able to construct a more prosperous society? Far from absolving the Revolution, this substantial human capital is what indicts it, this is what shows it to be a disaster as an economic system.

There is no country in the world, except Cuba, in which so many professionals sometimes go hungry or have to walk around in shoes that are in tatters. In all of Latin America, educated people are part of the middle classes, at least. Castro's unconditional friends insist that it's the fault of the American embargo, because this is an island under siege by its giant neighbor who harasses him on every front. They are ignoring the fact that on another side of the planet, Taiwan is also under siege by an implacable giant but has managed to rise above all obstacles, including military and diplomatic confrontations and embargoes, to become one of the most highly developed countries of Asia. In 1949, 60% of the Asian population was illiterate — in Chinese, which is a far bigger problem, since they have some 40,000 written symbols — and they had only one fourth of Cuba's population. At the dawn of the 21st century, the Taiwanese have ten times the population of Cuba and have totally eliminated illiteracy.

Castro's defenders forget that while the famous American embargo may have caused the government enormous losses, the 30 years of Soviet subsidies more than made up for that: more than $100 billion, according to audits conducted by Russian Irina Zorina. That is eight times the value of the Marshall Plan by which the Americans aided the reconstruction of Europe after World War II.

It is not the embargo that is to blame. It is the system that doesn't work — a system that penalizes creativity, crushes individual initiatives, and misspends the collective resources in a criminal way. Cuba has today — for example — more than a thousand geographers and geologists, many of them educated in the USSR. They have hundreds of engineers who specialize in locomotives and the organization of subterranean transportation, when the needs of the country could have been met with just a few dozen. What sense does it make for a nation the size of Cuba to have this endless horde of professionals?

Of course, the problem is not just Cuban: that is the stamp of a Socialist education system run by a bureaucrat to generate more bureaucrats. What difference does it make that, when a young professional leaves the university classroom with his diploma under his arm, he enters not an open society in which he can create something, but the opposite — a dull job with a salary that is barely related to his efforts? Why should astronomer Juan or ornithologist Pedro care about working toward a specialty with no economic future if he is going to be assigned an artificial responsibility anyhow, and a minimal salary, in some dark corner of the vast bureaucratic universe, regardless of whether his labor is useful? Osmany Cienfuegos, the second most important man in the corridors of power, once said to a visitor (the Mexican journalist Carlos Castillo Peraza) that the tragedy of the Revolution was that, along with the bourgeoisie, "it had thrown math out the window." And it is true: dedicated to accomplishing historic feats at a rate imposed by a slave-driver, Castro, they forgot that economic growth and development are a consequence of the relations between costs, benefits, savings and investments. When a society throws arithmetic out the window, it ends up discovering that it has in fact thrown itself into the void.

And sports? Cuba is, in effect, a sports super power, frequently winning medals in international competitions; it has thousands of coaches who were trained in East Germany and the USSR, also sports powers during the Cold War. But what does that prove? In reality, nothing, except perhaps — again —the country's scarce resources are put to the wrong uses. How much does it cost poor Cuba to earn those gold, silver and bronze medals that the athletes bring home? To Castro, it doesn't matter, because it allows him to transfer his endlessly competitive nature into the world of sports. Castro is a natural fanatic. He derives infinite emotional satisfaction from the confrontation between two adversaries; and he does not know how to lose. When Cubans leave the island to compete, the Revolution's honor is at stake. How the Revolution's honor is related to the number of times the ball goes through a hoop or how many meters a man can jump is another mystery. But related, it is. When his baseball team (baseball being Cuba's national sport) played against the Baltimore Orioles in 1999, Castro turned the matches into his own intergalactic war the galaxies. The Cubans, who have always been good players, lost the first match, held in Cuba, and they won the second, held in the United States. Upon the players' return, the *comandante* greeted them with honors and speeches. He cheered them as if they had defeated the Nazis at Leningrad. It was a defeat of imperialism, revenge for Grenada, evidence that the Revolution was invincible. Castro was asking the world to judge the Revolution on "feats" such as that — beating the Americans. How much sense does that make? Can you judge the government in Kenya by the awesome prowess of their long-distance runners or France or Mexico by their relative modest performance in sports?

What other achievements can the Revolution claim? One of the most often heard is "the dignity of the Cuban people." Those who hold that point of view feel that, by standing up to the United States, the Cubans have attained a special moral dignity that distinguishes them from the rest of Latin Americans, servile as they are. But first of all, it is hard to believe that the Cubans have voluntarily elected to confront the United States. Every time they can, they flee to that country and not to any other. By now, one of every six Cubans is living in the United States. To judge by the signs, half the country would like to do the same. And secondly, where is the "dignity" in a society that cannot freely elect the system under which it lives, where people cannot choose the leaders, the books, the friends, the place of residence, the workplace they really want? Are those Cubans who cannot go into the places marked "Tourists Only" more "dignified" than the rest of the Latin Americans? Are those who are arrested for walking down the street with a foreigner and warned that the government does not condone that type of relationship, because "the role of speaking to foreigners belongs to the tour guides"? Where does a person's "dignity" hide when he has to squelch his emotions, because showing feelings toward the persecuted is just another means of giving oneself away? Where is the dignity of the man forced to simulate hatred and revulsion and to participate in an act of repudiation, to insult a person or attack him, on the instructions of the Communist Party? How can a family have "dignity" when it has to watch the girls in the house prostitute themselves for the benefit of everyone, when even the parents and the grandparents lend their marriage bed as the symbolic raft by which to escape the miserable poverty that is consuming them all?

Well, and what about race? At least communism has brought black Cubans the dignity that was denied to them by the dominant whites had. It is true that in the private quarters of pre-Revolutionary Cuba — schools, clubs, entire workplaces and unions — blacks were few or nonexistent. That is sad, but it was that way in a good part of Latin America until the 1950s, and it was especially so in the United States. It is also true that the official practice discrimination was minimal. Public schools and universities were open to all; so were the Parliament and the Armed Forces. Batista, a mulatto himself, was President of the Republic, and at least in 1940 he won the position in a relatively clean election. The problem was in the ambiance of civil society. Whites were excessively anxious about blacks becoming senators or judges. The prejudice surfaced in places where people got together. There, the habits and customs that maintained the racial tension concentrated on a very common phrase: "Blacks have to know their place." Each race had its place. There was no implacable system of segregation like in the United States — with separate water fountains, bathrooms, bus seats — but it did exist.

Fortunately, the Revolution did accelerate the end of that unjust situation. It would have happened anyway, the way it happened in the United States, but there can be no doubt that Castro tried to give more opportunities to black Cubans. However, along with that positive discrimination came two contradictory elements. The first was that the Castroists had a weak grasp of the subtleties of sociology, and they soon realized that despite the proclamation of equality under communism, there were barely any blacks in the Central Committee of the Communist Party, in the Council of Ministries or among the 125 generals who composed the leadership of the Armed Forces. The representatives of the ruling power continued to be white. Why? Because the power structures of Cuba were not based on meritocracy but on cooptation by the existing chieftains, who were invariably white. They recruited among friends, and looked for personal loyalty, and the circle of these relationships was always white. Originally, the only black in the higher ranks was Juan Almeida and he had very little power. Later, others came along, but they were always few.

The second contradiction had to do with ideology. Castro's Revolution "elevated" blacks to the category of whites, but it did not do so to correct an injustice, but as a special concession to Cuban blacks who were then expected to show their gratitude with their permanent militancy in the revolutionary ranks. Blacks and mulattos had to be enthusiastic Castroists or they would be traitors to the Revolution, to their race and to their country. A white anti-Castro person was simply a counterrevolutionary. A black anti-Castro person was, in addition, an ungrateful traitor, and the police would treat him accordingly. He'd better not display any negative feeling toward the government or ask to leave the country. Before, for being black, they had to stay away from the bourgeois nightclubs. Now, for being black, they had to avoid thinking with their own brains. They must not reach the conclusion that Marxism is nonsense or that Castro was destroying the country. Which of the two situations is more humiliating to a human being?

Another "achievement" of the Revolution, if we are to judge from the boastful claims, is the consolidation of a national consciousness. Cubans, the hypothesis goes, are more nationalistic today, and they are, of course, vis-à-vis the United States, because nationalism is always the reaffirmation of one's own identity in reaction to an element that threatens it. It is a shame that the history of the real Cuba totally contradicts this interpretation.

When Cuba debuted as a Republic in 1902, a certain percentage of society was annexationist. It was the Cubans, and above all, the Spaniards who wished that the island would be incorporated into the United States to salvage their interests and enjoy the institutional tranquility of that patronage. At that time, control of one piece of Cuban territory — the Isle of Pines — was being disputed by the United States, and the Cubans had been forced to accept the Platt Amendment as part of the post-war agreements that went with its achievement of sovereignty. A significant (and growing) proportion of the economy — the sugar industry, the banks, transportation — were in the hands of Americans, and the ambassador of the United States was meddling in the internal affairs of Cuba, a practice that reached its apex in the 1920s during Zayas's government, when even the make-up of the presidential cabinet had to be approved by the U.S. embassy.

But that influence in Cuban society was decreasing very rapidly. First, interest in annexation waned. Later the native (Criollo) bourgeois, impoverished during the War for Independence, slowly began to regain control of the economy. In 1925, the United States gave up the Isle of Pines. In 1934, the Platt Amendment was eliminated, and the American Marines never again disembarked on Cuba to put the house in order or to defend U.S. interests. In the 1950s, two thirds of the sugar plantations were in the hands of Cubans and Cuban private banks controlled more than 50% of the deposits; foreign investments barely generated 6% of the national gross product. On the other hand, Washington's influence in Cuban affairs had diminished so drastically that in 1952, the White House could not stop Batista's coup, even if it wanted to (as in had done in 1933, when it orchestrated Machado's downfall). And in 1958, even though the U.S. feared Castro's rise to power, it could not prevent it. From the period of *Los Autenticos* — 1944 to 1952 — Cuba was no more or less dependent on the United States than the rest of the countries in the Caribbean Basin. Little by little, without any traumatic events, Cubans had asserted their nationality and the society had won its own sovereignty. In those days, the Cubans were not thinking of emigrating anywhere, and on the contrary, the island was welcoming immigrants from diverse parts of the world.

What do we see now, in the early days of the 21st century? Twenty percent of the Cuban population has moved to the U.S.; no one has confidence in the island nation's future. The "Cuban-American" identity has been created, and it consists in a group capable of influencing Washington-Havana relations more broadly and more powerfully than the annexationists ever dreamed possible. Meanwhile, give the failure of the Cuban model, it is those same Cuban-Americans who have the greatest influence on the Cuban economy. They send in millions of dollars, while Castro only has one formula for alleviating the tremendous pressure on him: to negotiate with Washington for the concession of 20,000 annual visas. These are distributed through a lottery intended to keep the peace in a population whose most pleasant fantasy is to head out for that country that has been described to them for forty years as the source of all that ails Cuba. There is no doubt that Castro, far from revitalizing Cuban nationalism, has reversed a healthy trend that had existed until he took the helm. He himself has turned out to be the worst annexationist.

Lastly, there is the issue of the "women's liberation" brought by the Revolution, a myth that has been persuasively debunked by two astute Cuban essayists: Ileana Fuentes and Uva de Aragón. The truth is that few Western societies were ever as *macho* as Cuba under Castroism. The origins and the later manifestations of the general concept all point to the view of society as a group of warriors embroiled in an eternal battle. The language is bellicose: the "battle" of production, the "war" against imperialism or those ridiculous ritual shrieks with which they always end their speeches (Homeland or death! We will win! Socialism or death!"). And then there is the constant, cruel and neurotic persecution of homosexuals, and the concern to protect the honor of the men in the leadership (who are tipped off by the political police as to any infidelity on the part of their wives or partners, so that they can immediately separate and terminate a situation that denigrates the dignity of the Revolution).

All of that shows how little significance women really have in the decision-making circles in Cuba. As is the case throughout Latin America, there is a growing number of professional women, but in Cuba they almost never occupy positions of significance. They put up with crushing family burdens as a consequence of the high divorce rate — more than 50% of all couples divorce — and the family suffers increased poverty because the children almost always remain in the custody of mothers who have no resources. This contributes to another fact, already mentioned in this book: Cuban women have the highest suicide rate in the entire world. That truly is a mark of distinction that the Cubans would have never achieved without the influence of the Revolution.

VI

THE OTHER SHORE

"Why do you live in Miami?" Americans ask, sarcastically. They immediately answer their own question: "Because it's the closest city to the United States." The joke carries a veiled criticism and the acknowledgment of an obvious anthropological fact: a large section of southern Florida is actually culturally closer to the Hispanic world than to the United States. You only have to land at the airport to see that. This Hispanic world has been made up out of the shattered remains of various shipwrecks and disasters, most of them, of course, Cuban. The Nicaraguans and the Colombians followed, and now there are floods of Venezuelans who fear, with reason, an Armageddon in their homeland. Soon the steady and almost suicidal diet of this city will add the Venezuelan *arepa* to the Cuban sandwich and the Central American corn tortilla. And then Miami, in addition to being more obese, will be a little bit more cosmopolitan, more mixed in the cultural sense, more interesting, as these new immigrants (even without meaning to) enrich the habits and ways of life of this already complex mosaic of nationalities and ethnicities that glitter on television and give the city a unique profile among the urban centers of the United States, and even a graceful architectural style in pastel hues.

Miami is not the only Hispanic city in the United States. Los Angeles and San Antonio also are Hispanic, as are many others — but in a different way. In Los Angeles and San Antonio, despite the enormous demographic significance of citizens of Mexican origin, the dominant culture is "mainstream," American. In Miami, however, two cultures co-exist without mixing much: there are two mainstreams. Why? Because the legendary capacity of assimilation of American culture and society, which managed to ingest millions of Germans, Italians, and Central European Jews without much difficulty, has not had time to absorb the hundreds of thousands of Latin Americans who have arrived in successive waves. For these people to be integrated and Americanized, we will have to wait until the flow of new arrivals begins to ebb, and for the second or third generation, already educated in English, to dominate the Census. That will be several decades from now; it will be a slow digestion.

This radical change is to some extent a consequence of the Cuban Revolution. Miami was nothing like this in 1959. It was, fundamentally, a tranquil beach resort where wealthy Americans escaped the harshness of winter, a happy-go-lucky parade of people, mostly in their later years, with a discreet sprinkling of personalities from the mafia and the entertainment world. The city was not distinguished in the academic, industrial or commercial spheres. The scene was the beach, the coconut palms, and the piña coladas that people were then starting to drink by the barrelful.

For Cubans, however, Miami was a different sort of destination. It was a political refuge. It served as a refuge in the 1930s, when several dozen exiles from Machado's dictatorship settled in the city, and it did so again in the 1950s, when several hundred fled Batista's government. The latter exiles and the subsequent evolution of the city that is still going on, can be traced in the pages of a Spanish-language newspaper founded in 1953 by an enterprising Nicaraguan lawyer, Horacio Aguirre. He in some way predicted Miami's curious destiny as a haven for Latin American disaster victims, and since then, set himself the task of giving a voice to the persecuted. Anyone who wants to investigate how Miami became what it is today, a kind of Latin American capital in the Caribbean basin, can simply peruse the archives of *Diario Las Americas*. It's all there.

Given the experience of exiles during the Machado and Batista coups, it was a natural thing for those who fled Castro's regime in its initial stages to make this Florida city their point of arrival. Even in the early days of 1959, those who were returning to Cuba and those who were abandoning it would pass each other en route. Not too many were fleeing Castroism in those days, and the group classified as *Batistianos* probably did not number more than 10,000 — most of them officials of the armed and political forces who certainly were in danger of being imprisoned by the new government. Despite that, it is possible that in the initial six months the migration pattern was favorable to Cuba — more Cubans were returning to the island than were fleeing it. And of those returning, the majority were not even anti-Batista exiles. There were some economic immigrants who had come to the United States after World War II in search of better job opportunities. Many of them sold their houses, their goods and their cars, and jubilantly went home, fascinated with the new Cuba being touted in the mass media. These returnees arrived on the island filled with good faith, and as proof, they publicly and notoriously changed their hard-earned dollars — the savings of a lifetime — into Cuban pesos "to help the Revolution." A good number soon returned to the United States, empty-handed, to start over — profoundly disappointed.

The honeymoon didn't last long. Starting in the second half of 1959, the Cuban exodus began to increase. Those who fled were no longer *Batistianos*. By July of 1959, after Castro's confrontation with President Urrutia, it was becoming clear that Castro had decided to move toward a Communist dictatorship. The most prudent and best-informed families, generally the better-educated, began to move out, especially if they had the economic resources to do so. At that time almost no one believed that a Communist regime could consolidate and persist for four decades — people only thought it would be a period of months, or at the most maybe a few years — but they believed the country was headed for a civil war and a final confrontation with the United States.

At the time, the most urgent geopolitical analysis was summed up in a phrase repeated *ad nauseam*, as the exiled entrepreneur Fernando Vega Penichet recalls: "The United States will never allow a Communist government aligned with Moscow to exist just 90 miles from its shores." Almost no one noticed that, since 1933, the United States had had little success with its Cuba policy. When Machado fell, power unexpectedly ended up in hands unfriendly to Washington, and in 1952, Batista staged a military coup that went against the wishes of the State Department. In 1959, all of the United States' pressure and intrigues on Batista and the opposition failed to secure a transition of power in Cuba in a way that would serve U.S. interests. But the Cubans saw things differently. Imbued with the memories of the beginning of the century, they continued to think of the United States as practically invincible, a power that always managed to impose its imperial will. The clever phrase circulated by the journalist Viera Trejo ended up being totally wrong: "Fidel says that history will absolve him; he doesn't realize that geography will condemn him." Geography, like the stars, suggested a probability but not a necessity.

Temporary Exile, Permanent Exile

At first, exile seemed to be a temporary state. Since it would not last long, there was no sense in dedicating oneself to building a solid foundation in the United States. But as 1960 came and went, a more worrisome reality was beginning to become apparent. Removing Castro from power was going to be harder than it had been with Machado or Batista. The political police never stopped detaining opponents or infiltrating the clandestine groups and popular militias; and the Committees for the Defense of the Revolution were already functioning. The government, generously equipped with supplies and ammunition from the East, armed its supporters and was quite willing to fight with live ammunition. As the tension mounted, and faced with increasing economic difficulties, tens of thousands of military professionals and business owners decided to leave the country.

It wasn't just the politically persecuted or those hurt by the crescendo of expropriations who were fleeing. People were leaving who simply did not want to live under a Communist dictatorship and who refused to turn themselves into officials and bureaucrats handled manipulated by "the new revolutionary class" rising under the protection of Castroism. And sometimes, those who felt trapped by family ties or obligations sent their young children on ahead, to "save them from the coming horrors," as essayist Leonardo Fernández Marcané described. Several thousand minors, without their families, sponsored by the Catholic Church, thus found themselves part of an operation known as Peter Pan. The secret plan was executed by anguished parents. Rumors were running rampant, saying that the government planned to take away the *patria potestad*, their rights over their children.

I have heard lawyer Ricardo Martínez Cid and editor Francisco "Pancho" Rodríguez say that it was a terrible experience. The children didn't know whether they would ever see their parents again, or whether they would ever be able to return to their country. Some children spent several years without meeting their relatives. Others were separated forever, or did not see each other again until they had become complete strangers. The writer Carlos Verdecia, who in exile became the editor of major publications, sent his oldest son, an adolescent, to the United States just one week before his own trip out of the country. The government then denied him permission to leave. He did not see his son until fifteen years later. This story was repeated in a thousand families, cruelly destroying homes and marriages, often irreparably; and that was (and is) the policy of the Cuban state.

Was this mass movement a hysterical and exaggerated reaction by the adversaries of Castroism? Not necessarily because, shortly after, in its zeal to construct the "new men and women," and with the excuse of training them in agricultural tasks so that they could collaborate in the homeland's prosperity, the Cuban government launched its "schools in the country" program. This was an experiment intended to liberate boys and girls from the influence of their parents and to place them under the moral tutelage of the state, which would take care of molding them according to the superior values and principles of Marxism. About a thousand of these "schools" were built, at an approximate cost of $1 million each. And while they may not have succeeded in incubating the "new men and women," they did succeed in sadly introducing them to sexual relations and promiscuity at an age when the ethical framework that should be part of such personal decisions was hardly formed. Those who travel to Cuba today and are surprised by the ease with which Cuban youth engage in sexual relations, or by the early age at which they start (conduct that is quite different from other Latin American societies) trace the origin of this notable change in the country's customs to these schools. The children enter at an early age, to discover communism, and without the attentive supervision of adults they end up, naturally, discovering sex.

After the failure of the Bay of Pigs in April of 1961, and after the dénouement of the Missile Crisis of October of 1962, it became clear that Castro's dictatorship was going to last longer than anyone had forecasted. At that point the "temporary" nature of exile started to give way to a different attitude. Those who were already outside of Cuba, as well as those ready to emigrate, knew that exile would be a prolonged or permanent way of life, and while that was a disheartening thought, it had its positive aspects. From that moment forward, Cubans experienced what some sociologists call "immigrant fever," a vital urgency to work furiously hard to make up for lost time and to successfully become part of the new society. And so, thousands of professionals, as they took on the typical jobs of immigrants — waiters, fruit packers, housekeepers — studied to renew their degrees (3,000 doctors among them), making Herculean efforts so that their children could go to good schools. The American government contributed generously, with special loans, while those who had experience in commerce and industry, after they were able to accumulate a certain amount of capital, took their first steps in new fields.

After a few years, the economic success of the Cuban community in the United States was evident — basically in Miami, New Jersey, Los Angeles, and the sister island of Puerto Rico where 50,000 exiles sought refuge. Little by little, it came to light that this was the Hispanic community with the highest index of per capita income and the one that generated the most businesses — some 42,000, in all sizes and fields of endeavor. And it was, in addition, the community that had penetrated the American corporate world most easily, with a notable number of top executives: Coca-Cola, Morgan, Kellogg's, and naturally, Bacardi, an empire created by Cuban exiles whose revenues exceed the value of the island's sugar harvest in the international market, $800 million. The statistical profile of Cubans was thus very close to the white American middle class. The Cubans in southern Florida alone, an estimated one million more or less, produced more goods and services than the 11 million who remained on the island, forced to live in a notoriously inefficient system. Rarely, in the history of the United States, had immigrants achieved so much success in so short a time. When Reagan took over the Presidency, he chose to celebrate and highlight two outstanding examples of entrepreneurial success: Carlos Pérez, a Cuban who had revolutionized the formula for the commercialization of bananas, and Armando Codina, a developer who had arrived in Florida in the Peter Pan children's exodus and had become a giant in urban construction.

An Escape Valve for Castro

The Cuban government, meanwhile, had a totally schizophrenic attitude toward the emigration. On the one had, Castro understood that it was a convenient bridge for the fleeing enemy — and he permitted it, as something that relieved a bit of the pressure — but on the other, he placed a whole range of obstacles in the way of those making their exit, and he inflicted humiliating punishment on those who manifested their desire to leave the country. Simultaneously, the emigration escape valve gave Castro the means to put pressure on the United States. In 1964, when the economic crisis worsened as a result of shortages and inflation, Havana stimulated an exodus via the port of Camarioca, by allowing hundreds of boats to come from Florida to pick up relatives who had not been able to leave the country through legal means. Washington was forced to accept thousands of unhappy Cubans. Faced with these events, the Johnson administration authorized the "Freedom Flights," and finally, more than 200,000 Cubans were able to come to the United States by that route.

Similar episodes were repeated twice more. In 1980, to end the outrageous and embarrassing fact that 11,000 people had sought refuge in the Peruvian embassy, Castro "opened" the port of Mariel and, except for young people of military age and university graduates, he allowed people to leave. This was during the Carter Administration. Some 125,000 Cubans arrived in America before the flow was stemmed.

Castro made sure he placed among the refugees a good number of men-tally unstable people and hardened criminals, taken from prison. His goal was to destroy the good reputation of exiles in the United States — that was always one of his passions — while at the same time freeing himself of the undesirables, and showing the world that those who were leaving the country were delinquents (or as he preferred to call them, *escoria*, scum. Fortunately, among the real refugees, not re-cruited by the government, was a large number of intellectuals and art-ists who later showed their worth, among them the writers Reynaldo Arenas, Carlos Victoria, Vicente Echerri, Andres Reynaldo, the Abreu brothers, and Roberto Valero, a notable poet who died prematurely, a few years later.

The last of these openings, a carbon copy of the others, occurred in the summer of 1994 as a result of the growing number of *balseros*, raf-ters, who fled the country illegally and found refuge in the United States. To end the favorable treatment given Cuban immigrants — pro-tected by a special law enacted during the Lyndon Johnson Administra-tion (a law that Castro believed actually stimulated emigration) — he allowed another uncontrolled exodus of *balseros*, and tens of thousands of Cubans took to the seas in anything that might float. Some 30,000 survived — and we will never know how many thousands died. The survivors were detained in the U.S. military base at Guantanamo until they were screened and allowed to travel to the United States. As a re-sult of this "persistent immigration blackmail," as the Spanish journal-ist Alberto Miguez classifed it, the Clinton administration agreed to accept at least 20,000 refugees annually, reiterating the paradox that it is in the United States that Castro finds the relief for the internal pres-sures that assail his government.

The total sum of refugees is as follows. One million Cubans have fled — including several thousand to Spain, Venezuela, Mexico and Costa Rica — and over the four decades they have given birth to a mil-lion children. Today, one of every six Cubans lives abroad. But accord-ing to estimates by diplomats stationed on the island, more than half of the population is willing to leave if could get a visa and find a way to finance the trip.

The exiles' economic success, however, has not been accompanied by a positive portrayal in the media. The stereotype, invented by skillful propagandists from Havana and helped along by Castroism's many sympathizers, has portrayed them as wealthy accomplices of Batista's dictatorship, passionate and intolerant; in reality, the great majority are people who initially supported the Revolution, who fled Cuba without a penny in their pockets. They were made into anti-Communists, whose direct experience of life in a totalitarian dictatorship inclined them to more conservative positions — an understandable phenomenon, similar to that which has happened to exiles from Hungary, Czechoslovakia and other victims of communist tyrannies. And few people realize how many of these exiles are active in the academic world. Some 3,000 professors have served in such diverse universities as Universidad National Autónoma de México, where Beatriz Bernal is an eminent legal expert; at Harvard, where Jorge Domínguez serves (as did Modesto Maidique, who today is president of one of the largest and best universities in the South); the University of Puerto Rico, which hosted Leví Marrero, author of a mammoth and unequaled encyclopedia on the history of Cuba; and the Madrid Conservatory, where José Luis Fajardo is a professor of piano music.

Leaving aside the skillful manipulations of the Cuban intelligence services, the distorted image of the exiles is largely attributable to the type of news that the press usually looks for — they always want something associated with a conflict or with violent political incidents between the exiles and the Cuban government. And so it was, in essence, during the 1960s and 1970s, when a large sector of the opposition enrolled in the armed struggle — the same methods Castro had used to achieve power — as the means to get him out. After Kennedy's death, when Johnson ended the subversive plots against the Cuban government, several independent groups carried out audacious but hardly effective commando operations. Tony Cuesta and Santiago Alvarez tried to sink a Soviet tanker en route to Cuba. Juan Miguel Salvat and several members of the Directorate machine-gunned a hotel hosting the Communist leadership. Others infiltrated Cuba to try to revive the guerrilla war in the mountains — among them the *comandantes* Eloy Gutiérrez Menoyo and Ramón Quesada (founders of Alpha 66, along with Nazario Sargén and Diego Medina) and spent more than 20 years in prison, and Vicente Méndez, who was executed.

But in 1970, it became obvious that Castro was practically unde-featable in the area of violence. His temperament and instincts served him well. According to General Domingo del Pino, who escaped from Cuba in 1987, it was in response to activities conducted by the exiles that former revolutionary *comandante* Aldo Vera was assassinated in Puerto Rico (by the Cuban intelligence services), and Rolando Masfer-rer was killed by a bomb under his car, while José Elias de la Torriente, who had developed what the government judged to be a dangerous military plan against the dictatorship and who was, above all, someone who had achieved a certain degree of unity among the opposition, was executed inside his own home by Castro gunmen who fired through the window.

The Elian Incident

The clearest view of the image problem confronting Cuban exiles around the world (and especially in the United States) springs from the case of the rafter child Elián González. Just six years old, he was res-cued at sea by two fishermen off the Fort Lauderdale coast on Novem-ber 25, 1999 — Thanksgiving Day — miraculously clinging to an inner tube. Three days earlier, Elián had left Cárdenas, a town on the north-ern coast of Cuba some 100 miles from Havana, aboard a fragile alumi-num boat propelled by an outboard motor that quit — just when they needed it most. He was traveling with his mother, Elizabeth Brotons (who was divorced from his father), her boyfriend Munero, and nine other people. After the little boat fell apart, the only survivors were Elián (who was placed on one of three inner tubes by his mother), and a young couple, who also managed to hang on until they were rescued, far from where Elián was found.

The news raced around the world. The image of Elián, an extraor-dinarily photogenic child, semi-conscious after floating for two days in the high seas, was a tough propaganda blow to the Cuban dictatorship. And emotions were further fueled when it became known, from the survivor's account, that his mother and stepfather had had the desper-ate courage (and love) to tie Elián to the inner tube that could have saved them; and they were lost. Newswires transmitted this sad tale of selflessness and the quest for freedom, in which dolphins were reported to have magically escorted the child until he was rescued; but Castro saw it as a good opportunity to reverse history. He transformed it into a battle for parental rights over Elián, whose father, Juan Miguel González (a young Communist without any special political significance) was still in Cuba. Urged by the Cuban government, he strenuously called for the return of his son. Meanwhile, in exile, Elián's great-uncle Lazaro González and Juan Miguel's uncle, a mechanic, had warmly accepted custody of the small shipwreck survivor, who had been given to him provisionally by the Immigration and Naturalization Service of the United States. Lazaro asked for political refuge for Elián, based on laws that do not specify an age requirement for lodging such a claim.

Everything seemed to be going in Uncle Lazaro's favor. Immigration (as it had done in so many similar cases, in accordance with its own regulations) granted political asylum to the child and provisional custody to his great-uncle. This did not close the door on the father's claims, which were then subject to a decision by a family court, after hearing arguments for and against the child staying in the United States or returning to Cuba (the country from which his mother wanted to "save" him, at the cost of her own life). But suddenly, Immigration authorities started to change course, and instead of allowing the case to be heard as a conventional custody case, in accordance with the wishes of many exiles and many Americans, including Vice President Al Gore, they announced their decision to hand over the child to the father, as soon as possible.

Why did their attitude change? There are two theories. First, in December of 1999, in a Louisiana prison, Cuban criminals rioted and took several hostages, threatening to kill them if they were not freed and sent to another country. These were prisoners who had already served their sentences, but because they were illegal aliens, the (absurd) immigration law required their repatriation to their country of origin. Since Cuba would not accept them, they were being held in custody indefinitely. All of a sudden, the Cuban government decided to resolve this grave problem and accepted that the return of the prisoners. In exchange for what? That was never publicly specified, but the *quid pro quo* seemed obvious: the child should be returned, just like the criminals. The second hypothesis was summarized by former American diplomat Richard Nuccio, former special adviser to Clinton on Cuban issues. The American government had clear indications that Cuba would unleash another overwhelming deluge of rafters if Elián were not returned, and quickly. "Send him back in 48 hours, or face the consequences," Castro warned. In an election year, the crisis could have had serious consequences — as Carter learned, in 1979.

Elián's father came to the U.S. to push his claim. Finally, in April 2000, during the pre-dawn chill of Holy Saturday, after the negotiations between Immigration and Elián's (ill-advised) exiled family failed to reunite the boy with his father, a force of armed agents took over. Looking more ready to face a pack of terrorists than a concerned family, they stormed the modest Miami home where Elián was staying. The agents threatened people with machine guns and sprayed demonstrators outside the house with pepper gas (hitting some of them); and they took the child to a military airport. Two hours later, Elián and his father were reunited, followed by an entourage of Communist teachers and sociologists sent to the United States to "deprogram" the child and eliminate any attachments or ideological harm produced by exiles and the corrupt American society. This process was to go on as long as the courts prevented the child's return to the island.

For those in exile, the Elián case was a rude shock. Castro had dragged them into a legal and public opinion battle that was hard to win, even if there were precedents that left space for some illusions. The most obvious popular intuition was that "with the mother dead, the child belongs with the father, Communist or not," and this reasoning was sustained by two thirds of people surveyed in the United States. But for exiles in Miami, a city in which there are literally thousands of *balseros*, political prisoners and families who have lost family members to shipwrecks and sinkings, the question was not a simple judicial debate but a serious moral and political problem. How could anyone permit Elián to be returned to a dictatorship, where he would surely have to start his new life by condemning the attitude of his mother lest he be turned into a political pariah? How could they fail to fight to save a child from the grip of a dictator who planned to deprogram him, to brainwash him until he became a dogmatic defender of a Revolution that has done so much harm to so many Cubans?

In defense of their cause, the exiles — although there were other important voices who defended and shared their points of view — employed demonstrations of civil disobedience and annoying traffic interruptions to make their point. However, they were shown scant sympathy by the country's media, which presented them as fanatics of the most recalcitrant right-wing. Perhaps the most vulgar attack appeared in the Spanish press, in the magazine *Cambio 16*, where the journalist over and over calls Cuban exiles "that mass of human shit," adding qualifiers like "drug traffickers," "pimps," etc. .Why this fury? Actually, no group of anti-Communist exiles, from the white Russians who fled the fledgling USSR after the Revolution of 1917 to the Nicaraguans of the 1980s, has ever found sympathy in the media. And this time, the cause was not very popular, and Castro's skillful manipulation had to be factored in.

A New Epoch

Once the armed struggle was discarded, and following obscure and reprehensible acts of terrorism that were never fully explained — like the blowing up of a Cubana Airlines plane in flight — many of the opponents began to explore other means to solve Cuban political conflicts. In 1978, banker Bernardo Benes makes contact with Castro, and after consulting with the Carter administration, he led several dozen exiles — some of whom, like Miguel González Pando, had fought bravely at the Bay of Pigs — to establish a dialogue with the Cuban government.

What were they after, in this delicate mission? First, the release of thousands of political prisoners who had spent almost two decades in prison. It was, in essence, a humanitarian mission. The exiles were also pleased to be able to return to visit the island and resume contact with their families. What did Castro want? He had three objectives. First, to consolidate officially his political legitimacy; if his enemies were willing to come flocking to his territory, in peace, it was obvious that they implicitly recognized their defeat and were ending the insurrection against his regime. Second, he could empty his prisons of some adver-saries who no longer had the opportunity to take up arms; it didn't make sense to keep them in jail anymore as a public warning, because the domestic situation in Cuba was totally under control. And third, it would start a sort of reconciliation with the United States, repeating what he had tried to do in 1963 with the return of the Bay of Pigs expe-ditionaries — an exchange of prisoners for good relations.

Carter's government was willing to end the old dispute between the two countries, but he demanded that Cuba stop its subversive aid to Central America and, especially, bring an end to the enormous Cu-ban presence in Africa. Castro was not willing to concede any of that; but he was willing to free prisoners. That was his *quid pro quo*: he would release thousands of prisoners and allow them (and even urge them) to leave the island, in exchange for which the United States would cancel its old policies toward Cuba.

A combination of factors kept Castro's strategy from succeeding. The greatest was the public impact made by the massive return of ex-iles. For twenty years, the government had bombarded the population with terrifying stories of the emotional distress and the failure of the *gusanos*, the worms, who had opted for exile. Castro had even prohib-ited contact with those undesirable people, who suffered all sorts of discrimination in American society. That was his official version. But suddenly, that caricature was exposed as a lie, when thousands of well-heeled exiles, loaded with gifts, descended from the airplanes and showered their families with stories of how they had achieved eco-nomic and social positions unattainable to those who had stayed be-hind in Cuba. This detonated an explosion of dissatisfaction that would be hard to miss. As it happened, the poorest of the exiles were living better in that demonic country than the most comfortable of the relatives who had remained in Cuba — unless, of course, they were part of the leading elite. As sociologist Juan Clark illustrates in his work, *Cuba: Myth and Reality*, the distance between the quality of life of the peo-ple and the Revolution's chiefs was abysmal.

A few months later, in 1980, events at the Peruvian embassy — those 11,000 people who occupied every inch of space in the big house and gardens — and the subsequent Mariel exodus seem to be the logical sequels to those visits. Cubans on the island had always known they were faring poorly, but when they contrasted their life, filled with tension and shortages, with that of their relatives, many wept in frustration. Others, more practical, ran to exile. Ironically, while Benes and those who accompanied him on his humanitarian mission were accused of being "traitors" (by exiles who did not want any contact with the dictatorship), the Cuban government profoundly regretted having allowed that minimal opening. The re-establishment of family ties and the exchange of information had pulverized twenty years of endless propaganda.

In those years, the end of the 1970s, the international public perception of exiles began to change, in intellectual publications. In the summer of 1979, several Cuban exile writers were invited to a writer's congress convened in the Canary Islands by the narrator J. J. Armas Marcelo — a Spanish novelist who, without renouncing his progressive positions, had no sympathy for Castro's dictatorship and was not shy to say so. Cuba's political issues were discussed and passionately debated. The majority of the participants — Communists and those who are pathologically anti-American were abundant — still backed Castro, but voices of condemnation were also heard, among them Federico Jiménez Losantos, Fernando Sánchez Dragó, and other young leftist writers who had broken with communism.

Encouraged by that experience, that same year the First Congress of Dissident Cuban Intellectuals was convened in Paris, joined by a dozen first-rate figures such as Fernando Arrabal, Alain Ravennes, Bernard Henri-Lévy, Phillippe Sollers, Paul Goma and Vladimir Bukovsky. Eugene Ionesco, Jean-François Revel, Néstor Almendros, Juan Goytisolo, and Jorge and Carlos Semprún lent their enthusiastic support. The poet and essayist Miguel Sales and the Cuban-French writer Eduardo Manet coordinated it along with the painter Siro del Castillo and the agrarian expert Mario Villar Roces. Several dozen Cuban intellectuals travel to Paris from all over the globe. Pedro Ramón López Oliver — a rare and efficient combination of storyteller, banker and social democrat ideologue — generously helped out with a large contribution of the necessary funds; editor Ramón Cernuda did the same. Novelist Hilda Perera, a finalist of the *Planeta* prize in 1972, twenty times recognized in literary contests, wrote some of the documents that were later circulated. Psychologist Marian Prío oversaw much of the logistics.

This collaboration proved that the European democratic intelligentsia not only opposed and condemned Castro, but also supported the opposition movement and identified with the dissident Cuban intellectuals. The intention was to break the isolation and even the rejection that numerous Cuban intellectuals and artists have experienced for vigorously opposing the regime. At this congress, some of the great Cuban writes who had been silenced and even discredited by Castroism were honored: Lidia Cabrera, Gastón Baquero, Lino Novas Calvo. If the Padilla case marked the beginning of a rupture between Castroism and the democratic intellectuals of the West, then this congress in Paris signaled a rapprochement and moral endorsement of the opposition.

This experience was followed by others, equally successful, in New York (1980), Washington (1982), Madrid (1986) and Caracas (1987). In New York, at Columbia University, playwright Iván Acosta and professors Julio Hernández Miyares and Modesto Maidique convened members of the academic world. At the top of the list was sociologist Irving L. Horowitz. In Washington, the organizers were Oilda del Castillo, Frank Calzón and Marcelino Miyares, a publicist well-versed in politics and a good communicator. Here in the U.S. capital, the important thing was to capture the attention of the political class with an analysis of the Cuban situation that would transcend the conventional views. The goal was achieved, resoundingly. In the Madrid conference, there were two notable additions: the novelist César Leante, who had recently defected in Spain, disgusted by the police repression during the events of Mariel, and the poet Armando Valladares, who had been freed following a vigorous campaign by Fernando Arrabal — who practically forced French President François Mitterrand to ask Castro for his freedom. The influential intellectual media in Paris were seething with indignation over the fate of the Hispanic-French playwright. In Venezuela, the only congress organized in Latin America, had the support of Christian syndicates led by Emilio Máspero, and was attended by parliamentarians Ramón Guillermo Aveledo, José Rodríguez Iturbe and Carlos Raúl Hernández, all three of them first-rate writers and analysts, and also by the Cubans Silvia Meso, Fausto Masó and Roberto Fontanillas Roig.

Mas Canosa and the Cuban-American Lobby

In the late 1970s, while the Cuban intellectuals in exile met in Paris with their European counterparts, another development of great significance was taking shape among the exiles. Jorge Mas Canosa, accompanied by Raúl Masvidal and Mario Elgarresta, among others, were cementing the bases for what would become the most effective lobby created by exiles to exert influence over American politicians. Mas Canosa was soon joined by businessmen like the Moreiras, father and son, and Diego Suárez. The life of Mas Canosa, whose story has been written by Alvaro Vargas Llosa in a noteworthy and generous book entitled *The Indomitable Exile*, was an example of the talent for entrepreneurial activity and the passion and total dedication to the fight against Castro's dictatorship. Exiled before the age of twenty, and a participant in the Bay of Pigs expedition — he was in one of the contingents that never got to disembark — Mas Canosa started his career as a milk delivery man and was able to amass a fortune of several hundred million dollars, without ever losing sight of his objective of ending communism in Cuba.

That militant political vocation took him through a diversity of ideological grounds and different strategies until he became convinced that the best way to influence Cuban developments, given the impossibility of defeating Castro in an armed struggle, was to exercise pressure on American politicians. The electoral influence of Cuban-Americans was a valuable weapon, and so was the considerable economic clout of that faction of exiles who supported him. For Mas Canosa, there were three power factors at play: Havana, Moscow and Washington. Since it was impossible to influence the first two, the best and only option was Washington. This was not a new idea in the history of relations between the United States and Cuba, since already in the middle of the 19th century, during the administration of President Franklin Pierce, a similar lobby was established. In those years, it was dedicated to trying to evict Spain from Cuban territory.

Even if Mas Canosa intuitively understood the significance of such an institution, he needed an accredited "Americanologist" to supervise the delicate carpentry of setting up a lobby, someone who knew well the idiosyncrasies of the American political class and the serpentine ways in which power flows in Washington. Experience had taught him that, in the United States, there was no one unequivocal center where authority reigned. To some extent, the institutional game of checks and balances did succeed in dispersing power. The White House was one, and the House and the Senate, the State Department, the security organizations — the CIA, the National Security Council, the Pentagon — the media and the academic community all had to be taken into account, and with all of those factors, a dialogue had to take place if the goal was to construct a Cuba policy that would lead to the annihilation of Castroism.

The "Americanologist" of choice turned out to be Frank Calzón, a respected activist in the field of human rights and a graduate of Georgetown University. He had been living in Washington since the 1970s and, in his student days, had been a militant in the youth organization Abdala (created by Gustavo Marin). Many young exiles who later became noted professionals and intellectuals had participated in that group, among them Ramón Mestre, Laura Ymayo, José Antonio and Silvia Font. Thus, Calzón had the necessary contacts and he knew that an energetic combination of financial contributions to candidates — something American law allows and stimulates — and the presentation of reasonable options would provoke an important result. For the first time, the leading class of the United States would take into account the opinion of Cubans, in the opposition, in designing its policies toward the island.

The timing for the creation of the Cuban American National Foundation (CANF) couldn't have been better. It was launched during the last days of Carter's administration, when Reagan began his first term and was looking for a new approach to the Cuban question, one that was more daring than that of his predecessor. It was then that the CANF proposed to create a radio station that would transmit to Cuba all the information and analysis that the Castro government was hiding from Cubans. It would be similar to Radio Liberty or Radio Free

Europe, which operated against the dictatorships of Eastern Europe. The proposal took almost five years to materialize, but finally, in 1985, the station was inaugurated under the name Radio Martí. Since then it has maintained a high level of credibility and a large audience among Cubans.

Later, the CANF lobby would achieve an even more far-reaching measure. Democratic congressman Robert Torricelli, a legislator who is to the left of the center of his party and who had developed strong personal ties to Mas Canosa, sponsored a bill, the Torricelli law, to strengthen the prohibitions on commerce between Cuba and the United States. This reinforced the so-called "embargo" (as the Americans call it); the Cuban government calls it a "blockade," giving it a rather more violent emphasis.

This is most revealing because there is a generalized belief that the "embargo" — we have to call it something — is the most conclusive expression of Washington's hostility against the Cuban government. But that is not correct. It is a policy sustained by the capacity for intrigue and the persuasive talent of the exile opposition, capable of influencing Democrats and Republicans who harbor scarcely any anti-Castro sentiment, especially since most members of this turn-of-the-century American ruling class were children when Castro came to power.

It's true that Eisenhower decreed the first restrictions on commerce between the two countries; and Kennedy did harden them after the Missile Crisis. But, since Johnson, every American president has been tempted to normalize economic relations between the two countries. That hasn't happened, principally, because of Castro's stubborn resistance to showing flexibility on his positions every time an emissary from the White House has tried to obtain some concession from Havana that would facilitate the change in policy. Even Reagan, the harshest of all, was willing to completely modify his policy toward Cuba, if Havana would stop helping terrorists and subversive agents in Central America — the White House's biggest worry at that time — but his envoy, General Alexander Haig, was rebuffed. "Fidel Castro never gives an inch when it comes to revolutionary principles."

The Cuban-American Congressmen and the Embargo

Almost at the same time that the exiles were gaining some indirect political power in Washington through the Cuban lobby, another hallmark event took place that would impact relations with Cuba. Cuban-Americans started to win election to Congress. First was Ileana Ros-Lehtinen, a woman beloved by Miamians; then came Lincoln Díaz-Balart — his aunt Mirta, ironically, had been Castro's first wife — a lawyer with the mettle of a statesman and a talent for polemics; and finally, Roberto "Bob" Menéndez. The first two are Republicans and the latter a Democrat from New Jersey. Menéndez also occupies the third position in his legislative group, which gives some idea of his position within the hierarchy in Congress.

The election of these three Cuban-American members of Congress, especially after the death of Mas Canosa in 1997 and the loss of his personal influence as a dynamic and attractive leader, has special significance. It has caused "a displacement of the center of dialogue," according to Leopoldo Cifuentes, a prominent exile in Spain (while he lived in Cuba, he owned some of the best cigar factories in the country). Washington now thinks it can reach a consensus, with these representatives, on its Cuba policy. Greater attention is paid to the opinions of these three legislators (and to the unofficial representation of the Cuban American community that is attributed to them) than to what is said by organizations formed by exiles, even though one of those congressmen, Bob Menéndez, has been elected in a district that barely has any Cuban voters. This — the great leverage of these three members of Congress — explains the approval of the Helms-Burton legislation, which through the mediation of Díaz-Balart codifies all the previous presidential decrees on the embargo and places Cuba policy in the hands of Congress, hampering any tenant in the White House who might want to change relations with Havana. Now, Congress alone controls the possibility of eliminating the embargo, and inside that institution there are three zealous guardians ready to defend this measure.

How do these three Congressmen uphold the embargo? With a combination of judicial, moral, strategic and political arguments, which we will examine. They clarify that the embargo does not prohibit any country in the world from doing business with the Castro government, or from intervening in Cuba to extend credits, soft loans or donations to the regime. And the proof is that some of the United States' best allies — Canada, Spain, France, Israel — constantly engage in this sort of commerce. If, inside Cuba (according to official figures in Havana) more than 350 foreign enterprises are functioning, and if Cuba's debt with the West surpasses *$11 billion,* is because the country is not, of course, economically isolated.

The truth is that all Cuba products of quality, if appropriately priced, always find a foreign market. That includes, basically, sugar, seafood, tobacco, nickel and some biotechnical products. And the truth is that everything that Cuba needs, if it has the money or obtains the credit to pay for it, Cuba can buy in Europe, Japan, Korea, Taiwan or Latin America, including products made in the U.S.A. That becomes clear to anyone who visits a tourist shop on the island. The Helms-Burton law is limited to prohibiting Americans from negotiating with Cuba — it is the American businesses that are hurt — and it leaves the door open to court procedures or to the denial of a U.S. visa to anyone who benefits from or takes possession of Americans' property confiscated in Cuba without indemnification.

On the other hand, it is also false that the Cuban government lacks access to the American market. All it has to do is fill out a licensing form, and 99% of the time, the application is approved. And indeed, the U.S. is the partner that helps the Cuban people most. According to an official report prepared for Congress by Roger Noriega, an aide to Senator Helms, from the approval of the Torricelli law in 1992 until 1997, private and church donations reached almost *$2.4 billion,* a figure that is at least twenty times the contribution of the European Union. If one adds to this number the *hundreds of thousands* of dollars that Cuban-Americans send annually to their families, or the humanitarian approval of 20,000 immigrants a year, a more realistic picture is given of relations between the two countries. The United States, far from being the cause of Cuba's economic problems, ends up being its chief source of relief — and almost its only one.

Neither does the extraterritorial application of the Helms-Burton law represent any contradiction from the judicial standpoint. In an era when the globalization of penal codes is accepted — consider the arrest of Pinochet, in London, by petition of a Spanish judge who was resolved to punish him for crimes committed in Chile; or the fourteen countries that declared war on Yugoslavia for the genocide that was committed within its own territory — it seems perfectly coherent that a country would decide to sanction or to allow court action by its judges against those who have profited from the stolen property of its citizens.

The moral arguments that the Cuban-American congressmen usually brandish are also worthy of consideration. A country — in this case, the United States — has the ethical obligation to impose sanctions and economic punishment on nations that violate human rights, especially if these are governments that don't show any willingness to make amends. This was done with South Africa's racist apartheid and against the Haitian narco-dictatorship. And the fact that the sanctions are unilateral, not approved by the UN, may not be significant. The UN also did not approve the bombing of Yugoslavia — but that did not keep the leading democracies on the planet from taking action. At the same time, it's absurd to discredit the embargo against Cuba by contrasting it with the United States' economic policies toward China. This is a case of selective justice, it is true, but it is not in the case of Cuba that it is wrong, but in the case of China. The United States has the wrong policy toward China — based on the size and the population of that country — but we cannot remedy that by making the same mistake in Cuba.

But, how can we defend the moral argument, when the embargo affects the Cuban people more than its government? First of all, that is a false premise, contradicted by reality. The embargo hurts the government, but not society. Paradoxically, it is probable that the embargo ends up benefiting society. 40 years' experience shows that Cubans have only seen their misery alleviated when their government, overwhelmed by the lack of resources, has been forced to allow private activities — among them *paladares* (little restaurants set up in private homes), small farmers' markets, and certain jobs and professions — whereas, when it thinks it has sufficient economic resources, it has strengthened its statism and official control of citizens. If state farms have today been turned into cooperatives, or if it is no longer illegal to use the dollar — so that exiles can help their families — or if Castro has been forced to reduce the size of his armed forces or his repressive apparatus, or if he has had to curtail his aggressive internationalism, it has only been a consequence of the government's financial crisis. This is the foundation of the belief that lifting the embargo would only help the government and hurt the population.

There are also political and strategic reasons for the permanence of the embargo. It is true that in forty years, the embargo hasn't toppled Fidel Castro, but according to the three congressmen's analysis those who say the embargo is ineffective probably said the same about the policy of containment, applied to the USSR. . . until the day, in 1989, when the Communist world came crashing down. In any case, that is an element that will most certainly not lure Castro to the negotiating table — this stubborn character has no concept of the verb "compromise" — but it will be useful when he is gone from the scene and a more realistic person succeeds him in governance. On the other hand, it is logical that an opposition movement that resists any form of participation with Cuba, and which cannot or does not want to resort to violence to end the dictatorship, should hold onto the only instrument of legitimate pressure left within its reach. If they gave that up, the members of Congress think, what weapons will e left that the opposition can use to defend their rights and to bring about democracy in the country?

The Democratic Platform and the Reconciliation

While the Cuban members of Congress represent the constituents of their districts before the United States government and, at the same time, unofficially, they represent a large sector of the Cuban exiles, naturally they do not cover the entire complex range of a community of two million people nor can they establish dialogues with all the many governments and institutions outside the United States. In recognition of that fact, in August of 1990, the liberal exiles (under the labels of *Sociodemocrats* and *Demochristians*) met in Madrid to build what was called the Cuban Democratic Platform, a coalition or association of democratic political parties linked to these movements through their international counterparts.

The purpose of this gathering was obvious: to prepare a nonviolent path to democracy. That's why Madrid was chosen for the meeting. The Spaniards had achieved a miraculous transition after Franco's death, in the second half of the 1970s, and since then the country has become a political landmark for those who wishing to contribute to peaceful change in societies where a certain model of governance has been exhausted. On the other hand, the fall of the Berlin Wall and the collapse of the Communist regimes in Europe led to the sense that something similar could and should happen in Cuba, sooner rather than later, so that the most reasonable thing to do would be to create an institutional channel capable of conducting or helping to conduct an efficient process that (at that moment) seemed immediate and inevitable.

The founding document — the Declaration of Madrid — renounced violence and proposed reasonable formulas that could lead to a democratic outcome, with guarantees to all sides. It bore the signatures, among others, of many exiles who had substantial pedigrees in the political and international arenas: José Ignacio Rasco, Roberto Fontanillas-Roig, Juan Suárez-Rivas, Uva de Aragón Clavijo, Felícito Rodríguez — a man who was very close to the Cuban ecclesiastical hierarchy — Marcelino Miyares, Enrique Baloyra, René L. Díaz, Ricardo Bofill, Emilio Martínez Venegas, the filmmaker Miguel González Pando (who would later premier two excellent documentaries about the history of the exile phenomenon) and Fernando Bernal, author of an interesting memoir of the time he spent in the Sierra Maestra and the early years of the Castro government.

The *Plataforma* was immediately and warmly greeted by the most important Western governments, and in a period of three years, practically every president of Latin America, the Russian chancellery and certain European leaders like Felipe González of Spain had opened their doors and offered expressions of political and diplomatic support. It was obvious that there was genuine interest in stimulating a peaceful change in Cuba, and the civilized proposals offered by the "Platform" had a reassuring measure of good sense. Only, Castro was not willing to admit the impossibility of sustaining the Cuban Communist project forever, and he turned his propaganda guns against the "Platform", characterizing it as "a CIA plot", when the whole world knew it was a totally independent initiative on the part of exiles who wanted to take the Cuban problem out of the Havana-Washington boxing ring and place it in an international arena where other players — European and Latin American — could collaborate in the difficult process of the building the country's democracy.

Curiously, Castro's attacks against the "Platform" coincided with criticism from other sectors of the exile community, but for different reasons. From the right, the Patriotic Council — a large and longstanding coalition of political and civic organizations, with strong roots among exiles of a certain age group, and the Cuban American National Foundation leveled accusations on the radio and in the press, claiming that the "Platform" was collaborating with the enemy and wanted to save Castroism at its worst moment. They presented as something reprehensible the Platform's explicit renouncement of violence and willingness to sit down with Castro to search for a peaceful way to make the passage to democracy. Meanwhile, a small sector of Castroists in exile repeated the Cuban slogan that "the *Plataforma* proposals were nothing more than an extension of the Foundation, invented by the CIA as a political ruse".

In effect, there is a group of Castro sympathizers in exile, a small minority with scarcely any bearing on public opinion, but with some presence in the media. Three of the most noted figures are Francisco Aruca, Andrés Gómez and Max Lesnik Menéndez. In his youth, Aruca was a Catholic leader, and shortly after the establishment of Castro's dictatorship, he began to conspire against it. He was jailed and accused of being a terrorist, but he fled prison, disguised as a child — he was thin and beardless, at that time — and after seeking asylum in an embassy, he was able to find exile. He studied business and became a professor in that the field, but he evolved into a successful entrepreneur in the travel industry and soon started taking passengers to Cuba. Little by little, his counterrevolutionary past evaporated until he became an unofficial spokesman of sorts for the Cuban government in exile. He speaks every afternoon on a Miami radio station, a fact that, on its own, disproves the theory that Cubans in that city are largely violent and intolerant.

Gómez arrived in exile when he was still practically a child; he studied in a Miami university. As happened with many young Americans in the 1960s and 1970s, he experienced a process of radicalization that led him to discover Marxism and to re-evaluate his analysis of the Cuban issue. He adopted the viewpoints of the Castroists, with a fidelity that displays an almost astonishing lack of originality and imagination. As a part of that conversion, he created the Antonio Maceo Brigade, a small (obviously) organization for dissident children and grandchildren of exiles who opt for communism; they admit that in their ranks are some of other origins, who are equally lured by the "virtues" of totalitarism. Lesnik, on the other hand, is a much rarer case — he developed a late vocation for Castro — this, from someone who spent his life affirming, everywhere he went and half the papers that he published, that Fidel Castro, in addition to being an enemy of his youth, was a detestable gangster; now, at almost the age of 70, Lesnik says that is false and asserts exactly the contrary view.

These people — whom Castro surely detests and will never trust — play a sad role in politics: their job is to repeat, outside of Cuba, the interpretations, fabrications and lies that the "apparatus" makes up in order to discredit its enemies. And especially, they spread the accusation that Castro's adversaries both inside and outside of Cuba, the dissidents and opponents of the regime, are paid and manipulated by the American intelligence services. Since the Cuban government's opinions about their enemies lack credibility, the testimony of these supposed exiles serves as "impartial corroboration" of the accusations they invent. This dirty game is clearly seen in a book that is sympathetic to Castro, written by the Spanish novelist Manuel Vázquez Montalbán, *And God Entered Havana*, when the Cuban intelligence officer in charge of propaganda operations, Luis Báez — identified by Major Rodríguez Menier — suggests to the author that he use Lesnik as an informant. (He will say exactly what the Cuban government wants him to say, and the source, clearly, will not be official. Furthermore, he will say exactly what Vázquez Montalbán wants to hear, since he is not interested in finding the truth or in exploring differing opinions). Vázquez Montalbán doesn't even try to see other sides of the story, perhaps because he is a novelist, even though he is presumably writing history. His only concern is to quickly and carelessly write a book that is useful to the Cuban dictatorship, the last stronghold of those Stalinist paradises the Catalonian writer never ceases to applaud even when they disappear under the weight of history.

Castro's political police invented the story that all exiles want to return to take vengeance on those who remained on the island, and to take away their scarce belongings (something that hasn't happened in Nicaragua nor in any country in Eastern Europe, and will never happen in Cuba). Nonetheless, despite their efforts to stop it, what is happening at the turn of the century is a rapprochement between the two Cuban societies, that of exile and that of the island, under a slogan that Orlando Gutiérrez, the young leader of the Revolutionary Directorate, never stops repeating. "We are one people."

And so, the texts of Zoé Valdés, Daína Chaviano, Luis Ricardo Alonso and Marcos Antonio Ramos are voraciously read on the island, and the preferred music is by Gloria Estefan, Celia Cruz, Paquito D'Rivera, Marisela Verena, Luisa Maria Güell, Elsa Baeza, Lucrecia, Willy Chirino, Flores Chaviano and Marianella Santurio — all of them prominent exiles. And in turn, among the exiles, books by Pedro Juan Gutiérrez, Abilio Estévez and Leonardo Padura are circulating, as are the writings of professors Pedro Monreal and Julio Carranza — who are received with open arms, whatever their opinions — against a backdrop of music by Carlos Varela and Pedro Luis Ferrer, because it is evident that there is a process of healing and reconstruction under way.

The same is evident in the growing collaboration between the academic communities of Cuba and the exiles, propelled by organizations like the Institute of Cuban Studies led by María Cristina Herrera, the Center for Cuban Studies at Florida International University, and the association of economists founded, against all the odds, in Cuba — the Cuban Institute of Independent Economists, which has its counterpart in exile in the imposing (by the quality of its work) Association for the Study of the Cuban Economy, a work group or think tank that includes one of the most noteworthy concentrations of talent in the history of the Cuban nation: Ernesto Hernández-Catá, Plinio Montalván, Rolando Castañeda, Carlos Quijano, Sergio Díaz Brisquets, Jorge Sanguinetti, José Salazar Carrillo, Juan del Aguila, Carmelo Mesa Lago and

Roger Betancourt, to mention just a dozen of the hundred names that make up the group.

What does all of this foretell? Something important: Cuban society, despite the stumbles and rumbles, is overcoming the immense fracture of the Revolution. The pieces are slowly falling into place. When the process is complete, the country will begin to move in the right direction: that of democracy and the market economy, like the twenty most prosperous nations in the civilized West. The direction that corresponds to Cuba's history and its geography.

EPILOGUE
THE DAY FIDEL CASTRO DIED

A short, sharp pain in the back of his neck, and Fidel Castro blacked out. He fell face-first onto the desk, where he was found by his aide, Chomi Miyar, whose medical training made it quite clear that *el comandante* was dying. And that was perfectly predictable, given the two previous strokes (the first in 1989). Over the age of 70, hypertensive, quick-tempered, a former smoker, arteriosclerotic — it was only a matter of time. And so it happened. Two hours later, at dawn, Castro's heart stopped, in spite of all the efforts to revive him. At his bedside were his wife Delia del Valle, three of his children, and his brothers Raúl and Ramón. Raúl — the one with the worst reputation, yet the most sentimental — was in tears. In a way, Ramón had assumed the strong-man role; he gave support to the rest of the family. Their sister Agustina deliberately had not been notified. She was not to be trusted, and they needed to keep this very quiet.

In the next room six people, all upset and nervous, were talking — almost in a whisper — José Machado Ventura, Ricardo Alarcón, Casas Regueiro, Abelardo Colomé Ibarra, Juan Almeida and Carlos Lage. Eusebio Leal showed up, unexpectedly. No one knew who had told him, but no one had the discourtesy to ask him. He clearly did not belong in the group; he was an outsider. Alarcón gave him the coldest of greetings. Lage was more civil and friendly, though well within his usual detached and proper demeanor. Leal bore his second surname, Spengler, with almost insolent pride. It was too aristocratic, too affected. You could smell from a mile away that his ties with the Revolution were the result of a comic twist of fate. He had been a seminarian and what would have actually fit him best was a cardinal's hat.

Raúl pulled himself together and addressed the small group. "Fidel is dead," he said. "Operation Alba is on." Operation Alba had been scheduled for the moment the inevitable news came. The Chief of Staff would immediately confine all army troops to the barracks and would place them on maximum alert, ready to respond. Officially, this was labeled a precautionary measure against a potential Yankee attack, but in truth it was to prevent any possible adventurism on the part of any disaffected officers who had not been neutralized by the counterintelligence forces.

Gen. Colomé Ibarra, Interior Minister, would mobilize all the police and parapolice forces, especially the anti-riot battalions, and the Committees for the Defense of the Revolution. A force of 10,000 agents would go out at dawn to make preventive arrests of dissidents, reinforce security at foreign embassies, and protect radio and television stations and civilian airports. Dr. José Machado Ventura — the great *apparatchik* — would be in control of the Communist Party, whose chiefs from each province would have to report to the Central Committee offices at 7:00AM to receive instructions. Carlos Lage would summon the cabinet and Juan Almeida would notify the State Council. Ricardo Alarcón would do likewise with the National Assembly of People's Power, since it would have to confirm Raul's predictable succession as Head of State. Felipe Pérez Roque, the none too skillful Minister of Foreign Relations, would of course summon the diplomatic corps and would handle the foreign press.

In order to give the impression of total calm, it was decided that the news of Castro's death would first be given by Radio Rebelde. At 5:00AM, military marches and political anthems would run to prepare the population. All stations would broadcast the same material. At 6:00AM — once Operation Alba was complete — a discrete announcer would give the news briefly: "At dawn today. . . etc.," ending with an announce that Raúl Castro would address the people at 8:00AM. Classes would be suspended and a 30-day period of national mourning would be declared. The first three days included the closing of workplaces, so that the people could mourn and attend the funeral.

Indeed, at 8:00AM sharp, at the office of the State Council, with its 30 members present, Raúl Castro, with a broken voice, read a two-page document establishing three fundamental facts. First, Fidel, the father of the nation, the teacher, the unequaled leader, had died of a devastating cerebral episode; second, the mechanisms of succession had been followed in accordance with the law and everything was under absolute control; and third, the Revolution would continue its uninterrupted socialist direction, now more than ever, in honor of the deceased hero. After Raúl's speech, it was announced that the funeral would take place 48 hours later at Revolution Square, where a mausoleum would be built very close to José Martí's statue.

The reaction of the Cubans, as seen on television, ranged from shock to hysteria, with tears, screaming, contortions. Groups from the Communist Youth shouted, *"Fidel, seguro, a los yanquis dale duro"* (Fidel really hit those Yankees hard), as if the slogan could bring him back to life. Those who sympathized with the opposition, those who were disaffected or indifferent — that is, the great majority of the population — prudently stayed home, to avoid confrontations with those who, for no known reason, angrily supported Castro. CNN correspondent Lucía Newman, despite her efforts, could find no critical opinions or disgruntled citizens to film. The correspondent for Notimex, Mexico's official agency, didn't even try. The people who were closer to disapproving of the regime merely shrugged and, with a finger to their lips, called for silence. Fear was the prevailing feeling — a huge fear of the unknown. It was as if an enormous and prolonged eclipse had begun, stunning an ignorant people. The sun had suddenly disappeared.

The day of the funeral, when Raúl Castro stepped up to the dais, the square was packed. He was the sole speaker, though all the famous faces of the Revolution sat on the front row. The intention was to project a credible image of unity. His emotional words, carefully chosen, reiterated the message that the succession was a fact; the Revolution continued its course; men died, but the Party was immortal. He acknowledged, however, that the country's economical situation was extremely difficult. The speech hardly lasted 45 minutes and it was more notable for what he didn't say than for what he repeated. There was not, for instance, any challenge to the United States nor to the Western model. The most astute experts on Castro's politics immediately noticed that the tone had changed. As they were leaving, in a soft voice, Raúl gave Lage an order: "Summon the State Council tomorrow; important events are taking place." He seemed terribly preoccupied.

After the horrible funeral of his brother Fidel, Raúl Castro made it to the meeting of the State Council; the huge bags under his eyes that were not the result of any hepatic ailment but of lack of sleep and the enormous tribulations weighing upon him. The Yankees had not landed in Cuba, but equally grave events were happening. For instance, the General Directorate of Intelligence had already notified him that less than eight hours after the news was known, numerous partners, Cuba's representatives and agents abroad had started to take possession of the island's assets outside the country — like a game of *piñata* gone out of control, everyone with a stick was taking a swing at the goodies.

Earlier, *Forbes* magazine had published an article claiming that Fidel Castro had a fortune abroad estimated at $1.4 billion — which Fernando Arrabal declared was another triumph of the Revolution, since Batista had only been able to take $200 million — but the fact was that this sum was split up among dozens of bank accounts in Panama, Switzerland, London, Luxemburg and Liechtenstein. Like vultures, insensitive elements had begun to loot the sacred tomb before the body was even cold, and due to the secrecy surrounding the source of the money, the Ministry of Foreign Trade could do nothing to stop the plundering. The money wasn't exactly Fidel's. It was for Fidel's use, to fund the Revolution's indirect activities. *Forbes* would have never understood the concept. In general, these were companies that negotiated Cuban exports abroad — sugar, tobacco, rum, nickel — but the operations had become more complex and now included hotels, restaurants, institutions that "laundered money" in complicity with the Financial Bank of Cuba, and even a Madrid restaurant frequented by thugs.

More worrisome by far was the attitude of the British, French and Swiss brokers who used to make advance payments in foreign currency against future sugar deliveries. Suddenly, they all turned cold, cautious, and noncommittal. Confidence is everything in the international financial community, and their new hesitance was devastating. Everybody was paralyzed, taking a wait-and-see attitude that thrust Cuba into an even greater financial crisis. A "terminal" crisis, as Raúl Castro himself described it, using an abused Anglicism.

Carlos Lage elaborated on the desolate economical situation with impressive detail: sugar production would again fall short of four million tons, and oil imports, given the paltry amount of foreign currency available and the total absence of credit, would hardly be sufficient to buy three million tons, unless Venezuela chose to grant an unsecured line of credit. That is half the minimum required for the country to operate, which meant dramatic cuts would be required in power generation and in transportation, and food production would drop precipitously. The tourism infrastructure (in places other than Varadero and Cayo Coco, where a certain level of comfort could still be expected) would also be diminished. The only significant income would be the $800 million sent by the exiles to their families, but this was a poisoned gift that discouraged local work, generated inflation and demolished the system's ethical foundations. The island was on the verge of a famine and a health disaster like the one suffered in North Korea after the death of Kim Il Sung.

The explanation given by Colomé Ibarra, Interior Minister, was equally somber. The crime rate was going up exponentially. If the food ration were to be reduced even more, assaults could be expected on the dollar shops and on confused tourists. The danger of public disorder and social eruptions came not from the well-known dissident opposition — which was perfectly under control and thoroughly infiltrated by the political police — but from the poorest, most helpless segment of the population, especially the blacks, who had less access to foreign currency since there were few exiled Afro-Cubans able to help their families.

Julio Casas Regueiro, the general who was closest to Raúl Castro, acknowledged that discontent was running high among the armed forces and eventually could prompt conspiracies and defections. First, there was the undeniable fact that the once-powerful Cuban army, ninth in the world when it scored its victories in Angola and Ethiopia, was now a mere economic entity that farmed land and owned half-empty hotels and financial institutions. Its colonels no longer dreamed of military glory, but of simply driving a taxi for tourists or running a *paladar*, a home-restaurant that could serve foreign patrons.

The Navy fleet had turned into scrap metal. The Air Force could hardly count 30 air-worthy planes. Mobile artillery and combat vehicles were grounded due to the lack of batteries and fuel. In the event of a confrontation with the United States, bacteriological warfare would be the only effective weapon; and, obviously, one never intends to resort to such methods on one's own territory. It was doubtful, in case of open war, that Cuban planes could make it across the Florida Straits. In sum, the armed forces were no longer the arm of the Revolution, but an inefficient conglomerate of economic activities without vision or mission.

Then Eusebio Leal spoke. With a trembling voice, Havana's historian dared to express what everyone was thinking. "Gentlemen, in this situation, it is not morally justified to impose more sacrifices on the Cuban people. What would be the point? To make tomorrow even worse? We made a glorious Revolution, at the wrong time, in the wrong place. We have resisted for more than 40 years. Nobody could defeat us. Yet, we must not continue sinking our country into misery. Cuba cannot become the political and economic exception in the West. It makes no difference whether or not we are right. It's a matter of survival, the survival of our people." The first who dared applaud was Alfredo Guevara, followed by Casas Regueiro, who had always thought it was stupid to cling to dogmas that were constantly denied by reality. He had even discussed it once with his father-in-law, Carlos Rafael Rodríguez, who had expressed a similar opinion. Ricardo Alarcón slightly smiled and joined in the applause. Raúl Castro assented with a gesture of resigned fatigue.

After an oath of eternal loyalty to Fidel Castro's memory, the Political Bureau took just six hours to come up with a new strategy. It was an obvious path. It called for an attempt, at the earliest possible juncture, to effect a reconciliation with the United States. Such an approach was all it would take to send the right message to the world that Cuba was starting a period of real and profound change. At the same time, the United States was the only power on Earth capable of organizing a swift rescue operation, directly or indirectly. With the goodwill of the American people, oil from Saudi Arabia or Kuwait could arrive to replenish the oil reserves — which, including those of the military, could scarcely carry the country for 48 days. European food products and Japanese capital equipment could only arrive with Washington's encouragement.

The person in charge of that task would be Ricardo Alarcón. He was the expert on U.S. affairs and he had dreamed of playing such a role his entire life. Washington was notified through a discrete conversation with the American woman diplomat who headed the U.S. Interests Section in Havana. The first contact was disguised as a routine continuation of the periodic meetings on immigration issues held in the U. S. capital, although the most knowledgeable observers must have noted that the U.S. delegation was headed by two no-nonsense officials with direct access to the White House, down-o-earth people who spoke clearly and to the point.

Alarcón began by describing the country's frightful economic situation, and immediately added that if things went on that way, it could cause instability and yet another uncontrolled exodus of rafters. With Fidel Castro dead, there was no one with the authority to stop such a phenomenon. That was his implicit blackmail. This was a clear hint — the Cuban government was ready for a political opening, based on two conditions. First, the United States was to make a commitment not to intervene militarily. Second, a "rescue operation", even larger than the one carried out in North Korea, was to be launched under Washington's initiative and coordination. In summary, and paraphrasing the Israeli term ("peace for land"), it was as simple as "democracy for help," a *quid pro quo* arrangement that would give the United States an obvious benefit — a hiatus in the migrations along its volatile Caribbean border.

The U.S. delegation was prepared for the proposal. It was important, however, that the Cuban government understood the American position quite clearly. In the first place, the Helms-Burton Act — fair or unfair, cruel or beneficial — allowed some room for this type of maneuver. Yet any agreement had to follow the spirit and the letter of that legal document. Secondly, for more than 40 years the Cuban community in the United States — two million people — had achieved a presence in the U.S. political and social life that meant their interests and wishes could not by totally ignored. For electoral reasons, neither Republicans nor Democrats would allow that to happen. Just as had happened in twenty other countries that had changed systems in the last few decades, the Cuban government would simply have to pass muster with its domestic and external opposition. There was no other way.

At the same time, the U.S. delegation knew all too well that, just as in Spain's transition to democracy, there were three steps that the Cuban government would have to adopt unilaterally beforehand, in order to initiate the process of opening up. It would have to decree a broad amnesty for prisoners of conscience; it would have to allow freedom of political association and freedom of expression; and it would have to authorize the return of political exiles who wished to rejoin the nation's public life. And a fourth step, to be taken a little later on, would be to hold a government-opposition forum to discuss the nation's destiny; 200 prominent leaders of the international democratic world linked to the large Western political families — Christian Democrats, Liberals, Social Democrats and conservatives — would be invited to participate. Such an event, with the presence of the most important political leaders of the United States and Latin America as well, would bear evidence of the firm commitment of all democracies to the Cuban transition, and would send a loud and clear message to the economic community of developed countries.

Once the change was initiated and a plan for the economic reconstruction of Cuba was underway (already sketched out under the Clinton administration), the United States could throw its weight behind a formula that would reconcile all Cubans without the need to resort to vengeance or retaliation. Fortunately, there were precedents in Uruguay and Argentina, where a "closure law", democratically undersigned by the voters, had helped turn a black page in the history of those countries. No one expected that the past would be forgotten, but what was needed was a collective, universally exculpatory forgiveness of sorts. Democracy was an excellent method to heal wounds and to legitimize such legal actions. If Raúl Castro had to abandon power as part of the transition, he could do so with full guarantees, which would not be such a sacrifice in any event since, after all, he was indeed a very ill man.

Did the change mean that the Communist Revolution would disappear? Very likely, though not under duress from the United States, but by sheer electorate will. It was the predictable scenario since Cuba could not and did not to escape its Western and Latin American destiny. The Island should follow the 25 most developed and happiest nations on the planet, organizing its public life in accordance with democratic principles and methods. Its economic model must not be anything but that of free enterprise, private property and the market economy, as Cubans themselves would surely decide in a free election. Only — as has happened in Eastern Europe — the new model would be implemented within such a broad framework that the former Communists would enjoy ample space to go on with their lives in dignity and without peril — a space they themselves never granted their adversaries.

Finally, the prisons were opened. As the poet once said, there is no greater joy than on the day when prisoners are set free. In silence — exhausted, their heads bowed — hundreds of thousands of Cubans from every corner of the earth embarked on their journey homeward. The nation came together in a long, silent, close embrace. It was like being born again.

BIBLIOGRAPHY

AA. VV. *El presidio politico en Cuba comunista*. Collective work. Icosov Ediciones. Caracas, 1982.

Aguila, Juan del. *Cuba: Dilemmas of a Revolution*. Westview Press. Boulder, Colorado, 1984.

—————. "The Cuban Armed Forces: Changing Roles, Continued Loyalties". *Cuban Comunism*. Ninth Edition. Transaction Publisher. New Brunswick and London, 1998.

Aguilar León, Luis. *Cuba 1933: Prologue to Revolution*. Cornell University Press. Ithaca, 1972.

—————. *Todo tiene su tiempo: Tiempo de llorar, tiempo de reir, tiempo de soñar y tiempo de pensar*. Ediciones Universal. Miami, 1997.

Aguirre, Rafael A. *Amanecer. Historias del clandestinaje: La lucha de la resistencia contra Castro desde Cuba*. Ediciones Universal. Miami, 1996.

Alarcón Ramírez, Daniel y Elisabeth Burgos-Debray. *Memorias de un soldado cubano: Vida y muerte de la revolución*. Tusquets Editores. Barcelona, 1997.

Alberto, Eliseo. *Informe contra mi mismo*. Extra Alfaguara. México, 1997.

Almendros, Nestor y Orlando Jiménez Leal. *Conducta impropia*. Editorial Playor. Madrid, 1984.

Alonso, José F. "The Ochoa Affair and Its Aftermath". In *Cuban Communism*. Transaction Publishers. New Brunswick and London, 1998.

Alvarez Bravo, Armando. *Cabos sueltos*. Ediciones Universal. Miami, 1997.

Amaro, Nelson. "De-centralization, Local Government and Participation in Cuba". *Cuban Communism*. Ninth Edition. Transaction Publishers. New Brunswick and London, 1998.

Amnistía Internacional. *Cuba: Ofensiva renovada contra las críticas pacíficas al go-*

bierno. AI: AMR 25/29/97/s. Amnesty International. London, August 1997.

Anderson, Jon Lee. *Che: a Revolutionary Life*. Grove Press. New York, 1997.

Apuleyo Mendoza, Plinio. *La llama y el Hielo*. Planeta Colombiana Editorial. Bogotá, 1984.

Aragón Clavijo, Uva de. *El Caimán ante el espejo*. Ediciones Universal, Miami, 1995

Arcocha, Juan. *Fidel Castro en rompecabezas*. Ediciones Erre. Madrid, 1973.

Baloyra, Enrique A. "Political Control and Cuban Youth". *Cuban Communism*. Ninth Edition. Transaction Publishers. New Brunswick and London, 1998.

Barquín, Ramón M. *El día que Fidel Castro se apoderó de Cuba: 72 horas trágicas para la libertad en Las Américas*. Editorial Rambar. San Juan, 1978.

―――――. *Las luchas guerrilleras en Cuba de la Colonia a la Sierra Maestra*. Vols. 1 y 2. Editorial Playor. Madrid, 1975.

Batista, Fulgencio. *The Growth and Decline of the Cuban Republic*. Devine-Adair Co.. New York, 1964.

Benemelis, Juan F. *Castro, subversión y terrorismo en Africa*. Editorial San Martín. Madrid, 1988.

Bernal, Beatriz. "La administración de justicia". *40 años de revolución: el legado de Castro*. Ediciones Universal, Miami, 1999.

Betancourt, Ernesto. *Revolutionary Strategy: A Handbook for Practitioners*. Transaction Books. New Brunswick, NJ, 1991.

―――――. "Castro's Legacy". *Cuban Communism*. Ninth Edition. Transaction Publishers. New Brunswick and London, 1998.

Bonachea, Rolando y Nelson Valdés. *Che: Selected Works of Ernesto Che Guevara*. MIT Press. Cambridge, MA, 1969.

―――――. y Marta San Martín. *The Cuban Insurrection 1952-1959*. Transaction Books. Brunswick, NJ, 1974.

Bonsal, Philip W. *Cuba, Castro and the United States*. University of Pittsburgh Press. Pittsburgh, 1971.

Breuer, William B. *Vendetta! Fidel Castro and the Kennedy Brothers*. John Wiley. New York, 1997.

Brune, Lester H. *The Cuban-Caribbean Missile Crisis of October 1962*. Regina Books. Claremont, California, 1996.

Bunck, Julie Marie. "The Politics of Sports in Revolutionary Cuba." *Cuban Communism*. Ninth Edition. Transaction Publishers. New Brunswick and London, 1998.

Burks, David D. *Cuba under Castro*. Foreign Policy Association. New York, 1964.

Calzón, Frank. *Castro's Gulag: The Politics of Terror*. Council for Inter-American Security. Washington, DC, 1979.

Carbonell, Néstor T. *And the Russians Stayed: The Sovietization of Cuba*. William Morrow & Company. New York, 1989.

Carranza Valdés, Julio. "Economía cubana: Reformas, socialismo y mercado". *Cuba hoy: Desafíos de fin de siglo*. LOM Ediciones. Santiago, 1995.

Carrillo, Justo. *Cuba 1933 — estudiantes, yanquis y soldados*. Instituto de Estudios Interamericanos. University of Miami. Miami, 1985.

Castañeda, Jorge G. *Compañero: Vida y muerte del Che Guevara*. Vintage Español. New York, 1997.

Casuso, Teresa. *Cuba and Castro*. Random House. New York, 1961.

Clark, Juan. *Cuba: Mito y Realidad*. Saeta Ediciones. Miami-Caracas, 1990.

Colomer, Josep M. "After Fidel, What?: Forecasting Institutional Changes in Cuba." *Cuban Communism*. Ninth Edition. Transaction Publishers. New Brunswick and London, 1998.

Conte Agüero, Luis. *Fidel Castro: Vida y Obra*. Editorial Lex. La Habana, 1959.

—————. *Los dos rostros de Fidel Castro*. Editorial Jus. México, 1960.

Córdova, Efrén (editor). *40 años de revolución. El legado de Castro*. Ediciones Universal. Miami, 1999.

Crassweller, Robert D. *Cuba and the U.S.: The Tangled Relationship*. Foreign Policy Association. New York, 1971.

Cuesta, Leonel de la. *Las constituciones cubanas*. Ediciones Exilio. Madrid, 1976.

Debray, Régis. *La guerrilla del Che*. Siglo Veintiuno Editores. México, 1975.

Dewart, Leslie. *Christianity and Revolution: The Lesson of Cuba*. Herder and Herder. New York, 1963.

Díaz-Briquets, Sergio. "Labor Force and Education in Cuba." *Cuban Communism*. Ninth Edition. Transaction Publishers. New Brunswick and London, 1998.

Dinges, John. *Our Man in Panama*. Random House. New York, 1990.

Domínguez, Jorge I. "Why the Cuban Regime Has Not Fallen". *Cuban Communism*. Ninth Edition. Transaction Publishers. New Brunswick and London, 1998.

—————. *Cuba: Order and Revolution*. The Belknap Press of Harvard University Press. Cambridge, 1978.

Dorschner, John and Robert Fabricio. *The Winds of December*. Coward, McCann & Geo-ghegan. New York, 1980.

Dorta-Duque, Manuel. *Alejandro (alias) Fidel*. Ediciones Joyuda, Inc. Puerto Rico.

Draper, Theodore. *Castro's Revolution: Myths and Realities*. Frederick A. Praeger. New York, 1973.

—————. *Theory and Practice*. Frederick A. Praeger. New York, 1965.

Duarte Oropesa, José. *Historiología cubana desde 1944 hasta 1959*. Ediciones Universal. Miami, 1974.

Dubois, Jules. *Fidel Castro. Rebel, Liberator or Dictator?* Bobbs-Merrill. Indianapolis, Ind., 1959.

Dumont, René. *Is Cuba Socialist?* Translated by Stanley Hochman. Andre Deutsch. London, 1974.

—————. *Socialism and Development*. Grove Press. New York, 1970.

Encinosa, Enrique. *Cuba en guerra*. The Endowment of Cuban American Studies, Miami, 1994.

El presidio político en Cuba comunista: testimonios. Obra colectiva. ICOSOCV Ediciones, Caracas, 1982.

Fagen, Richard R. *Cubans in Exile: Disaffection and the Revolution*. Stanford University Press. Stanford, California, 1968.

—————. *The Transformation of Political Culture in Cuba*. Stanford University Press. Stanford, California, 1969.

Falcoff, Mark. "Cuba and the United States: Back to the Beginning". *Cuban Communism*. Ninth Edition. Transaction Publishers. New Brunswick and London, 1998.

Falk, Pamela. "Political and Military Elites". *Cuban Communism*. Ninth Edition. Transaction Publishers. New Brunswick and London, 1998.

Fauriol, Georges and Loser, Eva. *Cuba. The International Dimension. Transaction Publishers*. New Brunswick, 1991.

Fermoselle, Rafael. *Política y color en Cuba: la guerrita de 1912*. Editorial Colibrí, Madrid, 1998.

Fernández, Alina. *Alina: Memorias de la hija rebelde de Fidel Castro*. Plaza & Janés. Barcelona, 1997.

Fibla, Alberto. *Barbarie: Hundimiento del remolcador "13 de marzo"*. Rodes Printers. Miami, 1996.

Figueroa, Javier. "Leví Marrero y Manuel Moreno Fraginals ante el Espejo de Clio". *Apuntes Posmodernos/Postmodern Notes* 6. Nº 2-7, 1996.

Fogel, Jean-Francois y Rosenthal, Bertrand. *Fin de siglo en La Habana*. Anaya & Mario Muchnik. Madrid, 1993.

Fontaine, Roger W. *Terrorism: The Cuban Connection*. Crane, Russak & Company. New York, 1988.

Fraide, Martha. *Ecoute, Fidel*. Denoël. París, 1987.

Franqui, Carlos. *Diary of the Cuban Revolution*. Translated by Georgette Felix, Elaine Kerrigan, Phyllis Freman and Hardie St. Martin. The Viking Press. New York, 1980.

—————. *Family Portrait with Fidel*. Random House. New York, 1984.

—————. *Vida, aventuras y desastres de un hombre llamado Castro*. Editorial Planeta. Barcelona, 1988.

Fuentes, Ileana. *Cuba sin caudillos. Un enfoque feminista para el siglo XXI*. Linden Lane Press. Princeton, 1994.

Fursenko, A. and Timothy J. Naftali. *One Hell of a Gamble: Khrushchev, Castro, and Kennedy, 1958-1964*. Norton. New York, 1997.

Geyer, Georgie Anne. *Guerrilla Prince: The Untold Story of Fidel Castro*. Little Brown. Boston, 1991.

Giuliano, Maurizio. *El caso CEA: intelectuales e inquisidores en Cuba*. Ediciones Universal, Miami, 1998.

Golden, Tim. "Health Care in Cuba". *Cuban Communism*. Ninth Edition. Transaction Publishers. New Brunswick and London, 1998.

Goldenberg, Boris. *The Cuban Revolution in Latin America*. Praeger. New York, 1965.

González, Edward. *Cuba under Castro. The Limits of Charisma.* Houghton Mifflin. Boston, 1974.

————. "Actors, Models and Endgames". *Cuban Communism.* Ninth Edition. Transaction Publishers. New Brunswick and London, 1998.

————. *Cuba's Dismal Post-Castro Futures.* Rand. Santa Monica, California, 1996.

————. and David Ronfeldt. *Castro, Cuba and the World.* Rand. Santa Monica, 1986.

Gouré, León. "War of all the People: Cuba's Military Doctrines". *Cuban Communism.* Ninth Edition. Transaction Publishers. New Brunswick and London, 1998.

Grupo Cubano de Investigaciones Económicas. *A Study on Cuba.* University of Miami Press. Coral Gables, Florida, 1965.

Gugliotta, Guy and Jeff Leen. *Kings of Cocaine Inside the Medellín Cartel. An Astonishing True Story of Murder, Money and International Corruption.* Simon and Schuster. New York, 1989.

Halperin, Ernst. *Castro and Latin American Communism.* Center for International Studies, Massachusetts Institute of Technology. Cambridge, MA, 1963.

Halperin, Maurice. *The Rise and Decline of Fidel Castro: An Essay in Contemporary History.* University of California Press. Berkeley and Los Angeles, 1972.

Hernández Miyares, Julio E. *Narrativa y libertad: Cuentos cubanos de la diáspora.* Ediciones Universal. Miami, 1996.

Horowitz, Irving L. "Military Origin and Evolution of the Cuban Revolution." *Cuban Communism.* Ninth Edition. Transaction Publishers. New Brunswick and London, 1998.

————. "Political Pilgrimage and the End of Ideology". *Cuban Communism.* Ninth Edition. *Transaction Publishers.* New Brunswick and London, 1998.

————. *Cuban Communism.* Third Edition. Transaction Books. New Brunswick, 1977.

James, Daniel. *Che Guevara: A Biography.* Stein and Day. New York, 1969.

Jiménez Leal, Orlando. *8-A. La realidad invisible.* Ediciones Universal. Miami, 1997.

Johnson, Haynes, with Manuel Artime, José Pérez San Román, Erneido Oliva and Enrique Ruiq-Williams. *The Bay of Pigs: The Leader's Story of Brigade 2056.* W. W. Norton & Company. New York, 1964.

Jorge, Antonio y Robert David Cruz. "Foreign Investment Opportunities in Cuba: Evaluating the Risk." *Cuban Communism, op. cit.*

Karol, K.S. *Guerrillas in Power: The Course of the Cuban Revolution.* Translated by Arnold Pomerans. Hill & Wang. New York, 1970.

Kennedy, Robert F. *Thirteen Days: A Memoir of the Cuban Missile Crisis.* Norton & Company. New York, 1969.

Kirk, John M. And Peter McKenna. *Canada-Cuba Relations: The Other Good Neighbor Policy.* University Press of Florida. Gainesville, 1997.

Khrushchev, Nikita. *Khrushchev Remembers.* Little Brown. Boston, 1970.

La economía cubana en 1996: Resultados, problemas y perspectivas. Centro de Estudios de la Economía Cubana. Universidad de La Habana. La Habana, 1997.

La Vesque, Jacques. *The U.S.S.R. and the Cuban Revolution: Soviet ideological and strategic perspectives.* Praeger. New York, 1978.

Le Riverend Brusone, Julio. *Economic History of Cuba.* Book Institute. La Habana, 1967.

Leiken, Robert S. *Soviet Strategy in Latin America.* The Washington Papers/93 Volume X. Praeger Publishers and the Center for Strategic and International Studies. New York, 1982.

Levine, Barry B. *The New Cuban Presence in the Caribbean.* Westview Press. Boulder, Colorado, 1983.

López Fresquet, Rufo. *My 14 Months with Castro.* The World Publishing Company. Cleveland, 1966.

Lowenthal, Abraham F. *Partners in Conflict: The United States and Latin America.* The Johns Hopkins University Press. Baltimore, 1987.

Luxenberg, Alan H. "Eisenhower, Castro and the Soviets". *Cuban Communism, op. cit.*

Llerena, Mario. *The Unsuspected Revolution: The Birth and Rise of Castroism.* Cornell University Press. Ithaca, 1978.

Mallin, Jay. *Che Guevara on Revolution.* University of Miami Press. Coral Gables, Florida, 1969.

Marrero, Levi. *Cuba: Economía y Sociedad.* 15 volúmenes. Editorial Playor. Madrid, 1976-1990.

Masó y Vázquez, Calixto. *El carácter cubano: Apuntes para un ensayo de psicología social.* Ediciones Universal. Miami, 1996.

Matthews, Herbert L. *Fidel Castro.* Simon and Schuster. New York, 1969.

—————. *The Cuban Story.* George Braziller. New York, 1975.

Mesa Lago, Carmelo. *Revolutionary Change in Cuba.* The University of Pittsburgh Press. Pittsburgh, 1971.

—————. *Dialéctica de la revolución cubana: del idealismo crismático al pragmatismo institucionalista.* Biblioteca cubana contemporánea. Editorial Playor. Madrid, 1979.

—————. *The Economy of Socialist Cuba.* University of New Mexico Press. Albuquerque, 1981.

—————. *La economía en Cuba socialista: Una evaluación de dos décadas.* Editorial Playor. Madrid, 1983.

—————. "¿Recuperación económica en Cuba?". *Encuentro de la Cultura Cubana* Nº 3. Madrid, invierno de 1996/1997.

—————. "Cuba's Economic Policies and Strategies for the 1990s." *Cuban Communism. op. cit..*

————— and June S. Belkin. *Cuba in Africa.* Center for Latin American Studies. University Center for International Studies. University of Pittsburgh. Pittsburgh, 1982.

Miná, Gianni. *Un encuentro con Fidel: Entrevista realizada por Gianni Miná.* Oficina de Publicaciones del Consejo de Estado. La Habana, 1987.

—————. *Fidel.* Edivisión. México, 1991.

Montaner, Carlos Alberto. *Informe secreto de la revolución cubana.* Sedmay. Madrid, 1975.

—————. *Fidel Castro y la revolución cubana.* Editorial Playor. Madrid, 1983.

—————. *Cuba: Claves para una conciencia en crisis.* Editorial Playor. Madrid, 1983.

—————. *Cuba, Castro and the Caribbean: The Cuban Revolution and the Crisis in Western Conscience.* Translated by Nelson Durán. Transaction Books. New Brunswick, 1985.

—————. *Castro en la era de Gorbachov.* Instituto de Cuestiones Internacionales. Madrid, 1990.

————. *Cuba hoy: La lenta muerte del Castrismo.* Ediciones Universal. Miami, 1996.

————. *Cuba: The country of 13 million hostages.* Internacional Liberal. Madrid, 1996.

Morán Arce, Lucas. *La revolucion cubana (1953-1959): Una visión rebelde.* Imprenta Universitaria, Inc. Ponce, Puerto Rico 1980.

Mujal-León, Eusebio. "Higher Education and the Institutionalized Regime." *Cuban Communism, op. cit..*

Navarro, Antonio. *Tocayo.* Sharock Publishing Company. Sandown Books. Westport, Conn., 1981.

Nelson, Lowry. *Cuba: The Measure of a Revolution.* University of Minnesota Press. Minneapolis, 1972.

Oppenheimer, Andrés. *La hora final de Castro. La historia secreta detrás de la inminente caída del comunismo en Cuba.* Javier Vergara Editor. Buenos Aires/Madrid/México/Santiago de Chile/Bogotá/Caracas, 1992.

Orozco, Román. *Cuba roja.* Cambio 16. Madrid, 1993.

Padilla, Heberto. *Fuera del juego.* Ediciones Universal, Madrid, 1999.

Pardo Llada, José. *Memorias de la Sierra Maestra.* N.p. La Habana, 1960.

————. *El "Che" que yo conocí.* Editorial Bedout. Medellín, 1969.

————. *Fidel.* Plaza & Janés. Bogotá, 1976.

Pérez, Louis A. *Army Politics in Cuba, 1898-1958.* University of Pittsburgh Press. Pittsburgh, 1976.

————. *Cuba and United States: Ties of Singular Intimacy.* University of Georgia Press. Athens, GA, 1997.

Pérez-Firmat, Gustavo. *El año que viene estamos en Cuba.* Arte Público Press. Houston, 1997.

Pérez-López, Jorge F. "Cuba's Socialist Economy: The Mid-1990s." *Cuban Communism, op. cit..*

Pflaum, Irving Peter. *Tragic Island: How Communism Came to Cuba.* Prentice-Hall. Englewood Cliffs, NJ, 1961.

Prado Salmón, Gary. *Cómo capturé al Ché.* Ediciones B. Barcelona, 1987.

Quirk, Robert E. *Fidel Castro.* W.W. Norton. New York, 1993.

Rabkin, Rhoda. "Human Rights and Military Rule in Cuba". *Cuban Communism, op. cit..*

Ramos, Marcos Antonio. *Panorama del protestantismo en Cuba.* Editorial Caribe, Miami-San José, 1986.

Recarte, Alberto. *Cuba: Economia y Poder (1959-1980).* Alianza Universidad. Madrid, 1981.

Ripoll, Carlos. *Harnessing the Intellectuals: Censoring Writers and Artist in Today's Cuba.* Freedom House. New York, 1985.

Ritter, Archibald R.M. "Challenges and Policy Imperatives to the Economy". *Cuban Communism, op. cit..*

Robbins, Carl Anne. *The Cuban Threat.* The Cuban Threat. New York, 1983.

Roca, Sergio G. "Managing State Enterprise in Cuba". *Cuban Communism, op. cit..*

——————. *Cuban Economic Policy and Ideology.* Sage. Beverly Hills, 1976.

Rodríguez, Carlos Rafael. *Cuba en el tránsito hacia el socialismo 1959-1963.* Siglo Veintiuno Editores. México, 1978.

Rodríguez Menier, Juan Antonio. *Cuba por dentro: el MININT.* Ediciones Universal, Miami, 1994.

Rojas, Marta. *La Generación del Centenario en el juicio del Moncada.* Editorial Ciencias Sociales. La Habana, 1973.

Rojas, Rafael. "La disección del pasado". *Apuntes Posmodernos/Postmodern Notes 6.* Nº 2-7, 1996.

Rojo, Ricardo. *My friend Che.* Translated by Julian Casart. The Dial Press. New York, 1968.

Roque Cabello, Marta Beatriz and Arnaldo Ramos Lauzurique. *Documentos del Instituto Cubano de Economistas Independientes.* CSA Occasional Paper Series, Vol.2, Nº 3. University of Miami. Miami, 1997.

Ros, Enrique. *Años críticos: Del camino de la acción al camino del entendimiento.* Ediciones Universal. Miami, 1996.

Roy, Joaquín. *España, la Unión Europea y Cuba: La evolución de una relación especial a una política de gestos y presión.* Cuban Studies Association. Miami, 1996.

Ruiz, Ramón Eduardo. *Cuba: The Makings of a Revolution.* The University of Massachusetts Press. Amherst, MA, 1968.

Salazar-Carrillo, Jorge. "The Cuban Economy as Seen Through Its Trading Partners." *Cuban Communism, op. cit..*

Salinger, Pierce. *With Kennedy.* Doubleday. New York, 1966.

San Martín, Marta and Ramón Bonachea. "Guerrillas at War". *Cuban Communism, op. cit..*

Schlesinger, Arthur M. Jr. *Robert Kennedy and His Times.* Houghton Mifflin Company. Boston, 1965.

Smith, Earl, E.T. *The Fourth Floor: An Account of the Castro Communist Revolution.* Random House. New York, 1962.

Smith, Wayne E. *The Closest of Enemies: A Personal and Diplomatic Account of U.S.-Cuban Relations Since 1957.* W.W. Norton & Company. New York, 1987.

Solchaga, Carlos. "Cuba: Perspectivas económicas". *Encuentro de la Cultura Cubana.* Nº 3. Madrid, invierno de 1996/1997.

Solidaridad de Trabajadores Cubanos. *La crisis nacional y el movimiento de trabajadores: Una propuesta económica y social de la Solidaridad de Trabajadores Cubanos.* STC. Caracas, 1997.

Sorel, Julian B. (pseudónimo). *Nacionalismo y revolución en Cuba 1823-1998.* Fundación Liberal José Martí. Madrid, 1998.

Sorensen, Theodore C. *Kennedy.* Harper & Row. New York, 1965.

Suárez, Andrés. *Cuba: Castroism and Communism, 1959-1966.* MIT Press. Cambridge, Mass., 1967.

Suchlicki, Jaime. *University Students and Revolution in Cuba.* University of Miami Press. Coral Gables, Florida, 1969.

—————. *Cuba, Castro and Revolution.* University of Miami Press. Coral Gables, 1972.

—————. *Cuba from Columbus to Castro.* Pergamon-Brassey's. Washington, 1986.

Szulc, Tad. *Fidel: A Critical Portrait.* William Morrow and Company. New York, 1986.

The Cuban Economic Research Project. *A Study on Cuba: The Colonial and Republican Periods; The Socialist Experiment; Economic Structure; Institutional Development; Socialism; and Collectivization.* University of Miami Press. Coral Gables, 1965.

Thomas, Hugh. *Cuba: La búsqueda de la libertad.* (3 volúmenes). Grijalbo. Barcelona, 1973.

Travieso-Díaz, Matías F. *The Laws and Legal System of a Free-Market Cuba. A Prospectus for Business.* Quorum Books. Westport, Conn. 1997.

Vázquez Montalbán, Manuel. *Y Dios entró en La Habana.* El País/Aguilar, Madrid, 1998.

United States House of Representatives, Committee on Foreign Affairs. *U.S. Response to Cuban Government Involvement in Narcotics Trafficking and Review of Worldwide Illicit Narcotics Situation.* U.S. Government Printing Office. Washington, DC, 1984.

Urrutia Lleó, Manuel. *Fidel Castro & Company, Inc.: Communist Tyranny in Cuba.* Frederick A. Praeger, Publisher. New York.

Valls, Jorge. *Twenty Years and Forty Days: Life in a Cuban Prison.* Americas Watch. New York, 1986.

Vázquez Montalbán, Manuel. *Y Dios entró en La Habana.* El País/Aguilar, Madrid, 1998.

Vives, Juan. *Los amos de Cuba.* Emecé Editores. Buenos Aires, 1982.

Walker, Phyllis Greene. "Political-Military Relations from 1959 to the Present." *Cuban Communism, op. cit.*.

Weyl, Nathaniel. *Red Star over Cuba: The Russian Assault on the Western Hemisphere.* The Devin-Adair Company. New York, 1962.

Wiarda, Howard J. "Crises of the Castro Regime". *Cuban Communism, op. cit.*.

Wilkerson, Loree. *Fidel Castro's Political Programs: From Reformism to Marxism-Leninism.* University of Florida Press. Gainesville, Florida, 1965.

Wyden, Peter. *Bay of Pigs. The Untold Story.* Simon & Schuster, 1979.

Name Index

Also from Algora Publishing:

CLAUDIU A. SECARA
THE NEW COMMONWEALTH:
FROM BUREAUCRATIC CORPORATISM TO SOCIALIST CAPITALISM

The notion of an elite-driven worldwide perestroika has gained some credibility lately. The book examines in a historical perspective the most intriguing dialectic in the Soviet Union's "collapse" — from socialism to capitalism and back to socialist capitalism — and speculates on the global implications.

DOMINIQUE FERNANDEZ
PHOTOGRAPHER: FERRANTE FERRANTI

ROMANIAN RHAPSODY — *An Overlooked Corner of Europe*

"Romania doesn't get very good press." And so, renowned French travel writer Dominique Fernandez and top photographer Ferrante Ferranti head out to form their own images. In four long journeys over a 6-year span, they uncover a tantalizing blend of German efficiency and Latin nonchalance, French literature and Gypsy music, Western rationalism and Oriental mysteries. Fernandez reveals the rich Romanian essence. Attentive and precise, he digs beneath the somber heritage of communism to reach the deep roots of a European country that is so little-known.

IGNACIO RAMONET

THE GEOPOLITICS OF CHAOS

The author, Director of Le Monde Diplomatique, presents an original, discriminating and lucid political matrix for understanding what he calls the "current disorder of the world" in terms of Internationalization, Cyberculture and Political Chaos.

TZVETAN TODOROV
A PASSION FOR DEMOCRACY – BENJAMIN CONSTANT

The French Revolution rang the death knell not only for a form of society, but also for a way of feeling and of living; and it is still not clear what we have gained from the changes. Todorov examines the life of Constant, one of the original thinkers who conceptualized modern democracy, and in the process gives us a richly textured portrait of a man who was fully engaged in life, both public and private.

MICHEL PINÇON & MONIQUE PINÇON-CHARLOT
GRAND FORTUNES – DYNASTIES OF WEALTH IN FRANCE

Going back for generations, the fortunes of great families consist of far more than money— they are also symbols of culture and social interaction. In a nation known for democracy and meritocracy, piercing the secrets of the grand fortunes verges on a crime of lèse-majesté . . . Grand Fortunes succeeds at that.

JEAN-MARIE ABGRALL

SOUL SNATCHERS: THE MECHANICS OF CULTS

Jean-Marie Abgrall, psychiatrist, criminologist, expert witness to the French Court of Appeals, and member of the Inter-Ministry Committee on Cults, is one of the experts most frequently consulted by the European judicial and legislative processes. The fruit of fifteen years of research, his book delivers the first methodical analysis of the sectarian phenomenon, decoding the mental manipulation on behalf of mystified observers as well as victims.

JEAN-CLAUDE GUILLEBAUD
THE TYRANNY OF PLEASURE

A Sixties' radical re-thinks liberation, taking a hard look at the question of sexual morals in a modern society. For almost a whole generation, we have lived in the illusion that this question had ceased to exist. Today the illusion is faded, but a strange and tumultuous distress replaces it. Our societies painfully seek a "third way", between unacceptable alternatives: bold-faced permissiveness or nostalgic moralism.

SOPHIE COIGNARD AND MARIE-THÉRÈSE GUICHARD
FRENCH CONNECTIONS – THE SECRET HISTORY OF NETWORKS OF INFLUENCE

They were born in the same region, went to the same schools, fought the same fights and made the same mistakes in youth. They share the same morals, the same fantasies of success and the same taste for money. They act behind the scenes to help each other, boosting careers, monopolizing business and information, making money, conspiring and, why not, becoming Presidents!

VLADIMIR PLOUGIN
RUSSIAN INTELLIGENCE SERVICES. Vol. I. (AD 882—1054)

Mysterious episodes from Russia's past – alliances and betrayals, espionage and military féats – are unearthed and examined in this study, which is drawn from ancient chronicles and preserved documents from Russia, Greece, and Byzantium. Scholarly analysis and narrative flair combine to give both the facts and the flavor of the battle scenes and the espionage milieu, including the establishment of secret services in Kievan rus, the heroes and the techniques of intelligence and counter-intelligence in the 10th-12th centuries, and the times of Vladimir.

JEAN-JACQUES ROSA
EURO ERROR

The European Superstate makes Jean-Jacques Rosa mad, for two reasons. First, actions taken to relieve unemployment have created inflation, but have not reduced unemployment. His second argument is even more intriguing: the 21st century will see the fragmentation of the U. S., not the unification of Europe.

ANDRÉ GAURON
EUROPEAN MISUNDERSTANDING

Few of the books decrying the European Monetary Union raise the level of the discussion to a higher plane. European Misunderstanding is one of these. Gauron gets it right, observing that the real problem facing Europe is its political future, not its economic future.

CLAUDIU A. SECARA
TIME & EGO – Judeo-Christian Egotheism and the Anglo-Saxon Industrial Revolution

The first question of abstract reflection that arouses controversy is the problem of Becoming. Being persists, beings constantly change; they are born and they pass away. How can Being change and yet be eternal? The quest for the logical and experimental answer has just taken off.

PASCAL BRUCKNER
THE TEMPTATION OF INNOCENCE – Living in the Age of Entitlement

"Gracefully erudite, deliciously mordant, Bruckner takes on a recent species of human self-deception: infantilism and victimization, the idea that powerlessness is a virtue without responsibility. This highly insightful essay dissects the culture of dependency and its damaging effects on the moral fiber of society, from corporate welfare to affirmative action.." *PublishersWeekly*
Académie française Prix 2000; Medici Prize for Essays

PHILIPPE TRÉTIACK

ARE YOU AGITÉ? Treatise on Everyday Agitation

The 'Agité,' that human species that lives in international airports, jumps into taxis while dialing the cell phone, eats while clearing the table, reads the paper while watching TV and works during vacation – has just been given a new title. "A book filled with the exuberance of a new millennium, full of humor and relevance. Philippe Trétiack, a leading reporter for Elle, takes us around the world and back at light speed." — *Aujourd'hui le Parisien*

PAUL LOMBARD

VICE & VIRTUE — Men of History, Great Crooks for the Greater Good

Personal passion has often guided powerful people more than the public interest. With what result? From the courtiers of Versailles to the back halls of Mitterand's government, from Danton — revealed to have been a paid agent for England — to the shady bankers of Mitterand's era, from the buddies of Mazarin to the builders of the Panama Canal, Paul Lombard unearths the secrets of the corridors of power. He reveals the vanity and the corruption, but also the grandeur and panache that characterize the great. This cavalcade over many centuries can be read as a subversive tract on how to lead.

RICHARD LABÉVIÈRE

DOLLARS FOR TERROR — The U.S. and Islam

"In this riveting, often shocking analysis, the U.S. is an accessory in the rise of Islam, because it manipulates and aids radical Moslem groups in its shortsighted pursuit of its economic interests, especially the energy resources of the Middle East and the oil- and mineral-rich former Soviet republics of Central Asia. Labévière shows how radical Islamic fundamentalism spreads its influence on two levels, above board, through investment firms, banks and shell companies, and clandestinely, though a network of drug dealing, weapons smuggling and money laundering. This important book sounds a wake-up call to U.S. policy-makers." — *Publishers Weekly*

JEANNINE VERDÈS-LEROUX

DECONSTRUCTING PIERRE BOURDIEU — Against Sociological Terrorism From the Left

Sociologist Pierre Bourdieu went from widely-criticized to widely-acclaimed, without adjusting his hastily constructed theories. Verdès-Leroux suggests that Bourdieu arrogated for himself the role of "total intellectual" and proved that a good offense is the best defense. A pessimistic Leninist bolstered by a ponderous scientific construct, Bourdieu stands out as the ultimate doctrinaire more concerned with self-promotion than with democratic intellectual engagements.

HENRI TROYAT

TERRIBLE TZARINAS

Who should succeed Peter the Great? Upon the death of this visionary and despotic reformer, the great families plotted to come up with a successor who would surpass everyone else — or at least, offend none. But there were only women — Catherine I, Anna Ivanovna, Anna Leopoldovna, Elizabeth I. These autocrats imposed their violent and dissolute natures upon the empire, along with their loves, their feuds, their cruelties. Born in 1911 in Moscow, Troyat is a member of the Académie française, recipient of Prix Goncourt.

DEBORAH SCHURMAN-KAUFLIN

THE NEW PREDATOR: WOMEN WHO KILL — Profiles of Female Serial Killers

This is the first book ever based on face-to-face interviews with women serial killers. Dr. Schurman-Kauflin analyzes the similarities and differences between male and female serial killers and mass murderers.

JEAN-MARIE ABGRALL

HEALING OR STEALING — *Medical Charlatans in the New Age*

Jean-Marie Abgrall is Europe's foremost expert on cults and forensic medicine. In his recent work, he examines the benefits and shortcomings of alternative medicines, helping the public to discern therapists from quacks. While not all systems of nontraditional medicine are linked to cults, he does suggest that many are futile if not downright harmful, and indeed can be used as an avenue of cult recruitment. The crisis of the modern world may be leading to a new mystique of medicine, where patients check their powers of judgment at the door.

RÉMI KAUFFER

DISINFORMATION — *US Multinationals at War with Europe*

"Spreading rumors to damage a competitor, using 'tourists' for industrial espionage. . . Kauffer shows how the economic war is waged." — Le Monde
"A specialist in the secret services, Kauffer notes that, 'In the CNN era, with our skies full of satellites and the Internet expanding every nano-second, the techniques of mass persuasion that were developed during the Cold War are still very much in use – only their field of application has changed.' His analysis is shocking, and well-documented." — La Tribune

CARL A. DAVIS
PLANE TRUTH — *A PRIVATE INVESTIGATOR'S STORY*

"Raises new questions about corporate and tribal loyalties, structural engineering, and money and politics, in a credible scenario that makes my flesh creep. . . I think I'll take a train, next time. Or walk." — Western Review
"Takes us around the world and finds treasure under stones that had been left unturned After reading these 'travels with Carl,' (or is he Sherlock Holmes?), my own life seems very flat." — Book Addicts

JENNIFER FURIO

LETTERS FROM PRISON — *VOICES OF WOMEN MURDERERS*

Written by incarcerated women, these incredibly personal, surprisingly honest letters shed light on their lives, their crimes and the mitigating circumstances. Author Jennifer Furio, a prison reform activist, subtly reveals the biases if the criminal justice system and the media. The words of these women haunt and transfix even the most skeptical reader.

CHANTAL THOMAS

COPING WITH FREEDOM

40 million American women of marriageable age are single. This approachable essay addresses many of their concerns in a profound and delightful way. Inspired by the author's own experiences as well as by the 18th century philosophers, and literary and historical references, it offers insights and the courage to help us revel in the game of life, the delight of reading, the art of the journey, and the right to say "no" to chains of obligations and family.

Printed in the United States
6386